Enduring Injustice

Governments today often apologize for past injustices and scholars increasingly debate the issue, with many calling for apologies and reparations. Others suggest that what matters is victims of injustice today, not injustices in the past. Spinner-Halev argues that the problem facing some peoples is not only the injustice of the past, but that they still suffer from injustice today. They experience what he calls enduring injustices, and it is likely that these will persist without action to address them. The history of these injustices matters, not as a way to assign responsibility or because we need to remember more, but in order to understand the nature of the injustice and to help us think of possible ways to overcome it. Suggesting that enduring injustices fall outside the framework of liberal theory, Spinner-Halev spells out the implications of his arguments for conceptions of liberal justice and progress, reparations, apologies, state legitimacy, and post-nationalism.

JEFF SPINNER-HALEV is the Kenan Eminent Professor of Political Ethics at the University of North Carolina at Chapel Hill. He is the author of *The Boundaries of Citizenship: Race, Ethnicity and Nationality in the Liberal State* (1994) and *Surviving Diversity: Religion and Democratic Citizenship* (2000), and co-editor of *Minorities within Minorities: Equality, Rights and Diversity* (Cambridge, 2005).

Enduring Injustice

JEFF SPINNER-HALEV
Kenan Eminent Professor of Political Ethics
University of North Carolina at Chapel Hill

CAMBRIDGE
UNIVERSITY PRESS

CAMBRIDGE UNIVERSITY PRESS
Cambridge, New York, Melbourne, Madrid, Cape Town,
Singapore, São Paulo, Delhi, Mexico City

Cambridge University Press
The Edinburgh Building, Cambridge CB2 8RU, UK

Published in the United States of America by
Cambridge University Press, New York

www.cambridge.org
Information on this title: www.cambridge.org/9781107603073

First published 2012

Printed in the United Kingdom at the University Press, Cambridge

A catalogue record for this publication is available from the British Library

Library of Congress Cataloging-in-Publication Data

Spinner-Halev, Jeff.
   Enduring injustice / Jeff Spinner-Halev.
      p.   cm.
   ISBN 978-1-107-01751-1 (Hardback) – ISBN 978-1-107-60307-3 (Paperback)
1. Justice.   2. Social justice–Philosophy.   3. Social change–Political aspects.
4. Reconciliation–Political aspects.   I. Title.
   JC578.S685 2012
   320.01′1–dc23

                                                                2011046103

ISBN 978-1-107-01751-1 Hardback
ISBN 978-1-107-60307-3 Paperback

*I dedicate this book to the memory of George Rabinowitz,
a model colleague and friend, and Professor and mentor.
George was a gentle man, full of wisdom and grace,
and he is missed by many.*

Contents

Acknowledgements

I began this book (before I knew it was a book) while I was at the University of Nebraska. I am grateful for all the institutional and collegial support I received while I worked there. My friend and colleague there, Elizabeth Theiss-Morse, graciously did not throw me out of her office on the morning that I barged in, announcing that we needed to co-author an article, and that perhaps we could do so now, maybe even starting that day. Elizabeth did agree to co-author that article, but rather bemusedly suggested that perhaps we could start on a different day. That article, "National Identity and Self-Esteem," hovers over much of this book. Working on that article convinced me that the basis for many liberal nationalist and multiculturalist arguments, which is self-respect, is misguided. While this book is not directly about multiculturalism and nationalism, there are certainly implications for those debates here, some of which I draw out explicitly in the concluding chapter.

When I arrived at the University of North Carolina, I was welcomed into an intellectually vibrant and exciting political theory community. I particularly thank Mike Lienesch and Susan Bickford for being such great colleagues, and for patiently listening to my arguments in this book, sometimes over and over again. The graduate students have helped me enormously, for their insightful questions at the workshops where I presented portions of this book, and in the graduate classes I taught. I want to specifically thank Amanda Barnes Cook, Josh Miller, Carl Najdek, and Tamar Malloy for their research assistance.

I began to think of this project as a book while spending a year in Jerusalem. I thank the Lady Davis Fellowship Trust and the Institute for Advanced Studies for inviting me to spend a year away from my teaching duties at the Hebrew University of Jerusalem. Earlier versions of parts of this book were presented to several audiences, whom I thank for their questions and comments: the Conference on the Study of Political Thought in Toronto, the political theory workshops at Washington University in St. Louis, University of Virginia, Columbia

University, and at UNC; the Department of Political Science at the University of California, San Diego, the Duke-UNC political theory group, the Geography Department at the University of North Carolina at Chapel Hill, Tel-Aviv University, Queen's University in Canada, the Einstein Forum in Germany, the Center for the Study of Democracy, Toleration, and Religion at Columbia University, the Religion and Diversity Project at the University of Ottawa, the Duke Working Group on Justice, and to the Law and Pluralism group at the Institute for Advanced Studies at the Hebrew University in Jerusalem. I also thank the organizers for inviting me to present my work in progress.

Many people commented on parts of the manuscript, sometimes in much earlier forms, including Jonathan Allen, Jean Cahan, Mary Dietz, Avigail Eisenberg, Will Kymlicka, Duncan Ivison, Margaret Moore, Sarah Song, Bernard Yack, Melissa Schwartzberg, Patti Lenard, Jürg Steiner, Milada Vachudová, Mariah Zeisberg, Suzanne Dovi, Nancy Heltzel, Niraja Jayal, Gurpreet Mahajan, Gary Shiffman, Mark van Roojen, Mark Gibney, John McGowan, and Melissa Williams. Rob Reich swiftly read one chapter at the last minute. A particular thanks to Susan Bickford, Rachel Bearman, Michael Lienesch, Hollie Mann, Anna Stilz, and Jonathan Weiler who waded through the entire manuscript. Susan and Hollie actually read parts of the manuscript twice, sometimes under ridiculously tight deadlines, for which I am especially grateful. Two anonymous reviewers for Cambridge University Press gave me excellent suggestions on how to improve the manuscript. I thank John Haslam, my editor at Cambridge, for his patience and encouragement for this project.

Some of the arguments here have appeared in earlier forms, though several have been reworked and revamped. Much of Chapter 3 originally appeared as "From Historical to Enduring Injustice," *Political Theory* 35, no. 5 (2007): 550–73. Small parts of Chapter 3 and Chapter 5 first appeared in "Hinduism, Christianity, and Liberal Religious Toleration," *Political Theory* 33, no. 1 (2005): 28–57. Both are reprinted with permission from Sage Publications. Parts of Chapter 5 and Chapter 6 are taken from "Feminism, Multiculturalism, Oppression, and the State," *Ethics* 112, no. 1 (2001): 84–113 and are reprinted with permission from the University of Chicago Press. One section in Chapter 7 is adapted from "Democracy, Solidarity and Post-Nationalism," *Political Studies* 56, no. 3 (2008): 604–28 and is reprinted with permission from Blackwell Publishing.

1 | Radical injustice

In 1829 gold was discovered on the land that the Cherokee Indians lived on and called home. The state of Georgia wanted the land for its own residents. Congress passed laws allowing for the removal of Indians, which President Andrew Jackson and later President Martin van Buren supported. The Cherokee, however, who declared themselves a sovereign and independent nation and established a written constitution, went to the US Supreme Court to protest the state of Georgia's attempt to impose its laws on them. The court ruled that it had no jurisdiction in the case; while the Cherokees won an indirect victory in another case, it didn't matter much, as the federal and Georgia government were intent on expelling the Cherokee and would not allow a judicial ruling to prevent them from taking the Cherokee's land. Soon enough the US government expelled the Cherokee from their land in Georgia. Forced to walk from Georgia to Oklahoma in the middle of winter, about four thousand tribal members died (approximately a quarter of the tribe) because of the inadequate food and clothing supplied by the US government on what is now called the Trail of Tears.[1]

In 1944 Stalin accused the Crimean Tatars of collaborating with Hitler (a few had, but most did not, and many Tatar men served in the Soviet army) and expelled the Tatars from their homeland in the Ukraine, sending them to exile in Soviet Asia. Estimates vary, but perhaps nearly half of the population died en route to exile or shortly afterwards. Some returned to the Crimea after the collapse of the Soviet Union, though they have done so in the face of some resistance from those who now live in the Crimea, and many are now impoverished; many other Tatars still live in exile, waiting for a propitious moment to return.[2]

---

[1] Theda Perdue and Michael Green, *The Cherokee Nation and the Trail of Tears* (New York: Viking Press, 2007).
[2] Greta Lynn Uehling, *Beyond Memory: The Crimean Tatars' Deportation and Return* (New York: Palgrave Macmillan, 2004).

Between 1869 and 1969, the Australian government routinely took Aboriginal children from their homes, or allowed churches to do so, and placed them with white families. Estimates suggest that between 10 and 30 percent of Aboriginal children were taken from their families. The intention of some of the lawmakers involved was benevolent, to help these children assimilate into a "superior" culture, but the policy was disastrous, and that it lasted until at least 1969 is surely testimony as to how colonialism can powerfully shape perceptions, convincing people that an obviously unjust policy is actually justifiable.[3]

The US federal government assured the Lakota Sioux rights to the Black Hills in 1850s by treaty. The Black Hills were and are considered particularly sacred to the Lakota, and special ceremonies were performed there. After gold was found on the land, the US convinced a few of the Sioux to sign another treaty to limit the amount of protected land. This second treaty, however, was made contrary to the stipulations in the previous treaty about treaty revisions, and so was illegal. This land too was, and still is, mined. The Sioux eventually sued, and won in the US Supreme Court, which found the treaties giving the land away to be fraudulent. But what the Lakota Sioux won was compensation (over $700 million today, including interest), not the return of the land. The Sioux have refused to accept the money, as they maintain that this sacred land cannot be bought.[4]

Hindu nationalism, present from India's birth, has often fueled violence against the Muslim community, sometimes with the backing of the local government. In 1992, Hindu militants tore down a mosque, the Babri Masjid, which sat on a site that the militants claimed contained an important Hindu temple, while Indian police watched passively, sending ripples of fear throughout the Muslim community, and leading to riots that killed up to 2,000 people, mostly Muslims, throughout India.[5] In 2002, Hindu militants accused

---

[3] Australian Human Rights Commission, "Report of the National Inquiry into the Separation of Aboriginal and Torres Strait Islander Children from Their Families, Bringing Them Home," www.hreoc.gov.au/social_justice/bth_report/report/index.html (accessed August 10, 2010). One story from this chapter in history is illustrated in the film *Rabbit Proof Fence*.
[4] Edward Lazarus, *Black Hills/White Justice: The Sioux Nation Versus the United States: 1775 to the Present* (New York: HarperCollins, 1991).
[5] www.bbc.co.uk/news/world-south-asia-11435240.

Muslims of setting a train full of Hindu pilgrims alight in the Indian state of Gujarat (the train was almost certainly accidently lit by the pilgrims themselves), setting off a several-day-long pogrom which resulted in over 2,000 Muslim deaths with thousands more injured. Many Muslim women were raped before being burned to death, the latter fate befalling many Muslim men as well. (The Gujarat police and government were not only idle during the pogrom, but actively encouraged the Hindu mobs in their rampages.) This pogrom hangs over India, unsettled, a reminder of the place of Muslims in India.[6]

Some of these injustices – and others like them – have recently and prominently surfaced in the political consciousness in the Western world, resulting in a spate, or perhaps a flood, of apologies. Here are but a few: in 1998, National Sorry Day emerged in Australia, after a government report entitled "Bringing them Home" about the stolen generations of Aboriginal children in Australia was published. In 2008 the Australian Prime Minister apologized to Aborigines for past injustices inflicted upon them, including the "stolen generations." Shortly afterward, the Canadian Prime Minister apologized to indigenous peoples for past government actions that placed some of their children in Christian boarding schools with the intent to assimilate them. The US House of Representatives passed a resolution apologizing for slavery and Jim Crow in the summer of 2008, while state legislatures in Alabama, Maryland, and North Carolina all issued apologies for slavery. In 1993 the US Congress apologized for the overthrow of the Hawaiian monarchy one hundred years earlier.

The academy and the politicians are moving in tandem on this issue, as scholars have increasingly addressed the issue of past injustices, calling for more remembering, apologies, and reparations. While a few scattered articles on the topic appeared in the 1970s, since 2000 a spate of scholarly literature on historical injustice has emerged. In many of the most recent publications, scholars have revealed their perspectives and politics in the very titles of their works: "History and Collective Responsibility"; "Coming to Terms with Our Past"; "Taking Responsibility for the Past"; "Sins of the Parents"; and "Sins of the Nation."[7] Political communities need to take responsibility for

---

[6] Martha C. Nussbaum, *The Clash Within: Democracy, Religious Violence, and India's Future* (Cambridge, MA: Harvard University Press, 2009).

[7] Thomas McCarthy, "Coming to Terms With Our Past, Part II: On the Morality and Politics of Reparations for Slavery," *Political Theory* 32, no. 6 (2004): 750–72;

their past, this literature charges, by which they mean that apologies and reparations are due to the injured communities. These arguments typically suggest that if political communities are to be moral, then they must remember the past – and not just the past they are proud of, but parts of the past that are shameful. Many of these arguments suggest, for example, that if the United States (or Australia, Canada, and so on) is to successfully confront racism, it must confront its racist past. If we – the dominant political communities in the New World, for example – are to treat indigenous peoples properly, then we must have a better understanding and accounting of the past. An apology is often part of the solution to past injustices, while reparations, compensation, and other remedies are also put forward. The path to a better future, these arguments contend, lies in a better understanding and appreciation of how the injustices of the past affect patterns of oppression today.

Why, however, should the history of an injustice matter? The advocates of repairing historical injustices have not adequately answered this pointed question. Many critics of taking past injustices into account say what should matter is current injustices, not past ones; others argue that they did not own any slaves or commit any atrocities, that they are not responsible for what others did long ago; and still others have argued that once we begin speaking about reparations or apologies for one or two past injustices, then we are open to many similar claims for many other injustices, which we can find aplenty throughout history. If an injustice exists now, the political community should be concerned, but why is the history of the injustice important? The usual answers have focused on the importance of remembering, or on responsibility; since certain current injustices are caused by past injustices, this argument maintains, they cannot be solved without taking responsibility for the past. Yet the examples used by the advocates of correcting historical injustices – typically indigenous peoples and African Americans – suffer from injustices now, and so they leave

Janna Thompson, *Taking Responsibility for the Past: Reparation and Historical Injustice* (Cambridge: Polity, 2002); Robert Sparrow, "History and Collective Responsibility," *Australasian Journal of Philosophy* 78, no. 3 (2000): 346–59; Danielle Celermajer, *The Sins of the Nation and the Ritual of Apologies* (Cambridge University Press, 2009); Brian A. Weiner, *Sins of the Parents: The Politics of National Apologies in the United States* (Philadelphia: Temple University Press, 2005).

the challenge of the critics unanswered: if an injustice exists today, members of the political community are responsible for helping to end it. What is gained by focusing on the history of an injustice? Indeed, since the past is littered with so many injustices, isn't a focus on historical injustice a recipe for paralysis? A plea for remembering past injustices does not help answer a key question: *which* injustices should a political community remember?

Too often these advocates of repairing past injustices focus on one historical injustice (occasionally they will look at two), and take it as obvious that it should be repaired. Most of these arguments turn on the importance of memory: if only the community would better remember the history of a particular injustice, it would be moved to do something about it.[8] Yet this sort of argument says little about which historical injustices should be of concern today; it says little about why the past matters today for some injustices, but why others should be ignored; it says little about why certain injustices persist. Oddly, few arguments by political theorists and political philosophers about historical injustice actually present a theory of historical injustice. Many arguments about past injustice focus on one case. The problem with this approach is that flaws in your argument may appear when you move from one case to several, something I hope to show in the following two chapters. An argument that works in one case, but not in several comparable cases, is not theoretical but simply ad hoc.

Instead of focusing on one or two cases, I want to reframe the issue of past or historical injustice and explain the relationship between injustice and liberal democratic theory and practice. To do this, I argue for the need to shift the conceptual ground away from historical injustice; the challenge for some peoples is not just the injustice of the past but that they *still* suffer from injustice. Together, they experience what I call enduring injustice. The injustice they endure today is

[8] Lawrie Balfour, "Unreconstructed Democracy: W. E. B. Du Bois and the Case for Reparations," *American Political Science Review* 97, no. 1 (2003): 33–44; William James Booth, *Communities of Memory: On Witness, Identity, and Justice* (Ithaca, NY: Cornell University Press, 2006); Burke A. Hendrix, "Memory in Native American Land Claims," *Political Theory* 33, no. 6 (2005): 763–85; Thomas McCarthy, "Vergangenheitsbewaltigung in the USA: On the Politics of the Memory of Slavery," *Political Theory* 30, no. 5 (2002): 623–48; McCarthy, "Coming to Terms With Our Past"; Gregory W. Streich, "Is There a Right to Forget? Historical Injustices, Race, Memory, and Identity," *New Political Science* 24, no. 4 (2002): 525–42.

connected to past injustices. Instead of urging citizens and governments to take responsibility for the past, I ask instead: which injustices
from the past persist today and cry out for remedy? Why are these
injustices the ones that call for the attention of the political community, but not others? Most arguments about historical injustice assume
that if citizens in liberal states had more understanding of the past,
these injustices would disappear. But I ask instead, liberal democracies
have so successfully conquered many injustices, so why have these
particular injustices persisted?

Reframing the issue as enduring injustice, instead of past or historical injustice, shows that certain past injustices matter because of
current injustices. By showing that the past matters because of its
connection to current injustice, my arguments need not grapple with
historical injustice in itself. This new framework of enduring injustice
has many implications for arguments about past injustice. It better
explains why some injustices endure than do arguments that focus on
the past. Enduring injustice is less interested in who caused the injustice than are arguments about past injustice; these latter arguments tie
causality to responsibility, but I aim to separate the two. Reframing
historical injustice as enduring injustice leads me to argue that the idea
of reparations for past injustices is mistaken. I will also argue that
many apologies for enduring injustices are often misguided and not
very meaningful, since the injustice is in fact ongoing. I argue instead
for acknowledging the injustice, which is a process, and not a single
act. Acknowledgement can lead to apology, but usually only after
a long process of overcoming the injustice. My argument is also a
response to many of the critics of repairing past injustices. These
critics contend that what matters is current injustice, not the pedigree
of the injustice. While I will argue that contemporary injustice should
drive a political community's concern with injustice, the past matters
for enduring injustice; it matters for how we should conceive of
injustices, and how we should think of solutions to them. I argue that
enduring injustices cannot be understood without recourse to their
history. Some injustices – like exile – only make sense if the history of
the injustice matters. If an injustice persists, this begs an important
question: why has it persisted? To answer this question, I will revise
some settled considerations about liberal justice, since liberal justice
has not been able to solve the problem. This leads to another way in
which history matters: I argue too that taking enduring injustice

seriously means that the history of liberal states will matter when it comes to the legitimacy of the state enforcing its own sense of justice on certain groups. When the history of a liberal state has sordid aspects, causing or contributing to an enduring injustice, it should not always readily be ignored when we argue about the legitimacy of the state implementing liberal justice.

1.1 Injustice

Enduring injustices have roots in what I call radical injustice. The origins of radical injustice can be many; I will broadly discuss three kinds here, though there may be others. One kind of radical injustice is the case of exile and dispossession. Sometimes return to the ancestral land is possible, other times it is not. Exile and dispossession cause radical and nearly always harmful changes in a community. While a common case that arises is indigenous peoples, there are other examples: the Crimean Tatars, Jews before the creation of Israel, and Palestinians, among others. Exile is a harm since the culture of so many peoples is tied to a particular land. It is not just that the Tatars do not want to be scattered across several Asian states, it is that their stories, their myths, their architecture, and clothing, and their sense of peoplehood, are tied to their ancestral land.

 Second is the case of pointed and harsh attempts to undermine the culture of a people, which can be called cultural dispossession. Exile can undermine a culture, so exile and cultural dispossession can be connected, but need not be. A case today of a culture being undermined is Tibet, where the Chinese government is sending many Han Chinese to settle in a short period of time. (In a different way, for a long time the Turkish government tried to stamp out a Kurdish identity.[9]) The result is that many Tibetans are losing recognition of their homeland; some are becoming disorientated, and many fear that they are losing control of the changes that every culture undergoes.

Third is when a community lives under pervasive discrimination, or even terror. The example of Indian Muslims that I mentioned above fits this description; so do Israeli Muslims and African Americans, and

---

[9] There has not been a flood of Turks moving to Kurdish areas, but for many years there were severe restrictions on speaking and teaching in Kurdish.

*mistrust +
liberalism*

the many Roma (gypsies) in Europe, although members of all these groups are victims of terror less frequently these days than previously. These cases are often straightforwardly violations of liberal principles, [but when deep-seated discrimination persists over time, the mistrust that results is often hard for liberal principles to account for.]

A radical injustice makes it hard for people to feel in Thomas Christiano's words "at home in the world."[10] Christiano borrows the term from Hegel, who argues that nearly all people in the modern world are not at home in the world, since we are alienated from the institutions of modernity, an alienation he thinks can be overcome.[11] Following Christiano, however, I use the phrase in a narrower way: to be at home, to live at ease is to "have a sense of fit, connection and meaning in the world one lives in." We all want to live in a society governed by principles that we see as our own, at least partly, other-wise we feel like we are living in someone else's home. "Living in a world that corresponds in no way to one's own judgment of how the world ought to be arranged is to live in a world that is opaque and perhaps even hostile to one's interests. It is to live in a world where one does not see how legitimately to make it responsive to one's interests. One is at a loss."[12] When one is part of a group where all feel that the world is a foreign place, run by other people for other people, and where there is no or little chance to make it responsive to one's needs, then it is likely that a radical injustice has occurred.

One might respond that American progressives did not feel at home when George W. Bush was president; it seems like some white Ameri-cans feel quite ill at ease with a Black man as President. To be at home in the world does not mean that one's political ideology governs the ruling bodies. The view I put forward means that if the political procedures make it so one feels like one's interests matter, and that one has a voice; or that if your particular voice is not heard, then the voices of people similar to yours are heard, then this is a sign that you are at home in the world. The disruption caused in one's life by an election is caused by a process that one believes in, that one is a part of. By contrast, those who do not feel at home in the world do not feel

---

[10] Thomas Christiano, *The Constitution of Equality: Democratic Authority and Its Limits* (Oxford University Press, 2008), 60–62.

[11] Michael O. Hardimon, "The Project of Reconciliation: Hegel's Social Philosophy," *Philosophy and Public Affairs* 21, no. 2 (1992): 165–95.

[12] Christiano, *Constitution of Equality*, 62.

part of the process that brings change with it, either because they are excluded from the process, or their concerns and interests are rarely regarded. People who feel at home in the world generally are empowered agents, who feel able to make changes in their own lives, and to press for change in the larger world. Empowered agents are not guaranteed success; but they do feel like success is possible. They feel like others will listen to them, enough others to make them feel part of the political process, and full citizens in society at large.

Radical changes often cause people to no longer feel at home in the world. Changes at elections are not the radical change I have in mind. Being expelled from one's homeland is a radical change; being forced to give up one's own ruling structures, to be replaced by those of foreigners is also a radical change. All ways of life change, and so my suggestion is not that change itself is unjust. The concern I want to highlight is the agent and scope of the change. One kind of radical injustice occurs when a people's conceptual universe is broken down so rapidly that it becomes hard to make sense of the world. The key here is the rapidity of the breakdown; when people have to make sense of drastic changes very quickly we move from the realm of cultural change, which every community undergoes, to cultural breakdown. Cultural breakdown is not the only kind of radical injustice, but it does highlight a key feature of radical injustice: that one community severely disrupts the lives of another community so the people of the latter do not feel at home in the world.

Liberal democratic theory speaks in the language of individual rights or perhaps distributive justice; it does not usually speak in the Hegelian terms of making people feel at home in the world. But when people are not at home in the world, they are unable to pursue their conception of the good; the dislocation of some may mean that they may not even be able to conceive of the good. The dislocation may mean they have a constant unfulfilled yearning that prevents them from reaching their conception of the good. Liberalism assumes that people can readily construct their own idea of the good, but this is often not the case when there is an enduring injustice. Feeling at home in the world is not part of liberal theory, but it does seem to be an assumption with liberalism: liberal theorists generally think that people are comfortable enough in the world to pursue their own good. Yet I do not want to make feeling at home in the world a particularly liberal idea, since one may feel at home in the world in a non-liberal society.

Feeling at home in the world may be an enabling condition for liberal values to be realized, but it also may be enabling in non-liberal societies.

Radical injustices become enduring when they continue; enduring injustices are those in which the original victims are now dead. Nahshon Perez defines historical injustices as those in which all the original wrongdoers, and all the original victims, have passed away. The wrong is also noteworthy enough to merit our attention; it is not a minor case of John's stealing Jane's wallet in 1725 in London. It is an event (or events) that we know took place, so issues of information are not a major obstacle to understanding the injustice. Historical injustices concern people who were *not* involved in the wrong.[13] They took place some time ago; the parties involved are now dead. I would add that historical injustices are injuries done to groups; it is the harm done to a group of people, targeted because of their identity, that commands attention. So the topic of transitional justice – how does a country move from a repressive regime to a democratic one and take account of the injustices of the recent past without crippling the present and future – is not one that I take up here. The efficacy and importance of Truth and Reconciliation Commissions or compensation to victims of radical injustices are not concerns of this book, since these are usually matters where the injustice is more recent, and where the victims or the relatives are alive. Reparations to Japanese Americans unjustly interned during the Second World War, or to Holocaust victims are not within the scope of this book, since reparations to victims who are alive present a different set of questions than those of enduring injustice.

A radical injustice can be thought of as enduring when the injustice lasts for at least two generations, and it seems like it will continue on without some clear change in policy or attitudes. There is no sure way to determine what time period is enough to pass before an injustice is called enduring. In authoritarian states, it is not surprising when injustices endure. But in liberal states we do expect justice, or at least a partial justice, to triumph. Before liberalism is termed a failure, there should be good reason to believe that liberalism is unable to alleviate

---

[13] Nahshon Perez, "On Compensation and Return: Can the 'Continuing Injustice Argument' for Compensating Historical Injustices Justify Compensation for Such Injustices Or the Return of Property?," *Journal of Applied Philosophy* 28, no. 2 (2011): 151–68.

what does this mean for the black experience in the U.S. ?

the injustice. (If after two generations matters are getting better, then it seems reasonable to give the liberal state more time; but if after two generations, the injustice appears embedded within society, then it may be time to search for other solutions to the problem.) One generation is clearly too short a time period in which to judge an injustice impossible to repair; it is unreasonable to expect a society to immediately treat all newcomers – or those considered to be different – like everyone else, for example. Yet four generations (something like one hundred years) seems rather long. If by the third generation, the grandchildren of the newcomers or those newly in contact with the liberal state, are living what appear to be unjust lives with little reason to believe that will soon change, then it appears as if the injustice is enduring. If the lives of immigrants and their progeny, for example, are improving, then they may live unjust lives, but not suffer from enduring injustice.

def.

An enduring injustice began as a radical injustice, but the original injustice may no longer be committed, or the injustice has tempered over time. Indigenous peoples are not hunted down today, expelled from their lands, and so on. Buffalo herds are being resurrected, not killed off. The Tatars are not being continually expelled. The injustices that the Dalits face are less today than in centuries past. Yet the effects of the radical injustice are still felt today; or the group still suffers from an injustice that is akin to or related to the radical injustice in important ways. The enduring injustice began as a radical injustice; the radical injustice was left to fester, and as it became enduring there were either no attempts to end it, or the attempts that occurred failed.

The present and future are implicated in an enduring injustice in at least three ways. First, there is good reason to think the present injustice is in important ways connected to past injustices. Causality arguments that stretch through decades or centuries are often hard to prove, but we can make reasonable suppositions. One could argue that the misery of Native Americans was caused by American policies that pushed indigenous peoples aside, shamelessly broke treaties with them, treated them harshly and so on. Yet we don't know what would have happened if Americans treated indigenous peoples with more respect and decency; it is hard to imagine that the traditional indigenous way of life would have survived once whites took to industrialization. It is likely that if indigenous peoples were treated with more respect, they would have had more control (not complete control) of the transformative process they encountered, and they would have

 # |

wrestled with modernity from a position of cultural coherence and not decimation. This almost surely would mean that their position today would be much different and better. Many indigenous peoples are suffering in many ways, and it seems likely that if they had been treated better by the colonialists and then the Americans, they would be better off today.

Second, it seems that without a change in the course of action, the injustice will persist. Nearly all the arguments on historical injustice share this assumption, though this does not mean this assumption is correct. There is no way to know the future with certainty – it is possible that imprisonment rates for Black Americans will suddenly plummet, while their educational attainment and income will begin to rise, but given current and past patterns, this seems very unlikely. Entrenched injustices do not have to stay that way, but we should not believe that an injustice that persists for two or more generations will fade.

Third, the pattern of past and current injustice will often (but not always) lead to a problem of trust. Trust correctly looms large in the literature on historical injustice. Leif Wenar argues, perhaps with some exaggeration: "Justice, taken as relations of mutual recognition and trust, cannot now go forward in these contexts because of the lingering presence of the past in the minds" of groups that are victims of historical injustice.[14] Mistrust may not be quite the barricade that Wenar suggests, but it surely makes it harder to achieve justice.

1.2 Liberal justice

Most arguments about past injustice work within standard theories of liberal theory; they accept liberal justice as the solution to injustice. The idea of liberalism, unfortunately, has different meanings in the academic and political worlds. By liberalism, I mean classical liberalism, the idea that individual rights should be protected, and that government should be limited; the government should be divided so the power of any one branch is circumscribed; liberalism is

---

[14] Leif Wenar, "Reparations for the Future," *Journal of Social Philosophy* 37, no. 3 (2006), 403; Thompson, *Taking Responsibility for the Past*, Part I; Melissa Williams, *Voice, Trust and Memory: Marginalized Groups and the Failings of Liberal Representation* (Princeton University Press, 1998); Duncan Ivison, *Postcolonial Liberalism* (Cambridge University Press, 2002).

characterized by the rule of law rather than of men and women. Fair procedures are needed to enact laws, to treat those accused with committing a crime impartially, and so on. Liberal citizens are equal to one another; they have the same political rights and hopefully something close to equality of opportunity. They also have equal liberty, more or less: each is able to pursue his or her plans and projects. Liberal governments should be strong, but limited.

I loosely work within the framework of what is called liberal egalitarianism. Egalitarian liberals see large inequities in terms of wealth and money as unjust, which justifies the redistribution of wealth, and moving resources toward education, since a good education is an important mechanism for social mobility.[15] Liberal egalitarianism often turns to economic redistribution and education as the key methods by which to reach equality. While libertarian views of justice, which are part of the classical liberal tent, tend to argue against state-directed economic redistribution, I will show how one of the most important libertarian views supports economic redistribution when the issue is enduring injustice.[16]

Another aspect of liberal justice that I assume here is the idea that liberalism is committed to the idea of equal respect and equal concern of persons. The moral equality of persons is central to many versions of liberalism, with liberal egalitarians arguing that an equal right to vote and equal individual rights is insufficient for equality. This idea is widely though not universally held; more controversial are the political implications that follow from these ideas. For most liberals, however, formal rights are insufficient to ensure equality, an assumption held by nearly all the thinkers I discuss in the following pages. The idea behind equal regard and respect suggests that safeguarding individual rights may be insufficient for equality if some people are left victims of severe discrimination or are impoverished. Equal respect, unlike individual rights, insists that everyone's voice should be heard

[15] Rawls's second principle of justice – that social and economic inequalities are to be arranged so that they are to be of the greatest benefit to the least-advantaged members of society – is a principle that is mostly interpreted in terms of economic redistribution. See generally Kymlicka's analysis of liberal egalitarianism in Will Kymlicka, *Contemporary Political Philosophy: An Introduction* (Oxford University Press, 2001), ch. 2.

[16] I examine Robert Nozick's libertarianism in Chapter 2. Robert Nozick, *Anarchy, State, and Utopia* (New York: Basic Books, 1974).

within the political community, and that all parts of the community ought to be treated with due concern.[17]

One issue I take up in the ensuing chapters is this: what happens when a group of people are consistently and for long periods of time not treated with equal concern and respect? Liberalism has no obvious answer to this problem. One might say that this is an issue for liberal practice, not theory, but I will argue that long-standing injustices have implications for liberal theory. I will argue here that in some cases justice and injustice are not congruent; that is, overcoming some injustices does not mean that liberal justice will triumph. More pointedly, I will also contend that a better defense of individual rights, and a modest or moderate redistribution of wealth will often not solve the enduring injustice.[18] While sometimes these things will help, I will also argue that the history of injustice often casts doubt on liberal solutions. If liberalism could solve the injustice readily, it would not have endured.

Part of my argument suggests that some kinds of enduring injustices are revealed on liberalism's own terms, but I will also argue that liberalism is blind to other kinds of enduring injustice. Several kinds of enduring injustice cannot be well understood without taking the collective narrative and the history of a group into account, which the presentist bias within liberalism typically overlooks. Liberal theory has a difficult time accounting for an exiled people's attachment to land. If the individual rights of the Tatars are protected, if they live in a just society, then liberal justice may be fulfilled. Yet living in exile may still be an injustice, one that has endured over time. Similarly, liberal theory cannot readily make sense of the idea of sacred land.

---

[17] See generally Chapter 3 of Kymlicka, *Contemporary Political Philosophy*. Equal concern and respect is implicit in the capabilities approach advocated by Amartya Sen and Martha Nussbaum. See Martha C. Nussbaum, *Women and Human Development: the Capabilities Approach* (Cambridge University Press, 2000).

[18] Iris Young criticized distributive justice in similar terms. Iris Marion Young, *Justice and the Politics of Difference* (Princeton University Press, 1990). Young's argument is not about enduring injustice (though past injustice does play a role in her argument). Still, one difference between her argument and mine is that she aims to expand upon the notion of justice, while I think justice is limited as a tool when it comes to enduring injustice. Young's argument against liberalism is also more totalizing than mine. Young sees liberalism as a failure, where I see it as having limitations.

Collective narratives also play an important role in the third example, the mistrust that many groups, like Indian Muslims or African Americans, have of their government. Stories of discrimination and prejudice help in the interpretation of current discrimination – random discrimination is one thing, but if people with a particular racial or religious identity routinely face this discrimination and have done so for years, that is quite another. An isolated incident may be troubling, but a long-standing pattern of discrimination against a particular group, is cause for mistrust.

This raises a puzzle. Liberals routinely argue that liberalism can see its own failures, or that problematic practices within liberal states do not necessarily mean a fault of liberal theory. This is a coherent approach, one without paradoxes. There can readily be a gap between theory and practice, and there is no reason to think that all failures within liberal states can or should be attributed to liberal theory. I will argue here, however, that non-liberal solutions are needed to tackle some problems of enduring injustice, an argument which certainly threatens to become paradoxical. How can liberalism recognize its failures, and accept non-liberal solutions to them?

I will follow three different approaches to the paradox of liberals endorsing non-liberal solutions to injustice. The first is familiar, and is what I will call the temporary detour from liberal justice. Here the potential paradox is solved by saying that liberal principles of justice in a particular case cannot be realized by liberal procedures of justice, so a detour from the procedures is needed. Once the principles of liberal justice are realized, then the detour can end, and liberal principles can be fulfilled. Affirmative action can be seen as an example of a detour, but I will point out others. The second approach is to say that some issues are simply not spoken to by liberalism. This is perhaps less a failure of liberalism than a silence of liberalism, but one that must be filled somehow. The best example of this is the issue of exile: a longing to return to one's ancestral homeland – and the idea of sacred land generally – is not an issue captured by the language of liberalism. Even many of the recent arguments about liberal nationalism and multiculturalism do not speak to these issues.[19] In these cases I will

---

[19] Most of these arguments assume that the nation is territorially concentrated, and wants to build up or retain the political institutions it currently has. See, for example, Chaim Gans, *The Limits of Nationalism* (Cambridge University Press, 2003); Will Kymlicka, *Multicultural Citizenship: A Liberal Theory of Minority*

argue that liberals can recognize an injustice, while endorsing solutions that do not violate liberal principles. Liberal justice does not encompass all of the possible human goods, and the denial of some of them – like return from exile – is an injustice. Part of the idea here is that liberal justice and injustice often move on different planes. What I mean by this is that the kinds of matters that liberal justice speaks to are much different than the harm of exile. Liberal justice is concerned with settled political institutions and how they interact with individuals. It does not to speak to the issue when a people is not living on its homeland, and lacks political institutions. While theories of liberal justice tend to be all encompassing, it is not paradoxical for liberals to recognize that some harms may take place outside the scope of liberal justice. Liberals readily recognize the importance of religion to many people; and if they can do that, they can recognize the importance of sacred land. Liberal theory is silent about this issue, but liberal democratic states and liberals themselves need not keep up this silence; if they do, then this silence becomes a failure.

The third approach to the paradox is the hardest for liberals to accept, that in some cases of enduring injustice the possible solution to the injustice may violate the dictates of liberal justice. In these cases, there has been a failure of liberalism, and sometimes the appeal to liberal principles in cases of failure is not effective. My argument here will be that liberals ought to recognize that when liberal states continually and over time fail to treat a group of people with equal (or, I will later argue, at least decent) regard, then their legitimacy to impose their view of justice on them is put into question. I will argue that liberals should accept that a long-standing failure of liberal practice does in fact cast doubt on the legitimacy of the liberal state. I will also argue that some of the failures of liberal practice can be partially attributed to liberal theory, or at least to some versions of liberal theory. In other words, liberal theory is partly (but not fully) to blame for some enduring injustices. In other cases, liberal states inherited injustices that liberalism cannot readily solve. The genesis of the problem may not be liberal, but if liberal tools cannot end the injustice, then liberals should recognize that non-liberal solutions may be needed.

Rights (Oxford University Press, 1995); Avishai Margalit and Joseph Raz, "National Self-Determination," *Journal of Philosophy* 87, no. 9 (1990): 439–61; David Miller, *On Nationality* (Oxford University Press, 1995).

Enduring injustices are not, by definition, easy to solve. My arguments for solutions are often modest and uncertain; the certainty that is either explicit or implicit in many arguments about historical injustice that more understanding of the past injustice will seamlessly lead to justice is, I will argue, misguided. More understanding is often a good goal to strive for, and I will argue that political communities should often do more to acknowledge the enduring injustices in their midst. But many liberals think the path to justice is often blocked by misunderstanding or a weak political will. This is surely sometimes the case, but I will argue that the path to justice in many cases of enduring injustice is uncertain.

In the latter part of this book, I suggest a tragic liberalism. A tragic liberalism does not think that one value can reign supreme or that liberalism can solve all injustices; sometimes, there will have to be trade-offs between different values. My argument for a tragic liberalism is influenced by Isaiah Berlin. Berlin teaches that there are several competing worthwhile values; that one value does not necessarily trump all others; and that balancing the different values is not always easy.[20] The approach I use here assumes that there are pluralistic worthwhile values that sometimes conflict with one another. A second part of a tragic liberalism is that it accepts a certain open-endedness about the future, since I do not believe we can be certain about how to solve many enduring injustices. It is possible that at some point in the future liberal justice will be able to reign fully. My argument does not rule out this possibility, but it does suggest that we liberals should be open to the idea that liberal justice will not fully unfold in a clear and obvious fashion in all cases. A tragic liberalism, I argue in the concluding chapter, should also be a chastened liberalism: one that is less confident about its ability to solve problems than its nineteenth-century counterpart.

One question to ask then is, why liberalism? If liberalism has failed in the cases of enduring injustice, why not turn to a different political theory altogether? There are undoubtedly limits to liberalism, but there are limits to every political theory, every theory of justice and every theory of human community. We should be wary of any political

---

[20] Isaiah Berlin, *Four Essays on Liberty* (Oxford University Press, 1969); William A. Galston, *Liberal Pluralism: The Implications of Value Pluralism for Political Theory and Practice* (Cambridge University Press, 2002).

theory that thinks that it can solve all or most of a polity's political problems. We can have theories of justice, and these will apply in many cases, but it is hard if not impossible to develop a theory of justice that will solve all the injustices of the world, since there are a rather large variety of injustices. To say then that liberalism has flaws does not mean it is completely flawed. Many of liberalism's rivals – post-modernism, radical feminism, Marxism – offer criticisms of liberalism but lack much in the way of substantive alternatives. Liberalism's core principles – individual rights, the moral equality of persons, the justification for the redistribution of wealth – are powerful if also limited. Liberalism's pluralistic nature allows it to more readily accept criticisms and amendments than other political theories. Finally, as I will argue in Chapter 2, the idea of historical injustice cannot appear in totalizing criticisms of liberalism like Marxism. It is liberalism's pluralism that reveals some of its failures.

Thinking about the limits and conflicts of justice and the prejudices of liberalism cannot take place in the abstract. My method is empirical, comparative and theoretical; different cases are used to highlight normative issues. A variety of cases is used to highlight my arguments in the following pages, though three particular countries dominate my examples: Israel, India, and the United States, with some attention to the Tatars and Tibet, among other cases. I look at the first two countries because they are both democracies with liberal elements, but they depart from some of the usual features of Western liberalism in important ways. Both Israel and India are democracies that were colonized by the British, reached independence about the same time, had very bloody births, have hostile neighbors, have their family law systems governed by religious law, have besieged Muslim minorities, are predominately non-Christian, and have strong right-wing political movements that are interwoven with the dominant religion. I look at the United States as a good example of a liberal democracy; it is simply a Western liberal country that I know well. I do look, however, toward Europe, Canada, Australia, and New Zealand on occasion.

Some of the examples I use are not from liberal states. Ukraine is something of a democracy, but hardly a liberal democracy; Turkey is not a robust liberal democracy in the same way as many Western European states are, though certainly more of one than China, which also appears in this book when I discuss Tibet. The examples I use from these countries all nonetheless pose challenges for liberalism; if these countries were to become (more) liberal we would want to know how they should respond to the enduring injustices I point to, since there is not an obvious liberal solution to them. We would want to know how liberal states should try to pressure these countries to act in these cases of enduring injustice. Nonetheless, that I have higher hopes for liberal states to try to end the enduring injustices within their midst than for non-liberal states is testimony to the moral standards of liberal states.

1.3 Outline of the book

Those who argue that historical injustice ought to be addressed treat the category as obvious, and so never ask why the category has now become so important. Until a few years ago, the problem of past injustices barely existed. In Chapter 2 I ask and answer this question: Why now, in this historical era, has the problem of past injustice arisen? Past injustices have almost always existed in the world, so why now are political communities concerned with this issue? The idea of historical injustice is relatively new and never occurred to earlier modern thinkers since they thought that all of history was unjust, except to the elite. I will argue that it is certain failures of the liberal idea of progress that reveal enduring injustice. The frustration that many face at this lack of progress leads them to argue that historical injustices are a problem that liberal states and liberal theory ought to face better, partly by better recognizing their failures. Yet their arguments are too backward looking, as I explain.

Chapters 3 to 5 show how history does and does not matter for enduring injustices. The third chapter explains in detail the idea of enduring injustice. It also challenges the idea of a country needing to take responsibility for the past, while arguing against the idea that only current injustice matters. In this chapter I explain why the history of certain past injustices matters, which leads me to redefine the idea of past or historical injustice as one of enduring injustice. Certain injustices only make sense if we take history – or collective memory – into account. A view of justice that ignores the past will simply not see some important injustices.

In Chapter 4 I try to show that the increasingly popular idea of apologizing for the past is often not thought through well, and urge instead that we think in terms of acknowledgement. Apologies are moments in time, but acknowledgement is a process that may, over time, lead to apology. Acknowledgement (and apology) also lie outside the usual liberal framework of justice, since it is not about rights, equality, or the redistribution of wealth. Acknowledgement should not just note the injustices of the past; the complexity of the past should also be acknowledged. The injustices of the past did not only produce terrible things; nor are the victims of enduring injustices always and only innocent. Further, acknowledgement ought to note the difficulty in resolving the enduring injustice; some trade-offs and compromises will have to be made to try to end some enduring injustices.

In Chapter 5 I show how the history of enduring injustices matters in a different way. Here, the history of the injustice casts questions over the legitimacy of the liberal state's rule over certain groups. In the first part of this book, I argue that certain kinds of injustice cannot be understood without taking their history into account. In Chapters 5 and 6 I argue that it is the history of liberal states that matters when we try to implement justice today. Liberal theories of justice are typically abstracted from the state that implements these principles, but here I bring them together. I begin Chapter 5 with a discussion of ideal and non-ideal theory, and then discuss a temporary detour from liberal justice, which can then secure the conditions for liberal justice. I then argue that in some cases of enduring injustice the liberal state lacks the legitimacy to impose its version of justice on all groups. This is one important way of acknowledging the enduring injustice. Acknowledging the history of an enduring injustice will mean taking into account the history of liberal practice in certain cases. The cases I use in Chapter 5 – Indian and Israeli Muslims, and indigenous peoples – also figure prominently in Chapter 6 (in which I also discuss Tibet). In Chapter 6 I argue that justice will be elusive in some cases of enduring injustice. In these cases, I argue that liberal justice should not be imposed on groups, but for the rules of these communities to be legitimate they must be imposed democratically. While I argue that some groups should retain their partial autonomy (or be able to exercise partial autonomy), questions of what makes their rule-making procedures legitimate need to be addressed. I argue for a democratic form of legitimacy that leaves open the possibility that these communities can eventually embrace liberal justice but does not insist that they do so. I also argue in this chapter that ending an enduring injustice does not mean the triumph of justice, that some-times ending the oppressive practices faced by a group does not mean that liberal justice will triumph within the group. Though it seems that ending an injustice should allow justice to flourish, this is not always the case. On a related note, I warn against romanticizing victims in this chapter.

In Chapter 7 I discuss some partial success stories, where enduring injustices have been partly repaired. These partial successes occurred because the victims pressed their claims, but also because the relevant government responded to these claims. I conclude with discussions of several implications of my arguments. I argue that liberals today should not have the same confidence in progress as earlier liberals; instead of assuming progress, I argue for a restrained view of hope. This leads me to suggest a chastened liberalism. Second, I argue that liberals should become more welcoming to pluralism, even to plural-istic conceptions of justice, and accept the idea of what I call overlap-ping communities. I then discuss the implications my argument has for pluralism and certain recent arguments about post-nationalism, in which memory and narrative play a diminished role. I suggest some cautionary notes about rushing toward post-nationalism. I end the book by revisiting the idea of feeling at home in the world, noting that many current liberal citizens do feel at home in the world. To make others feel at home will undoubtedly make many uncomfortable. I explain why this is the case, and why despite this being an obstacle to overcoming enduring injustice, the difficulty of doing so does not mean we should not try.

2 | *Which injustices? What groups?*

Why has concern about past injustices arisen recently? Calls for reparations did begin in the late 1960s, but did not pick up steam until two decades later. Academic articles about past injustices and reparations began with a very slow trickle in the 1970s and the 1980s (with most arguing against the idea). A few more academic works appeared in the 1990s, with the issue coming of age by the year 2000 in the academic literature, with a spate of articles and a smaller number of books published on the subject, along with a flood of government apologies. Many of these arguments maintain that (some) people today are responsible for the past, though there are important dissenters. I discuss the substance of these arguments in the next chapter, but here I want to ask two questions that are rarely posed, much less discussed. First, why in *this historical moment* has the issue of past injustice arisen? The idea of historical injustice never occurred to people in the nineteenth century (or earlier); so why has it arisen now as a concept? Second, of the countless past injustices, how does one pick which victims of past injustice deserve redress today?

The many arguments about historical injustice do not ask why there is now so much concern about the issue; nor can these many arguments help determine which past injustices should be of political concern and which should not. Why are Huguenots and Chinese Americans never or rarely mentioned as victims of historical injustice? Or Irish Americans? Or women or workers? The advocates of rectifying historical injustice argue that the shape of the history of injustice matters, and that governments have a responsibility to rectify injustices done in their name in the past. But this plea for more remembering is much too general and vague to be politically or theoretically useful.

There is a curious refusal to think about the idea of past injustice conceptually among the many theorists and philosophers who write about the issue. The idea of historical injustice is simply assumed to be a problem with which a political community should wrestle.

One strategy often taken up by some philosophers is to argue that there should be compensation or reparations for past injustices. This argument has spawned a discussion of identity – what if the victims of injustice would not exist but for the injustice? – that simply puts us off track: nearly all of us in the Western world, if not all of us, have ancestors that have suffered grievous injustices. The process of modernization was wrenching, violent, uprooting many, and full of injustice. Tracing wrongs through generations, and trying to sort out the identity problem is simply a misguided way to discern which injustices should concern us today.

A second approach focuses on the importance of memory, suggesting that if only the political community would better remember the history of a particular injustice, it would be moved to do something about it.[1] This model of historical injustice, however, says little to the many injustices of the past. The oppressors of the Tatars (expelled by Stalin from the Crimea) no longer exist; and it is unclear if and why Chinese Americans or French Protestants deserve compensation for the injustices their ancestors suffered, since they generally no longer suffer from these injustices. Of course, there are many other past injustices that are rarely or never discussed today. Moreover, these arguments do not tell us why the particular injustice they discuss is the one (or one among many) that should be of concern. Thomas McCarthy suggests that we Americans should be concerned about past injustices to Native Americans, Mexican Americans, Puerto Ricans, Alaskan Eskimos, and immigrants.[2] If that is the case shouldn't we also be concerned about women and workers as well? Perhaps we should reverse the lens, and determine which group is not a victim of historical injustice and work from there. This method, of course, would produce quite a small list. Yet if the concept of historical injustice encompasses almost everyone,

---

[1] Lawrie Balfour, "Unreconstructed Democracy: W. E. B. Du Bois and the Case for Reparations," *American Political Science Review* 97, no. 1 (2003): 33–44; William James Booth, *Communities of Memory: On Witness, Identity, and Justice* (Ithaca, NY: Cornell University Press, 2006); Burke A. Hendrix, "Memory in Native American Land Claims," *Political Theory* 33, no. 6 (2005): 763–85; Thomas McCarthy, "Coming to Terms With Our Past, Part II: On the Morality and Politics of Reparations for Slavery," *Political Theory* 32, no. 6 (2004): 750–72.

[2] Thomas McCarthy, "Vergangenheitsbewaltigung in the USA: On the Politics of the Memory of Slavery," *Political Theory* 30, no. 5 (2002), 624.

what good can it do? A theory of historical injustice ought to have a conceptual lens that helps us to see which injustices should be repaired, and which deserve less attention. The past is full of injustices, and so any argument that does not tell us which ones the political community should concern itself with is failing in a basic task.

My suggestion here is that we can best think about which historically victimized groups should be of concern today by answering the prior question of why the concept of past injustice is now a concern to so many. I locate the rise of historical injustice in the idea of progress, or rather the exceptions to progress. There is an assumption within liberalism that citizens within liberal states will be able to form and pursue their life's plans and projects, and be treated with equal respect. When this wasn't true for some groups, as it was not in the nineteenth century, most liberals assumed that it would be true soon enough. This idea of progress carried forward to the 1960s, when the civil rights era arrived, and many assumed that progress would once again sweep away injustice. Similarly, while many are frustrated by the discrimination against gays and lesbians, another powerful narrative is that over time this discrimination will fade away; one assumes that matters will get better for all soon enough. In one court case, the court declared: "In this case, as in *Perez* and *Loving,* a statute deprives individuals of access to an institution of fundamental legal, personal, and social significance – the institution of marriage – because of a single trait: skin color in *Perez* and *Loving,* sexual orientation here. As it did in *Perez* and *Loving,* history must yield to a more fully developed understanding of the invidious quality of the discrimination."[3] We live in a human rights era, where many people assume that people's rights, particularly of those in the Western democracies, will be protected, and that all citizens will be treated with equal respect. The exceptions to these expectations – when many assume that treating certain groups with equal respect is not about to occur – makes for the rise of the idea of historical injustice. The idea that surfaces in this chapter is that it is present concerns that drive the interest in past injustice.

---

[3] *Goodridge v. Department of Public Health.* 440 Mass. 309, 798 N.E.2d 941 (MA, 2003).

2.1 The limits of remembering

Some advocates of repairing historical injustice suggest that somehow the past calls us, or we are obligated to remember its injustices. Pablo De Greiff says: "We have an obligation to remember what our fellow citizens cannot be expected to forget."[4] Similarly, W. James Booth argues that the "past wants to be remembered." The past is there for us to remember, which we are called to do: "In invoking it, and giving it voice and remembrance, we answer its call. We do not make, or construct, this past."[5] Others argue that nations are intergenerational communities; their institutions and moral relationships persist over time and through generations. Members of these nations rightfully think they made demands on their successors; the same is true for obligations. A political community reaches from the past to the future, so we as a political community are responsible for the past just as it affects the moral character of our society. A typical argument is this: "Each generation of citizens, whether native or foreign-born, inherits the burdens of membership – the national debts, as it were – together with the benefits of membership." Janna Thompson says that: "To be worthy of respect, a nation has to be prepared to fulfill its historical responsibilities."Individual citizens ought to regard "the past of their nation as a source of obligation and entitlement."[6] By being part of a community with a history we become responsible for that history; and so if an injustice occurred in our political community's past, then we are responsible for that injustice, or so these arguments seem to suggest.

   Yet people cannot be expected to remember all historical injustices. The idea that the past calls us does not tell us which past is calling; which parts of the past we can remember must be chosen. The past in its entirety cannot be there waiting to be remembered, since we forget

---

[4] Quoted in McCarthy, "Vergangenheitsbewaltigung," 629.
[5] Booth, *Communities of Memory*, 258.
[6] McCarthy, "Coming to Terms with Our Past, Part II," 757; Janna Thompson, *Taking Responsibility for the Past: Reparation and Historical Injustice* (Cambridge: Polity, 2002), 68. For other arguments about history and responsibility, see Farid Abdel-Nour, "National Responsibility," *Political Theory* 31, no. 5 (2003): 693–719; Duncan Ivison, *Postcolonial Liberalism* (Cambridge University Press, 2002), Ch. 5; Brian A. Weiner, *Sins of the Parents: The Politics of National Apologies in the United States* (Philadelphia: Temple University Press, 2005); Chandran Kukathas, "Responsibility for the Past: How to Shift the Burden," *Politics, Philosophy and Economics* 2, no. 2 (2003): 165–90.

most of it, as we must: "it is impossible to recover or recount more than a tiny fraction of what has taken place." The content of the past is "virtually infinite."[7] I will not belabor the point, but history is boundless; it is beyond the recall capacity of any person or of a people to remember even a tiny part of history. To remember the past is to choose to remember a particular past: *remembering means choosing.* The idea that the nation is an intergenerational community and so in some sense is responsible for past injustices does not say much about which injustices we should remember or which past injustices need redress.

Workers, women, immigrants, people of the "wrong" religion, indigenous peoples, various ethnic and national groups: the list of victims of injustice throughout history is not merely long, but very, very long. Which historical injustices are the ones that deserve some kind of repair now? The literature on historical injustices usually focuses on two groups, indigenous peoples and Black Americans, but does not say why others are not included. If Canada restored rights to Aboriginal peoples, former Prime Minister Trudeau maintained in an argument echoed by some skeptics of repairing historical injustice, then Canada would have to grant rights to French-Canadians, the Acadians, and Japanese-Canadians, all of whom were treated badly at some point in Canadian history.[8] The US could add many more groups: not just Blacks and Native Americans, but Jewish Americans, Irish Americans, Italian Americans, Catholics, Asian Americans, and others. There is also an absurdity problem here: if all historical injustices deserve compensation, then we need to be prepared for many, many claims. The dean of an Egyptian law school recently announced that he is investigating suing all the Jews in the world for taking items from Egypt during the Exodus.[9] Though it would seem that the Jews

---

[7] David Lowenthal, *The Past is a Foreign Country* (Cambridge University Press, 1999), 214.

[8] Pierre Trudeau, "Remarks on Aborginal and Treaty Rights. Excerpts From a Speech Given August 8th, 1969," in Peter A. Cumming and Neil H. Mickenberg, eds., *Native Rights in Canada* (Toronto: Indian-Eskimo Association of Canada in association with General Pub. Co., 1972), 331–32. For the latter of these injustices, see Barry Broadfoot, *Years of Sorrow, Years of Shame: The Story of the Japanese Canadians in World War II* (Toronto: Doubleday Canada, 1977); for the Acadians see Geoffrey Gilbert Plank, *An Unsettled Conquest: The British Campaign Against the Peoples of Acadia* (Philadelphia: University of Pennsylvania Press, 2001).

[9] Bruce Birnbaum, "A Family Deposition: Should Egypt Receive Reparations for the Exodus?," www.theatlantic.com/doc/200401/birnbaum.

would have a more powerful case for compensation for their slave labor during their years under the Pharaohs, both cases seem silly. Skeptics of repairing historical injustice can argue that there are too many groups that have suffered from historical injustices to repair or compensate for them all, and so liberal states should forget about past injustices and concentrate on present injustices, of which there are plenty.

Arguments today that suggest that we are, somehow, called to remember the past overlook the fact that we forget most of history: how could it possibly be otherwise? Americans are often charged with being especially forgetful, but all peoples (and all people) forget most of the past. It's not that the past calls to us, it is that we today call to the past; but not to any past, only to particular pasts. The idea that many political theorists have assumed is that the past has a grip on the present, but I will argue nearly the opposite in this and the next chapter: that the current interest in historical injustice is fueled by present-day concerns and the future. This does not mean that people can do without the past, or that we are or can be ahistorical beings. That the past is important, however, does not mean it is simply out there waiting to be remembered. We all need the past, we all live in a narrative that has a past and a present and looks toward the future, but we construct the past in certain ways. Our collective narratives include certain events and exclude others; it makes sense of the past, the present and our view of the future by including some events and excluding others.

This construction of the past does not mean it is false or invented. Most of us do not simply make up the past (though perhaps this happens sometimes) but we must pick and choose from the past, as we shape it into a narrative. This is true for individuals and groups; and it is an ongoing process for both. The idea of historical injustice depends on how the past is interpreted, which in turn depends on perceptions of the present and future. History does not simply unfold for us in an obvious fashion that calls out to us to be remembered in an evident way. To decide that some past injustices but not others should be remembered and that some past injustices have normative force – that is, that some past injustices weigh on the present and call out for repair – assumes a certain interpretation of history and a certain view of the present and the future. If we say that past injustices confer obligations on us now, then it is not enough to simply describe historical events; we need an account of why some past events should command our attention while others can be ignored.

2.2 Problems with reparations

Arguments that try to focus on the historical nature of an injustice and the need for it to be redressed fail because they cannot say why any particular injustice ought to be of concern. Part of the problem is that these arguments implicitly assume that most of the past was just, which is surely a spectacularly false assumption. Such a false assumption is part of reparation arguments, which look backward and implicitly assume a mostly just past. One argument for reparations focuses on exploited labor, which is sometimes used as a reason for reparations for Black Americans. Some advocates note that members of the dominant community in the US benefited (and benefit) from the forced labor of slaves: "Our national inheritance was to a large degree unjustly acquired at the expense of African Americans. The issue is not whether someone has personally benefited from slavery, but if they share in and benefit from an unjustly acquired and unfairly distributed national inheritance. This is not a matter of collective guilt but of collective responsibility."[10] This argument can readily become the basis for a claim for reparations to African Americans. Renée Hill argues Black Americans "are still owed a debt for the labor of their ancestors for which there has not yet been payment." Hill's argument suggests that debts are inherited: "If person A borrowed money from the grandfather of person B and never paid the money back, the money would still be owed to the descendants of person B's grandfather. The wages would constitute a heritable debt which would be passed on to the next generation's legatees."[11] Consequently, the labor stolen from slaves is owed to their descendants. If the slaves die with a

---

[10] McCarthy, "Coming to Terms With Our Past," 758. See also Randall Robinson, *The Debt: What America Owes to Blacks* (New York: Penguin, 2001) and Daniel Butt, "On Benefiting From Injustice," *Canadian Journal of Philosophy* 37, no. 1 (2007): 129–52.

[11] Renée A. Hill, "Compensatory Justice: Over Time and Between Groups," *Journal of Political Philosophy* 10, no. 4 (2002), 411–12. See too Robert Westley, "Many Billions Gone: Is it Time to Reconsider the Case for Black Reparations?," *Boston College Third World Law Journal* 19 (1998): 429–76, and Bernard Boxill, "The Morality of Reparations," *Social Theory and Practice* 2, no. 1 (1972): 113–24. Generally, people do not inherit the debts of their

debt owed to them, their descendants inherit that debt. Though many advocates do not distinguish between compensation and reparation, Hill argues that this is not compensation for historical injustice, but a repayment of a debt. Those that benefit from this unpaid debt are liable to pay the debt back.

Black Americans are hardly the only group that has worked unjustly, however. The working conditions and wages in Western countries during the industrializing years were quite horrible; many workers were treated harshly, unfairly, and sometimes violently. Indeed, it was these working conditions that spurred on socialism; the intellectual architects of socialism were appalled at the working conditions of the laboring classes. In a well-known passage from *Capital* in the section called the "Working Day," Marx chronicles the working life of Mary Anne Walkley, who died after working twenty-six hours straight making dresses for the wealthy. She worked on average sixteen-and-a-half hours a day, often without a break. She worked "with 60 other girls, 30 in one room, that only afforded 1/3 of the cubic feet of air required for them. At night, they slept in pairs in one of the stifling holes into which the bedroom was divided by partitions of board."[12] After her death, a local newspaper decried "our white slaves, who are toiled into the grave, for the most part silently pine and die."[13] Walkley's death received an unusual amount of attention, but working conditions in the industrializing world in the nineteenth century were typically oppressive – and often in the twentieth century as well.

Strikes by American labor unions in the late-nineteenth and early twentieth centuries were often met with harsh violence, sometimes by American corporations, but also sometimes by federal or state troops. The killing of American workers by private or state soldiers was rarely prosecuted; indeed, the American court system routinely sided against labor during this time. Furthermore, company towns were common and limited the freedom of American workers in many ways.[14] On

---

ancestors, though these debts usually must be paid from the deceased's estate, and before any money is distributed from it to the deceased's inheritors.

[12] Karl Marx and Friedrich Engels, *Capital: a Critique of Political Economy*, Vol. 1 (Moscow: Progress Publishers, 1978), 244.

[13] *Ibid.*

[14] Philip S. Foner, *The Great Labor Uprising of 1877* (New York: Monad Press, 1977); David Ray Papke, *The Pullman Case: The Clash of Labor and Capital in*

another note, it may be hard for Americans to fully understand the violence and hatred that Chinese immigrants faced in the nineteenth century in the US, but it was tremendous: "no variety of anti-European sentiment has ever approached the violent extremes to which Chinese agitation went in the 1870s and 1880s."[15] Lynchings, riots, massacres: Chinese Americans faced these and more. "Decades of anti-Chinese violence, segregation, and discrimination" culminated in the Chinese Exclusion Act of 1882, which outlawed most Chinese immigration, and made it impossible for Chinese immigrants to become naturalized citizens.[16]

This is not to compare the injustice inflicted upon slaves to workers or Chinese Americans (though these comparisons were made),[17] but to say the wealth of all developed countries was built upon the backs of many different people and with many different kinds of oppression. One might argue that the slavery was horrible and unjust in ways that are unique in the history of the US and perhaps other countries as well; or slavery of Africans in the West generally was unique. Slaves were sold into their conditions like chattel, denied citizenship, and worked under unjust working conditions. Yet many indigenous peoples were also treated unjustly in terrible ways; I do not want to judge which was worse, which is surely a pointless exercise. Still, one might say that some historical injustices stand out as particularly horrible. Yet one needs an argument about why a particularly bad historical injustice needs compensation or reparations today, as opposed to those historical injustices that were merely bad.

If a country must pay reparations to the progeny of those who worked under unjust conditions in the past, the bill will be quite hefty; and the number of people and groups eligible for payments will be quite large. To be sure, one might say that if the bill to rectify past injustices is

Industrial America (Lawrence: University Press of Kansas, 1999); Lon Savage, *Thunder in the Mountains: The West Virginia Mine War, 1920–21* (University of Pittsburgh Press, 1990); David O. Stowell, *The Great Strikes of 1877* (Urbana: University of Illinois Press, 2008).

[15] John Higham, *Strangers in the Land: Patterns of American Nativism, 1860–1925* (New York: Atheneum, 1963), 25.

[16] Jack Chen, *The Chinese of America* (San Francisco: Harper & Row, 1980), 129. See also Jean Pfaelzer, *Driven Out: The Forgotten War Against Chinese Americans* (New York: Random House, 2007).

[17] A comparison between slaves and workers is in George Fitzhugh, *Cannibals All! Or, Slaves Without Masters* (Richmond, VA: A. Morris, 1857).

high, so be it; there is no reason to think that justice is inexpensive. In one of his arguments for reparations, Bernard Boxill argues that compensation for the unpaid labor of slaves deserves to be repaid; if the original victims are now dead, the right to compensation is inherited by their descendants. It does not matter, Boxill argues, if the descendants are now well off: "The inheritance argument, however, would be unaffected if slavery's long reach had ended some time ago and it no longer harmed the black population. It relies on the assumption that the U.S. Government owes the present black population a debt for an unjust loss it helped to cause, and such a debt is not revoked just because the creditor has recovered from the loss and is prosperous."[18]

What would happen, though, if we generalized Boxill's argument? One result would be many groups would have claims against the US government. It is hard to see who would not have a claim against the US – perhaps the descendants of wealthy immigrants and a few others. Given the vastness of the sea of past injustices in industrializing states, the idea that all past unjust labor should be repaid needs to be defended; focusing on one group in an argument about historical injustice evades this important issue. This is not merely a practical issue, that citizens will be unwilling to pay such a large bill to compensate for all past injustices. It is also an issue of justice: given scarce resources, compensation for past injustices may mean fewer resources to alleviate current injustices. It may mean transferring wealth from the poor to the wealthy as well. An argument that prioritizes historical injustice over present injustices – or insists that compensation be paid to the descendants of victims of all historical injustices – needs to defend the idea that descendants of victims, who may not be victims of injustice today, deserve compensation given scarce resources. This shows, again, the problem with focusing on one group: an argument for reparations for past unjust labor with one group in mind might make sense, but once that argument becomes generalizable, the argument often loses its footing.

2.3 The causal argument

A different argument for reparations is based on the idea of causality: past injustices are the cause of current injustices, and so to rectify the

---

[18] Bernard Boxill, "A Lockean Argument for Black Reparations," *The Journal of Ethics* 7, no. 1 (2003), 69.

latter we must repair the former. These arguments try to face the non-identity problem.[19] We can say that a particular person is owed reparations because her ancestor was a victim of an injustice long ago that was never rectified. The debt is in some way inherited. But what if the ancestor would not exist except for the injustice? In a widely accepted argument, Christopher Morris argues that it is likely that if the injustice in question did not occur, then the descendants of the victim of the past injustice would not exist. If slavery did not exist, the descendants of slaves would not exist. This is true for all past injustices, since any small injustice will affect the victims' procreation. Hundreds of millions of sperm cells are contained in a male's ejaculation so "any trivial difference affecting conception would ... [bring] it about that a different individual is conceived."[20] Not only is the amount of reparations hard to determine, but the descendants of the victims of the past would not exist but for the injustice. This is true for almost any injustices: the actual people who live today would almost certainly not exist but for the injustice.

One way to deflect this criticism is to argue that the rights violated are not only those of the original victims, but of their descendants as well. In other words, the injustice is not just from the past, but is ongoing. One version of this argument suggests that parents want to support their children, and that in fact they have a duty to do so. An injustice done to parents that inhibits their ability to care for the children as well as they would otherwise have done, is then also an injustice to the children. The injustice done to the parents also harms the children, and so the perpetrators also must compensate the children. This compensation is not endless; once the children have a certain level of welfare that is sustainable over time, the claims for redress fall away. A child whose welfare falls below a certain

---

[19] This problem arises in Boxill, "A Lockean Argument for Black Reparations" and George Sher, "Transgenerational Compensation," *Philosophy and Public Affairs* 33, no. 2 (2005): 181–200. Cohen tries to correct this problem in Andrew I. Cohen, "Compensation for Historic Injustices: Completing the Boxill and Sher Argument," *Philosophy and Public Affairs* 37, no. 1 (2009): 81–102.

[20] Christopher W. Morris, "Existential Limits to the Rectification of Past Wrongs," *American Philosophical Quarterly* 21, no. 2 (1984), 177. This argument is mentioned by others as well. See Stephen Kershnar, "Are the Descendants of Slaves Owed Compensation for Slavery?," *Journal of Applied Philosophy* 16, no. 1 (1999): 95–101, and Samuel C. Wheeler III, "Reparations Reconstructed," *American Philosophical Quarterly* 34, no. 3 (1997): 301–18.

minimum because her parents are unable to provide sufficiently for her due to an injustice inflicted upon them, is also a victim of that injustice. If as an adult she suffers because of this welfare deficiency – which is due to an injustice done to her parents – then she is owed compensation from the perpetrator of the injustice. If this person is not compensated, then she too is a victim of injustice; in this way compensable claims for injustice are passed down through the generations.[21]

One might also say that the non-identity problem leads to absurd conclusions, as Daniel Butt suggests. Butt points out that it is unlikely that the exact children born shortly after the Bhopal or Chernobyl disasters would have been born if these disasters had not occurred. Perhaps we can even say these children owe their existence to these disasters. Yet Butt poignantly asks, "would anyone seriously argue that, in the event of their suffering health problems, they should not be compensated on account of the non-identity problem?"[22] These children were harmed by an injustice, and so they are owed rectification for this harm. What we can say is this: if these unjust acts had not taken place, then almost certainly fewer children in the area of Bhopal or Chernobyl would have health problems than currently do, which is sufficient reason for compensation to be owed to the victims.

While I agree with Butt that the non-identity problem is a distraction that we should not take too seriously, there is a more fundamental identity problem in these arguments. How can we determine who deserves compensation? If the problem is that some people's ancestors suffered harm that may have been passed down, how are we to determine which people today deserve reparations? Andrew I. Cohen suggests that if the descendants of victims are under some level of welfare ("W"), then we can assume they are due compensation. Cohen talks about Luke and Jill and others in his argument, so it is

---

[21] Cohen, "Compensation for Historic Injustices." Daniel Butt makes a similar argument, contending that the failure to rectify a past injustice is unjust. Since the burden to rectify the past injustice is current, the injustice takes place today – and every day the past injustice remains without remedy is another day of injustice. Daniel Butt, *Rectifying International Injustice: Principles of Compensation and Restitution Between Nations* (New York: Oxford University Press, 2009), 183–88.

[22] Butt, *Rectifying International Injustice*, 106. Simmons also dismisses the causality argument, though very quickly. A. John Simmons, "Historical Rights and Fair Shares," *Law and Philosophy* 14, no. 2 (1995): 149–84.

uncertain how the argument transfers over to groups, which is what
he has in mind; indeed at the end of his article he discusses Black
Americans, as do nearly all arguments for reparations.[23] Yet how do
we move from Luke and Jill, to white and Black Americans? If some
Irish Americans are poor, do they have a claim for compensation? And
if they do, is the claim against the descendants of Irish landowners,
the Irish government or the US government? We could, of course,
extend this query to all poor people, trying to determine how they
arrived at their impoverishment, perhaps doing some kind of careful
genealogical research. This seems an impossible task, however. Cohen
notes these kinds of problems in reparations arguments: there are
"determinacy problems," "counterveiling moral considerations,"
and so on to weigh.[24] Yet Cohen dismisses them, because in "most
cases of plausible reparations claims, many generations of people have
suffered needlessly under the yoke of subjugation and now languish in
penury."[25]

This may be the case, but then why isn't the argument that the
American political community should focus on the injustices that
Black Americans face, because they face them *now*? If the injustice
that Black Americans face today is enough reason to ignore the
irritating details in determining how people today are responsible for
past injustices, why aren't injustices that Black Americans face today
enough cause to say that we ought to work to end this injustice?

Recall that Cohen argues compensation is due if the descendants of
injustice fall below a certain baseline of welfare. Most arguments for
reparations have a baseline, either implicit or explicit, since they want
to measure the well-being of victims, and show that they are below a
certain minimum. Most people in the political community are at or
above this minimum. The fact that many people of a certain group are
below that minimum shows they are victims of injustice. If this is a
reasonable way to characterize the causality reparations argument, as
I believe it is, it is unclear why the history of the injustice matters. On
this argument, it would seem that all people, regardless of group
membership and group history, deserve compensation if they are
below "W."

---

[23] Cohen, "Compensation for Historic Injustices," 102. Black Americans are used
as the example in all the articles cited here that discuss reparations.
[24] *Ibid.*   [25] *Ibid.*

Perhaps unsurprisingly, some reparation arguments actually speak about the present as motivating their arguments.[26] The typical reparations arguments begin with a list of the current inequalities between Black and white Americans – the large differences in income, wealth, living conditions, and the condition of the schools that many Black and whites attend.[27] The argument then moves to an explanation of these gaps, which is found in history: "It is impossible not to link the continuing economic disparity between the races to our history of race-based economic exploitation begun in slavery and continued through discrimination."[28] Another typical argument suggests that until the racial gaps on the measures of education, health, income, and wealth close, then the debt from the past injustice of slavery and racism "will not have been paid."[29]

If the racial gap did not exist, the implication is, then the past injustice would not matter. While these and other arguments about historical injustice mention the importance of current injustice of the group in question, this comment is usually introduced as an aside. What I am suggesting here is that this aside be put front and center. Responsibility for the past, reparations, being part of a community of obligations – all these concepts are backwards looking. Yet if Black

---

[26] Leif Wenar notes this in "Reparations for the Future," *Journal of Social Philosophy* 37, no. 3 (2006): 396–405.

[27] Rhonda V. Magee, "The Master's Tools, From the Bottom Up: Responses to African-American Reparations Theory in Mainstream and Outsider Remedies Discourse," *Virginia Law Review* 79 (1993), 863; Westley, "Many Billions Gone." A good primer on the reparations debate is Alfred L. Brophy, *Reparations: Pro and Con* (Oxford University Press, 2008).

[28] Magee, "The Master's Tools," 876. Similarly, Lawrie Balfour approvingly interprets W. E. B. Du Bois's argument for reparations because money is needed to address the *current* economic inequality between Black and white Americans. Balfour, "Unreconstructed Democracy," 43.

[29] Andrew Valls, "Reconsidering the Case for Black Reparations," in Jon Miller and Rahul Kumar, eds., *Reparations: Interdisciplinary Inquiries* (Oxford University Press, 2007), 114–29. See also Roy L. Brooks, *Atonement and Forgiveness: A New Model for Black Reparations* (Berkeley: University of California Press, 2004). Other backward looking arguments include Elazar Barkan and Alexander Karn, "Group Apology as Ethical Imperative," in Elazar Barkan and Alexander Karn, eds., *Taking Wrongs Seriously: Apologies and Reconciliation* (Stanford University Press, 2006), 18; Hendrix, "Memory in Native American Land Claims," 775; McCarthy, "Coming to Terms With Our Past," 751; Gregory W. Streich, "Is There a Right to Forget? Historical Injustice, Race, Memory, and Identity," *New Political Science* 24, no. 4 (2002): 525–42.

Americans did not suffer from current injustice, there would be little call for reparations. Reparations are called for because of *current* conditions, not because of the past. If there is not current injustice, the advocates of reparations would not make their case. This is why the non-identity problem is beside the point. The issue is not the often impossible one of determining if a people's suffering today can be traced to an injustice long ago. This method, which tries to work from the past to the present, frames the issue in the wrong way. Instead, we need to begin in the present, and ask who suffers from injustice? This is why the call for reparations is almost always argued for in the case of the African Americans, but rarely in other cases of historical injustices where the injustice is in the past, like in the case of Chinese Americans (and Italian Americans and Irish Americans and Jewish Americans, and so on).

Furthermore, the causality argument is not explored beyond the one case at hand. It is hard to imagine that most reparation advocates think that we must be able to identify a historical causal mechanism for the injustice in order to have cause for remedy. If people in a political community suffer from terrible living conditions, the political community is obligated to help them live better, regardless of the issue of causality. If a new policy unfairly harms a group, isn't the political community responsible for changing the policy? If refugees enter a country, isn't the host country responsible for trying to help them adjust to their new society, even if others are responsible for them being forced out of their native country? If a hurricane devastates an area, aren't other members of the political community responsible for helping those who lived in harm's way, even though the harm is quite new and no person was responsible for it? When Cohen argues that members of a historically disadvantaged group deserve reparations if they are below a certain minimum "W," one can ask: why should not *all* citizens below this minimum receive assistance until they are not impoverished?

Few scholars think that the repair for an injustice must always be connected to an agent who has a history of causing the injustice. An important exception is Robert Nozick, who argues that justice and injustice are both historical (I note another exception below). Nozick argues that if a holding is originally just, and is transferred by just means, then under most circumstances its current owner has a just claim to the property. If the original holding is unjust, or if a transfer is unjust, then reparations are called for. Under Nozick's account, justice and agency are closely intertwined. If you have less than others, if you live under conditions of inequality, that in itself is not a matter of (in)justice. Only if someone wrongly took some of your (or your ancestor's) holdings has an injustice occurred. How reparations are calculated, or what to do when nearly all holdings in a country are unjust – as most are in nearly every country in the world on Nozick's theory – is not addressed by Nozick in his remarkably brief comments on the subject. Nozick does say that in the case of large injustices the principle of rectification might call for transfer payments from rich to poor, but then he leaves the issue dangling, calling it complex and the proper subject for a full principle of rectification, which he does not offer.[30] While Nozick's theory does genuinely begin in the past, he cannot say how we move forward from the actual history of the world. Nozick calls his theory historical, but it is hard to see how it actually can take history into account. This may be one reason why few advocates of repairing injustice rely on Nozick; but another reason may be that they think that injustice ought to be repaired regardless of its pedigree.

One argument that parallels Nozick's is the suggestion made by some that since indigenous peoples were in a particular place first and their sovereignty over the land was wrongly usurped, they deserve in some way to have all or part of that sovereignty back. This is the idea behind James Tully's argument about the legitimacy of indigenous people's governmental structures at the time of contact with Europeans.[31] This argument focuses on original possession: since a certain group originally lived on some land, they deserve reparations or compensation (or the land itself) if it was unjustly taken from them.

---

[30] Robert Nozick, *Anarchy, State, and Utopia* (New York: Basic Books, 1974), 152, 231.

[31] James Tully, *Public Philosophy in a New Key: Vol. 1, Democracy and Civic Freedom* (Cambridge University Press, 2008), 234. The argument that some land should be returned to indigenous peoples because it was wrongly taken can be found in Simmons, "Historical Rights and Fair Shares." Simmons does argue that the land must be shared with non-indigenous peoples, but he is very short on specifics. Both Moore and Gans review and reject the argument from original possession. See Margaret Moore, *The Ethics of Nationalism* (Oxford University Press, 2001), 184–89; Chaim Gans, *The Limits of Nationalism* (Cambridge University Press, 2003), 104–07. One reason is that it is hard if not impossible to actually determine what people originated where, since human migration has always been quite common.

Yet this argument, as powerful as it seems in the case of indigenous peoples, is mistaken. There is no right to have a historical injustice rectified, even one as grave as expulsion from one's land: one needs to know why *this* past injustice should be rectified, and what the consequences of doing so will be. The implicit idea in many arguments about historical injustice is that if only the historical injustice had not happened, all would be well today. But there is actually no counterfactual to a history of injustice. We cannot imagine what the world would be like if injustice did not occur in the past since it is so ubiquitous. Danielle Celermajer looks at the Jewish tradition of apology, which teaches us that it is "through recognizing that one has strayed from the path that one cannot only return to it, but also identify it as one's path."[32] This is of course the path of justice; the implicit idea here is that the injustices committed against groups are the exception to a history of justice. This image, however, does not resemble the history of the world.

We cannot say that all would be just if we could only correct one or two injustices, since history is filled with injustices. To the extent that any of us believe that things are well today – I won't explore this assumption here – it is despite the many injustices of the past, or perhaps because of them. The process of modernization and industrialization was wrenching, uprooting, and, for many, terrible; yet it may be that the oppression of many of our ancestors enables us to live relatively comfortable lives. I want to emphasize this point, because in a world whose history is full of injustice, it is hard to make sense of the claim that past injustices should matter today, without some account of which should matter.

It is also the case that to pick out one historical injustice to repair may simply reveal another injustice. Many peoples over the long course of history have been expelled from their land; many have had their sovereignty usurped. Indeed, there were often wars between indigenous peoples over land and resources. The Aztecs, for example, excelled in warfare, and they conquered many peoples and forced them to pay tribute. They were eventually defeated by the Spanish, aided by the many native peoples who were quite happy to see the Aztec Empire fall. Was the defeat of the Aztec Empire an unjust act

---

[32] Danielle Celermajer, *The Sins of the Nation and the Ritual of Apologies* (Cambridge University Press, 2009), 83.

that wrongly ended Aztec sovereignty; was it an act of liberation; or was it simply one empire defeating another, whose original sovereignty and power was unjustly established through military conquest? Do the descendants of the Aztecs deserve reparations today because their empire was overturned by the Spanish? More to the point, the idea that we can determine original possession is almost surely wrong. Hobbes's comment that there is "scarce a commonwealth in the world whose beginnings can in conscience be justified," is explained by Hume: "Almost all the governments, which exist at present, or of which there remains any record in history, have been founded originally, either on usurpation or conquest, or both."[33] Peeling back one injustice when it comes to the origins of government will often just reveal another injustice.

The ubiquity of injustice is another reason why the non-identity approach to past injustice is mistaken. The argument that some people today would not be alive if it was not for injustice is misleading: *none* of us would be alive today if were not for injustice. Indeed, nearly all women who have given birth in the world up to this point have done so under conditions of injustice. Jeremy Waldron argues that there is no reason to think that if certain historical injustices had not occurred that we would now be living in conditions of justice: "Are we so sure that a smooth transition, untainted by particular injustice, from some early nineteenth-century status quo ante would leave us now where we actually want to be? Quite apart from particular frauds and expropriations, things were not marvelous in the nineteenth century. ... Why take all that as the baseline for our present reconstruction?"[34] This is not to condone injustice, or to suggest that injustice in the future is inevitable. Rather, the point is that the identity framework (and most arguments for repairing historical injustice) assume a counterfactual to injustice that does not exist. It assumes that some of us were conceived under just conditions, but we don't have to go that far back into history to realize that this assumption is mistaken.

Perhaps the difficulty of determining original just holdings is why Nozick devotes so little space to the issue, and why few advocates of

---

[33] Thomas Hobbes, *Leviathan* (Indianapolis: Hackett, 1994 [1651]), 492; David Hume, *Essays: Moral, Political, and Literary*, ed. Eugene F. Miller (Indianapolis: Liberty Classics, 1985 [1742]), 471.

[34] Jeremy Waldron, "Superseding Historic Injustice," *Ethics* 103, no. 4 (1992), 14.

repairing historical injustice work with Nozick's theory of justice. Since many of the advocates emphasize the unfair conditions in which some people live today, it renders their point about their injustice's history opaque. If the political community is obliged to all who have insufficient health care, income and/or wealth, or if large amounts of poverty concentrated in particular groups is unhealthy for a democracy,[35] then what is gained by calling the remedy for certain injustices a matter of reparation? Skeptics of repairing historical injustice often agree that political communities are responsible for remedying current injustices. These skeptics do not deny that African or Native Americans suffer from injustice today, and do not suggest that liberal states should ignore these injustices. An important part of the argument for repairing past injustice rests on finding the agent responsible for causing the injustice, but why discovering this responsible agent is necessary for ending the injustice is never explained well.

Some advocates do try to make some headway to explain why the history of an injustice matters, but by focusing on one or two cases they fail to help us understand what the general problem is in cases of historical injustice. Janna Thompson argues that the injustices suffered by indigenous peoples are often caused by the way treaties with them were ignored by Western governments. While treaties were wrongly ignored, Thompson's argument does not help us to understand the problem in other historical injustices. Indeed, when Thompson turns to Black Americans, she switches to a different argument, and says that the historical injustice there was the harm done to family lines. Perhaps if Thompson were to look at a third group – say the Crimean Tatars who were exiled from the Crimea by Stalin – she would present a third argument about why the history of the injustice matters. In the case of Black Americans, Thompson's argument is strained. She argues that the effect of slavery "continues to harm families" and resulted in "psychological damage to black Americans which has also had an effect on their material well-being."[36] One might think that many of the laws affecting Chinese Americans and the violence they faced would have affected their families as well. In the 1870s, laws were passed that made it nearly impossible for Chinese women to

---

[35] Balfour, "Unreconstructed Democracy," 43.
[36] Janna Thompson, *Taking Responsibility for the Past: Reparation and Historical Injustice* (Cambridge: Polity, 2002), 130, 139.

immigrate into the US, even if their husbands were already in the US. In the early 1880s, an anti-miscegenation law made it illegal for white women to marry Chinese Americans. These laws clearly affected the Chinese American family in the late nineteenth century, though their current effects are hard to determine.[37]

Similarly, the effects of slavery on current Black families are hard to test. It may be that the structure of many Black families results in psychological and material damage (or perhaps it is the obstacle to material success that leads to disrupted families and psychological damage), but the injustices against Black Americans over the last century or so are primarily about discrimination, which often has immediate financial effects, and then has *secondary* effects on family lines. The repair then, is not to families, but to end the discrimination suffered by Black Americans. If this is the case, what role does the history of the injustice done to Black Americans play in the argument? Thompson's argument assumes that the injustice to Black Americans is ongoing, since the harm to family ties has to be continuing for there to be a case of historical injustice. Many of the skeptics of repairing historical injustice would agree that the ongoing injustices suffered by Black Americans should be stopped. They would rightly be confused, however, by the gain in calling this injustice historical. What unites Thompson's arguments in the indigenous peoples and Black American cases is not the structure of the injustice, or their particular history, but the fact that these groups have suffered from injustice in the past and continue to do so.[38]

[37] Pfaelzer, *Driven Out*.

[38] Michael Ridge argues that we owe compensation to the actual victims of historical injustice. If they are dead, Ridge says, we can benefit them by satisfying their desires. There are many possible desires, though, like revenge, that may have negative consequences for innocent people today. To allay this objection, Ridge argues that the desires that can be satisfied must be worthwhile and not constitute a moral vice. Under these constraints, Ridge argues that the dead would want their descendants to flourish, which he interprets to mean promoting the welfare of the descendants in the standard liberal redistributive sense. On Ridge's account, it is hard to see how bringing in the interests of the dead actually produces a different account of justice than those that concentrate on the present. Michael Ridge, "Giving the Dead Their Due," *Ethics* 114, no. 1 (2003): 38–59. (I elaborate on this criticism of Ridge in Jeff Spinner-Halev, "From Historical to Enduring Injustice," *Political Theory* 35, no. 5 (2007): 550–73.) The ambiguity about the present and the past is also revealed in Tamar Meisels's contribution, where she devotes most of her article to arguing for the principle of restitution in cases of lost territory – she

2.4 Progress and its exceptions

My argument about which groups, and what past injustices arise, is based on the idea that our concern should begin with contemporary injustices. My argument in sum is this: the best way to make sense of the idea of historical injustice, and to explain why past injustices of some groups should be of political concern is because these groups have not mostly or fully been part of the progress of the Western world over the last two or three centuries. In other words, looking at history in a certain way, the present and the future, makes the idea of past injustice visible and important. What I hope to show is that the idea of progress and liberalism are linked, but I do not want to suggest that all versions of liberalism are interwoven with progress. Most versions of liberalism are linked to progress in important ways, however, and progress is an implicit assumption in most or perhaps all accounts of past injustice. The idea of liberal progress suggests that along with technological progress will come moral progress; that equality, the protecting of individual rights, and an increase in wealth will increasingly benefit all of society over time. The issue of historical injustice arises within a liberal narrative of progress, a narrative that can help answer the questions of this chapter: Which injustices? What groups?

Before I explain my argument, I want to briefly show how a traditional Marxist view of history does not reveal particular past injustices. Totalizing criticisms of liberal society do not see historical injustice as a particular problem to solve. A Marxist history might see the past as horrible (though inevitable), but it wouldn't see any one or two injustices that need special repair or attention; nor would it pinpoint a people as the perpetrator of injustice.[39] Rather, a Marxist would not suggest that liberal society ought to face up better to a

---

suggests the practice must be different when the lost land has current inhabitants – and adds a parenthetical qualification to her argument: "and/or where the group's objective situation is such that its members continue to suffer deprivation as a result of the injustice inflicted upon them in the past." It is not clear how much weight the parenthesis or the "and/or" should have, but skeptics would agree with the suggestion that absent current injustice, then past injustice matters considerably less. Tamar Meisels, "Can Corrective Justice Ground Claims to Territory?," *Journal of Political Philosophy* 11, no. 1 (2003), 76.

[39] Marxists don't really see injustice in the past. Workers are treated horribly, but that is different than being treated unjustly. See Allen W. Wood, "The Marxian Critique of Justice," *Philosophy and Public Affairs* 1, no. 3 (1972): 244–82.

particular historical injustice to try to alleviate it. A Marxist would think that all of bourgeois liberal society was flawed; it would not make sense to try to repair one or two injustices. A Marxist would see a need to change all of society. Marxism teaches that only a few benefit from bourgeois liberal society (and the societies before it), and so the idea of picking out certain historical injustices to repair would make little sense. To be sure, Marxists do have a view of progress, but unlike those who think that progress takes place within a liberal framework, Marxists see liberal bourgeois society as a necessary precursor to a different kind of society. The Marxist narrative would see Black and Native Americans as victims of exploitation; but they would see workers and many others in a similar light. Reparations for past injustices would make little sense to a Marxist for another reason: the terrible working conditions of the past were inevitable, and pave the way for a better future. Reparations and the idea of past injustice assume that matters could have been different. Marxists view history through the lens of progress, but progress will mean transcending liberal society, not repairing the injustices within it.

This Marxist understanding of history helps to explain why for many years the Chinese Communist government made little mention of the now infamous "Rape of Nanking" by the Japanese in 1937 at Nanking, where between one and three hundred thousand Chinese, most of them civilians, were killed and tens of thousands of women raped. Nanking was horrible, but the list of atrocities committed by imperialists is awfully long, and so for several decades from the Chinese Communist point of view there was no reason to focus on any one particular terrible imperialist event. Marxist theory teaches that life before communism is pretty awful everywhere. The main thing about Japanese and Chinese imperialists was that they were imperialists, and not their nationality; and their actions were horrible if unsurprising – imperialists obviously act horribly, how else would they act? Recently, however, as the idea of communism has receded in China, nationalism has come to the fore and there is now a special emphasis on Nanking in China. The perpetrators at Nanking are no longer viewed as imperialists by the Chinese government, but are now seen as Japanese. Chinese films and televisions portrayed the Nanking massacre for the first time in the 1990s; a popular traveling exhibit was created around the same time. On December 13, 1996, 59 years *after* the massacre, sirens wailed to commemorate the massacre for the *first* time, and now the sirens are an annual event.[40] The narrative in China about their history has changed, and so the way they remember particular events – and perhaps the events they remember – changed as well.

The idea of historical injustice would have made little sense to eighteenth- and nineteenth-century liberals. One might begin an explanation of why this is so with the ahistorical nature of liberal theory. State of nature theories ignore the particular histories of particular peoples, while Rawls's original position is similarly ahistorical. The liberalism of the Enlightenment was ahistorical and forward-looking. Yet other liberals like Mill and Kant argue that only certain societies at a certain stage of development were able to be liberal states. But historical injustice would not have made much sense to these more historically minded liberals either. It is not that the idea of the state of nature blinded liberals to the idea of historical injustice, but rather that the forward-looking nature of much of liberal (and some non-liberal) theory was based on the idea that the past was best kept where it was.

The idea of concentrating on particular historical injustices would have made little sense to most Enlightenment thinkers and to nineteenth-century liberals. These thinkers often had a rich sense of history, and thought history was full of injustices to nearly everyone, except for the ruling class. Late eighteenth- and nineteenth-century liberals argued that with the triumph of individual rights a progressive era would be established, and the spread of liberty and enlightenment would usher in an era of progress. History would unfold in a roughly linear fashion; the past was bad, the present is good, the future will be better, and it will be better for everyone. If you think society will progress, then acknowledging specific acts of injustice to a particular group makes little sense. It was not so much that these thinkers hoped that the future would be better, but that they assumed it would be; they were confident that humanity would progress.

The idea of progress in the nineteenth century was tied to techno-logical progress and to the idea of civilization. I will concentrate on John Stuart Mill's view of progress, but many other liberals also saw progress as inevitable. There is little novel in Mill's view, and he

---

[40] Takashi Yoshida, *The Making of the "Rape of Nanking": History and Memory in Japan, China, and the United States* (Oxford University Press, 2006).

clearly borrowed much from eighteenth-century thinkers, but his view can be used as an exemplar of an important school of thought within liberalism that is often implicitly accepted, though rarely acknowledged.[41] I will argue that progress inhabits much of liberalism today as well; in his book on pessimism, Joshua Foa Dienstag argues that "pessimists have in many cases been dismissed from the upper reaches of the canon of political thought."[42] Dienstag tries to recover a strand of pessimism within political theory, but that is exactly the point: the idea of pessimism is muted within political theory generally, and certainly within liberal thought.

Mill thought technology would help change the social and political structure of society, and its morality as well. He argued that industrialization would change not only Europe, but eventually the whole world: "All the nations which we are accustomed to call civilized, increase gradually in production and in population: and there is no reason to doubt, that not only these nations will for some time continue so to increase, but that most of the other nations of the world ... will successively enter upon the same career."[43] One of the effects of industrialization is the ability of society to educate large numbers of people. Education and increased urbanization lead to a more intelligent populace.[44] He argued that people were becoming better educated and were living ever closer together, which was enabling, even forcing, different kinds of political institutions. The aristocracy no longer had the right to rule, since they no longer had a monopoly on intelligence. Mill contended that there had been a "wonderful development of the physical and intellectual power on the part of the masses," that has not been matched by the fading aristocracy.[45] The

---

[41] Eighteenth-century views are well explored in David Spadafora, *The Idea of Progress in Eighteenth-Century Britain* (New Haven: Yale University Press, 1990). See also J. B. Bury, *The Idea of Progress: An Inquiry Into Its Origin and Growth* (New York: Cosimo Press, 2011 [1920]); Robert Nisbet, *History of the Idea of Progress* (New Brunswick: Transaction Publishers, 1994).

[42] Joshua Foa Dienstag, *Pessimism: Philosophy, Ethic, Spirit* (Princeton University Press, 2006), 3.

[43] John Stuart Mill, *Principles of Political Economy, With Some of Their Applications to Social Philosophy*, ed. J. M. Robson, Vol. III of Collected Works (33 vols.) (University of Toronto, 1965 [1848]), 706.

[44] John Stuart Mill, "The Spirit of the Age," in *Essays on Politics and Culture*, ed. Gertrude Himmelfarb (New York: Anchor Books, 1963 [1831]), 24.

[45] John Stuart Mill, "Civilization," in *Essays on Politics and Culture*, ed. Gertrude Himmelfarb (New York: Anchor Books, 1963 [1836]), 52.

increase in people's cultivation, he argued, means "mankind are capable of being better governed than the wealthy classes have ever heretofore governed them."[46] Mill thought history was moving in a certain direction. He was nearly certain that humanity would progress, and while he was less sure what ultimately that would mean, he was certain that it would include equality of treatment, of all people, regardless of gender or race:

> The entire history of social improvement has been a series of transitions, by which one custom or institution after another, from being a supposed primary necessity of social existence, has passed into the rank of a universally stigmatised injustice and tyranny. So it has been with the distinctions of slaves and freemen, nobles and serfs, patricians and plebeians; and so it will be, and in part already is, with the aristocracies of colour, race, and sex.[47]

The nineteenth-century notion of progress was underpinned by a particular notion of civilization.[48] For Mill, liberation and freedom is not merely a struggle against a regressive power; freedom can only take place in the context of a civilized or civilizing society. Freedom is not merely the right to act as one wishes; freedom should be used responsibly, to cultivate one's higher faculties. That is why notions of urbanization, technological progress and education echo throughout Mill's story of progress. Mill juxtaposes civilization with what he calls rudeness, barbarism, or savage life. Civilized society has a dense population, dwells in fixed places, and is marked by trade and agriculture. In savage societies people wander around in tribes, with little law or justice, hunting and gathering, greatly concerned about security, and typically having to rely on themselves or family members for protection. Civilized people act together for common purposes and enjoy the fruits of living and working together.[49] For Mill, it is unquestionably better to be civilized, to be cultivated,

---

[46] Mill, "The Spirit of the Age," 29.

[47] John Stuart Mill, "Utilitarianism," in *On Liberty and Other Essays* (Oxford University Press, 1991 [1861]), 200.

[48] Thomas McCarthy makes a similar argument, though he focuses more on Kant than Mill in *Race, Empire, and the Idea of Human Development* (Cambridge University Press, 2009). A different view of Kant, one that does not see Kant as imperialist is Sankar Muthu, *Enlightenment Against Empire* (Princeton University Press, 2003).

[49] Mill, "The Spirit of the Age."

to work with others in a common purpose, than to live a savage life as he suggests in this now infamous passage:

Nobody can suppose that it is not more beneficial to a Breton, or a Basque of French Navarre, to be brought into the current of the ideas and feelings of a highly civilised and cultivated people – to be a member of the French nationality, admitted on equal terms to all the privileges of French citizenship, sharing the advantages of French protection, and the dignity and prestige of French power – than to sulk on his own rocks, the half-savage relic of past times, revolving in his own little mental orbit, without participation or interest in the general movement of the world. The same remark applies to the Welshman or the Scottish Highlander as members of the British nation.[50]

Mill's idea is that the uncivilized will give up their way of life to join the civilized. Who would rather be savage than civilized, after all?

One important aspect of Mill's attitude about civilization, which was a widely shared view, is that it shows the ways in which progress can be used to excuse injustice.[51] The idea that civilization would triumph, and that it should triumph, was shared by many in the nineteenth century United States (and other colonial states), who saw the way of life of Native Americans as a relic of the past that would be overcome by civilization. A corollary of the view that society would progress was that civilization would overcome the primitiveness of the past. Many people in the nineteenth century understood that the US was acting unjustly toward Native Americans, but few thought that the traditional way of life was viable, at least not next to the civilization of the US. The injustice faced by the Indians

---

[50] John Stuart Mill, "Considerations on Representative Government," in *On Liberty and Other Essays* (Oxford University Press, 1991 [1861]), 205–467.
[51] This is a major theme in McCarthy, *Race, Empire, and the Idea of Human Development.* See too Tully's argument about how John Locke's views on property justified taking land away from Native Americans. James Tully, *Strange Multiplicity: Constitutionalism in an Age of Diversity* (Cambridge University Press, 1995), 71–78. For liberal imperialism, largely in the nineteenth century, see Uday Singh Mehta, *Liberalism and Empire: A Study in Nineteenth-Century British Liberal Thought* (University of Chicago Press, 1999). For liberal anti-imperialism, largely in the eighteenth century, see Muthu, *Enlightenment Against Empire.* How the idea of civilization was used in the US as a contrast between whites and Native Americans in ways that try to justify the superiority of the former is explained by Roy Harvey Pearce, *The Savages of America: A Study of the Indian and the Idea of Civilization* (Baltimore: Johns Hopkins Press, 1953).

(as they were called then) was inevitable, but would be short-lived. Progressives thought that Native Americans should, and with the proper encouragement could, assimilate into white civilization.[52] Others thought the Indians would simply disappear in the face of civilization.

Many liberals today assume that society has progressed over time; in other words, they think that eighteenth- and nineteenth-century liberals were right to assume progress. Many scholars locate a particularly liberal story of progress within the seeds of the Reformation. It was then that the idea of liberty of religious conscience was born, which over time became secularized. Perez Zagorin, for example, argues that the concept of religious toleration "underwent considerable secularization" during the Enlightenment. He argues that religious toleration "became largely separated from its religious roots" in the eighteenth century, when toleration "was now frequently extended to unite religious with intellectual freedom."[53] Religious toleration came to be seen as a right, and the idea of rights expanded beyond religious freedom, with the rise of the idea of human rights. Similarly, John Headley argues that the idea of natural law became secularized over time, and became a universal idea: "the extension of a rule of law in programs of human rights to all the peoples of the earth, born of the belief in an essentially uniform and rationally disposed humanity."[54]

This idea of the progress of religious toleration to individual rights is also captured by John Rawls. Rawls states that the historical origins of liberalism are the "Reformation and its aftermath," where "the modern understanding of liberty of conscience and freedom of thought began."[55] For Rawls, freedom of religion becomes simply freedom: "political liberalism assumes the fact of reasonable pluralism as a pluralism of comprehensive doctrines, including both religious

---

[52] Lucy Maddox, *Citizen Indians: Native American Intellectuals, Race, and Reform* (Ithaca, NY: Cornell University Press, 2005); David Wallace Adams, *Education for Extinction: American Indians and the Boarding School Experience 1875–1928* (University Press of Kansas, 1997).

[53] Perez Zagorin, *How the Idea of Religious Toleration Came to the West* (Princeton University Press, 2003), 292.

[54] John M. Headley, *The Europeanization of the World: On the Origins of Human Rights and Democracy* (Princeton University Press, 2007), 102.

[55] John Rawls, *Political Liberalism* (New York: Columbia University Press, 1993), xxiv.

and nonreligious doctrines."[56] Rawls sees his project of justice as fairness as one that can "complete and extend the movement of thought that began three centuries ago with the gradual acceptance of the principle of toleration and led to the nonconfessional state and equal liberty of conscience."[57] Once Luther established that the Bible could be interpreted in different ways, the idea of religious liberty eventually followed; and once religious liberty was established, then liberty, religious and otherwise, became established. We can see this too when we move from Locke to Kant and Mill. Locke was very concerned about Christianity when he spoke of religious toleration, which he withheld from atheists. Kant and Mill, however, are concerned with the freedom of all citizens.

Liberal states first granted religious toleration to all Christians, then to other religions, and then to the non-religious. After that, toleration becomes a shared principle, a matter of freedom, not something granted by the state in order to maintain peace. Freedom is not defined in religious terms; it becomes a secular notion that applies to all beliefs and to actions, with certain constraints. All citizens should be able to readily exercise this freedom. This story is a widespread one in the West. This is very much a teleological story, a story of progress that ends in liberty for all; freedom begins in a small way, but spreads over time and over space. The narrative of moral and technological progress and the narrative of unfolding toleration overlap with each other. All of these narratives are encapsulated by the idea of civilization: people working together, largely in cities, progressing morally and technologically in an ever-increasingly wealthy society. The idea of individual rights has more currency today in more places and in a more robust fashion than it did one and two hundred years ago. When there is justice in the present and the future looks hopeful, the injustice of the past is often eclipsed. When the narrative is triumphant, the injustice of the past is written about as a steppingstone or a stumbling block on the way toward a better future.

2.5 The irony of progress

The idea of historical injustice makes sense when viewed through the lens of progress. The idea of past injustice is revealed most clearly

---

[56] *Ibid.*   [57] *Ibid.*, 154.

when the narrative of progress is triumphant for many, but not for others. A society infused with liberal ideals often makes an implicit promise of progress to citizens. Historical injustice arises as a political problem when this promise is hollow for some groups. David Scott argues that many anti-colonial movements wrote history as a romance, with an inevitable triumphalist ending.[58] History is emplotted with a story of progressive change; the colonialists take over, there is the anti-colonialist struggle, there is victory which brings liberation, followed by freedom. Scott's reading of anti-colonial movements as romance is similar to eighteenth- and nineteenth-century liberal history. While Scott does not focus on past injustice in his work, what we can learn from his argument is that the issue of past injustices arises when the history of a group has turned out to be a tragedy within a larger romantic narrative. It is when the story of progress is hard to maintain for some groups, when it faces obstacles that are hard to surmount, that the category of historical injustice arises. Once the idea of progress is shown to be partially flawed, the exceptions come forth as injustices.

The idea of historical injustice did not occur to earlier liberals since they assumed injustice was so prevalent. But when justice actually has some success, then stark injustices stand out. One does not need to view the rest of society as completely just to perceive past injustices; but if one sees that justice has some success, and if one thinks that justice will continue and increase for some, then stark injustices that do not seem as if they will end do stand out. When the idea of progress is accepted, when the past is viewed not merely as a cascade of one injustice after another, but when justice extends its reach to include the previously excluded, our attention is called to those who are left behind. When one looks at a society through the lens of justice and progress, the exceptions stand out. It is this lens that most advocates of repairing historical injustices use (as do the skeptics).

Viewing these exceptions, one could think that liberalism is still in its infancy, and we just need to redouble our efforts to ensure that individual rights are respected; or one could suggest, as Melissa Williams seems to, that liberal democracy can move toward its

---

[58] David Scott, *Conscripts of Modernity: The Tragedy of Colonial Enlightenment* (Durham: Duke University Press, 2004). Despite my brief reference to Scott's book, I found his argument very rich and instructive.

promise with one important change (ensuring fair representation for women and African Americans, and perhaps others).[59] Absent these arguments, however, if one thinks that that the condition of women and workers is on a par with that of most Black and Native Americans – that is, that they were victims of deep injustices that continue to this day – then one would wonder if liberal society could correct these injustices. Iris Young's concern that these groups and others are oppressed in liberal society is what leads her to search for non-liberal solutions to this perceived problem.[60] The problem for Young is not the exceptions to liberal progress, but liberalism itself. This is why it is hard to take seriously McCarthy's aside that he won't treat many other possible victims of historical injustice: if he thought about all the groups together, and decided that all those groups are victims of injustice, then his solution – more understanding of the history of racism and its effects – might very well be quite different. If liberalism has failed nearly everyone, then calling for more understanding to reverse a particular injustice is a rather feeble solution to a large problem.

The idea of historical injustice makes sense in a liberal society where one assumes that progress has or will soon take care of most injustices. It is the injustices that progress leaves behind that arise as a particular problem to be solved. The progress that nineteenth-century liberals hoped for did not unfold as they would have predicted, but certainly there has been some progress. Religious discrimination in the West has faded over time; there is much less religious discrimination now than in the past. In the US, only white property-owning men first had the franchise; then all white men; then Black men were added; in the twentieth century women gained suffrage, while legislation denying rights to Chinese Americans was overturned. Discrimination faced by Catholics and Jews also faded over the twentieth century, while the Civil Rights Laws committed the US government to racial equality. The story of progress is a real historical experience for many.

Still, the twentieth century did not always see progress, but the Civil Rights Movement certainly resurrected the idea, and with it came the hope that an egalitarian regime of rights combined with affirmative

[59] Melissa Williams, *Voice, Trust and Memory: Marginalized Groups and the Failings of Liberal Representation* (Princeton University Press, 1998).

[60] Iris Marion Young, *Justice and the Politics of Difference* (Princeton University Press, 1990).

action would ensure that real equality between Black and white Americans was widespread. Several decades later, however, many have less faith that Blacks will be treated equally to whites; and that the lives of indigenous peoples will improve much. The turn to historical injustice, the move to ask Americans to better understand history and its connection to present injustice, is part of this frustration; it has resulted in a loss of faith of liberal progress for certain groups. Elizabeth Anderson, in her book arguing for racial equality and racial integration, states: "This book aims to resurrect the ideal of integration from the grave of the Civil Rights Movement."[61] The liberal ideal of equality seems to have stalled or disappeared when it comes to Black Americans; the idea of historical injustices arises to dislodge this stalled ideal, and move it forward once again.

Post-modernists criticize grand narratives like the narrative of progress, in part because of what they hide. While the narrative of progress genuinely describes the experience of many, the promise of civilization and liberal democracy has failed, or has been a mixed blessing, for some people. Not all have enjoyed the fruits of progress. Since the 1960s, histories of marginalized groups have become increasingly prominent.[62] The history of marginalized groups is in part a history of injustice. Although there is more to their histories than injustice, the interest in the history of the marginalized is often fueled by present concerns. The cases of Black and Native Americans arise in arguments about historical injustice less because of their history of oppression, and more because of their current living conditions are poor. Even though one can read a story of progress in the history of Black Americans, many perceive that progress to have stopped over the last two decades. The idea that once given liberty, formerly oppressed groups would readily become part of mainstream society may be partly true for some groups but clearly not for others. How to lift up the living conditions of Black and Native Americans; how to close the "achievement gap" in schools between these groups and others; how to reduce the large percentage of Black men entangled with the criminal justice system; how to improve their earnings; these

---

[61] Elizabeth S. Anderson, *The Imperative of Integration* (Princeton University Press, 2010), 1.

[62] Dorothy Ross, "Grand Narrative in American Historical Writing: From Romance to Uncertainty," *The American Historical Review* 100, no. 3 (1995): 651–77.

problems defy easy answers. (If one is unsure whether Black Americans are oppressed, consider this: African-Americans are 13 percent of the general population, but over 50 percent of the prison population. Blacks are incarcerated at a rate eight times higher than that of whites. One quarter of all Blacks are poor, compared to 8 percent of non-Hispanic whites. The median black household income is two-thirds that of the median white household income.[63]) The previous hope that these problems were conquerable, that equality of opportunity would be easy to engineer and that many good things would follow from that, is hard to hold now for certain groups. The confidence of the Enlightenment and the nineteenth century that progress would occur as a matter of course is hard to sustain for certain groups.

But there is an important irony here: historical injustice, or what I reconceptualize as enduring injustice in the next chapter, also reveals the failure of progress. My argument here is genealogical – that is, my aim in this chapter is to explain why the idea of historical injustice arose when it did. The narrative of progress reveals its failures that cannot easily be redressed within this narrative. Another way of saying this is that liberalism's success starkly reveals its failures: if liberalism was not much of a success, if progress was not a real historical experience for many, specific failures would not be revealed. Liberalism is a theory that promises much; it is, in a way, anti-tragic. One way to sidestep this irony is to show that liberal progress can resume and repair the historical injustices; it is also the case, however, that enduring injustices suggest the limitations to progress, and that we may need to replace the idea of progress with hope, an idea I touch upon in the conclusion.

A different kind of exception to progress is at work in other cases that I bring up here: the Tatars, the Tibetans, and the Palestinians. These groups lack self-determination, which is now an expectation for nations since the end of the Second World War, and particularly since

---

[63] Anderson, *Imperative of Integration*, 23–24. Other disparities: Black–white disparities in unemployment, for example, are 2–1; in nonmarital childbirth, 3–1; in infant mortality, 2–1; and in net worth, 1–5. See also David Cole, "Can Our Shameful Prisons be Reformed?," *The New York Review of Books* 56, no. 18 (2009), www.nybooks.com/articles/archives/2009/nov/19/can-our-shameful-prisons-be-reformed/ (accessed January 5, 2010). See generally Andrew Hacker, *Two Nations: Black and White, Separate, Hostile, Unequal* (New York: Touchstone, 2003).

the fall of the Soviet Union in 1989. Since that event, there has been a large scholarly literature defending the idea of liberal nationalism, though Isaiah Berlin noted the importance of national identity in the 1960s.[64] It seems normal that the Armenians, the Slovenians, the Hungarians, and so on should have their own state. When a national group does not have its own state, it is often the case that they have some group autonomy, like the Catalans and the Scots. And so the Palestinians are an exception to the general trend, as are the Tatars and the Tibetans. When national self-determination is the norm, then it appears strange when a nation lacks a state. My purpose is not to explain the rise of the nation-state, which arose with democracy,[65] but only to note that peoples without states are the exception, particularly when they live in exile or under the yoke of a different people or government.

Not every version of liberalism must be intertwined with progress. One might think that the liberal state ought to protect individual

---

[64] Berlin discusses national self-determination in his essay on two concepts of liberty. See Isaiah Berlin, *Four Essays on Liberty* (Oxford University Press, 1969) and in the essay "The Bent Twig," in Isaiah Berlin, *The Crooked Timber of Humanity: Chapters in the History of Ideas* (New York: Knopf, 1991), 238–61. The literature on liberal nationalism is large. See Ronald Beiner, ed., *Theorizing Nationalism* (Albany, NY: State University of New York Press, 1999); Rogers Brubaker, *Citizenship and Nationhood in France and Germany* (Cambridge, MA: Harvard University Press, 1992); Margaret Canovan, *Nationhood and Political Theory* (Cheltenham: Edward Elgar, 1996); Gans, *The Limits of Nationalism*; Ernest Gellner, *Nations and Nationalism* (Ithaca, NY: Cornell University Press, 1983); Will Kymlicka, *Multicultural Citizenship: A Liberal Theory of Minority Rights* (Oxford University Press, 1995); Neil MacCormick, "Liberalism, Nationalism, and the Post-Sovereign State," *Political Studies* 44, no. 4 (1996): 553–67; Neil MacCormick, "Nation and Nationalism," in Beiner, ed., *Theorizing Nationalism*, 189–204; Avishai Margalit and Joseph Raz, "National Self-Determination," *Journal of Philosophy* 87, no. 9 (1990): 439–61; David Miller, *On Nationality* (Oxford University Press, 1995); Moore, *The Ethics of Nationalism*; Kai Nielsen, "Liberal Nationalism and Secession," in Margaret Moore, ed., *National Self-Determination and Secession* (Oxford University Press, 1998), 103–33; Yael Tamir, *Liberal Nationalism* (Princeton University Press, 1993); Charles Taylor, "Nationalism and Modernity," in Beiner, ed., *Theorizing Nationalism*, 219–46; Bernard Yack, "Popular Sovereignty and Nationalism," *Political Theory* 29, no. 4 (2001): 517–36.

[65] I argue for a connection between the two in Jeff Spinner-Halev, "Democracy, Solidarity and Post-Nationalism," *Political Studies* 56, no. 3 (2008): 604–28. See also Michael Mann, *The Dark Side of Democracy: Explaining Ethnic Cleansing* (Cambridge University Press, 2005).

rights, or preserve toleration, or protect free markets, and not much more. These sorts of liberal ideologies do not necessarily presume progress. My argument is that the idea of historical injustice makes the most sense through the lens of a liberal narrative of progress, one that has been predominant in much of Western political life. Rarely do those involved in this debate argue for wholesale changes in the economic and political structures of liberal democratic states; they assume that the current political and economic structure is more or less sound, but needs to do better with exceptional cases.[66] My argument suggests the framework of progress is the right one in which to see historical injustice – or what I rename enduring injustice – but I will also paint a picture in which liberalism should become less optimistic about the future, and more tragic about the possibilities and trade-offs that must be made to try to end enduring injustices.

[66] The liberal framework comes through clearly in the work of some reparation advocates. Bernard Boxill works within an explicitly Lockean framework, taking a Lockean view of property, rights, and reparations. Lawrie Balfour argues that what motivates reparations for Black Americans is the material inequality they suffer from today. Similarly, when Andrew I. Cohen uses a minimum baseline welfare level for his argument, he is very much in the tradition of liberal theories of distributive justice.

3 | *Enduring injustice*

Even if there are exceptions to progress, the critics of working to repair past injustices might ask, why does the history of an injustice matter? Injustices today ought to be addressed, they argue, but why does the pedigree of the injustice matter? The critics are right in a narrow sense, that current injustice matters more than past injustice, but they are wrong to treat long-standing injustices in the same way as other injustices. Instead of discussing historical injustice, I want to build upon my argument about the exceptions to progress to reframe the issue as one of enduring injustice. Enduring injustice has roots in the past, and continues into the present day; an enduring injustice endures over time and often over space as well. What makes an enduring injustice particularly perplexing is how difficult it is to repair. This difficulty is rooted in the solutions offered by most versions of liberal justice, which typically focus on individual rights and a modest redistribution of resources. Cases of enduring injustice, however, often encompass matters of exile, mistrust, sacred land, and acknowledgement of the past, all of which lie outside the bounds of liberal justice, and all of which cannot be accounted for without taking the past into account, which is why a solely contemporary focus is insufficient.

The idea of enduring injustice helps to answer the question of why and which past injustices cry out for attention today. The answer is not just because the history of some groups was unjust, but because their present is also unjust, and the future appears to be unjust for them as well, without some changed in course of action. Part of what I hope to accomplish with the idea of enduring injustice is to turn our gaze away from beginning in the past and moving forward. Rather, I want to call attention to the way in which we should begin with present injustices, trace them backward and then project them forward. The account of enduring injustice that I present is a political one. My argument here helps to explain what cases of injustice should be considered as ones of concern to the political community; I point to

what kinds of injustices should be remembered, but this leaves
open other events that can be remembered, or perhaps should be
remembered for other reasons. My account of political memory is
not an exhaustive account, but one that spells out a certain kind of
minimum. There may be reasons for a political community to
acknowledge past events that are not enduring injustices, something
I leave aside here.[1]

Beyond not being able to determine which past injustices ought to
be of political concern, another key difference between the ideas of
historical injustice and enduring injustice is how each uses the past
and looks at responsibility. The advocates of repairing historical
injustice focus on two powerful cases of past injustice, Native Americans
and African Americans. These examples lead advocates to assume that
the political community in which the injustice persists through time,
and the ancestors of the victims and perpetrators can be roughly
identified, with the latter responsible for repairing the injustice. They
often link history to responsibility in terms of repairing the injustice,
but this leaves many enduring injustices beyond repair, since there is
not always a direct relationship between victims of historical injustice
and their current political community.

Instead of looking at history as a way of assigning responsibility,
I argue that history should be used to see why the injustice persists.
This means, in part, looking at why the history of the injustice
matters from the point of view of the victims. Doing so leads very
quickly to issues of collective narrative – a term which I sometimes
use instead of the more common "collective memory" – which plays
an important role in issues of governmental trust, ancestral connec-
tions to land, and dignity. Collective narratives tie the past to the
present, something the skeptics too readily overlook. But perhaps the
most important difference between historical and enduring injustice is
that the latter leads us to two important questions: Why has the
injustice endured, and how might it be repaired? Historical injustices
are many; but the exceptions to progress that continue to this day beg
for an explanation and often lead us past the solutions offered to us
by liberal justice.

---

[1] Two instructive accounts of the ethics of memory of political community are
Jeffrey Blustein, *The Moral Demands of Memory* (Cambridge University Press,
2008); Avishai Margalit, *The Ethics of Memory* (Cambridge, MA: Harvard
University Press, 2002).

3.1 Enduring injustice

The reason why the examples of indigenous peoples and African Americans are so powerful is not only that they have suffered from injustice in the past, but also that these historical injustices continue on to the present. The problem for some peoples is not only that they suffered injustices in the past, but that they *still* suffer from injustice. Together, this constitutes what I call *enduring* injustice. Enduring injustice has a historical and a contemporary component. All enduring injustices are also historical injustices, but the reverse is not true, since many historical injustices no longer persist today. One might point out that all injustices have a history; and liberal justice readily solves many injustices. Yet once an injustice persists through time, and it does not seem like it will be solved, it can be seen as enduring. By shifting to enduring injustice, the problem of injustices with historical roots is better defined. It too suggests why there is a problem – that the regime at hand has a hard time resolving this particular injustice. (I will now shift my language to discuss enduring injustice instead of historical injustice since I believe this accurately describes the issue at hand.) The intractability of the injustice helps answer a question dangling from the last chapter: which groups can count as victims of enduring injustice?

The idea of anything enduring in modern or post-modern times can be hard to grasp. In important ways, we can be fairly sure that the world will be different in a few years from now than it is today; certainly the world will look considerably different in twenty or thirty years from now. The rise of Chinese, Indian, and Brazilian economic power was hard to foresee in the 1970s; the place of computers and the internet would also have been hard to anticipate. Yet despite the changes that may come, it seems safe to predict that the condition of African Americans and Native Americans, relative to other Americans, will not change much unless important policy changes are implemented. This prediction about the future is of course something of a guess. It seems reasonable, however, since despite the changes since the Civil Rights era, African and Native Americans lag far behind many other Americans on important indices of well-being.[2] One could point

---

[2] There is a large literature on the gap between African Americans and whites on many indices of well-being. See for, example, Elizabeth S. Anderson, *The Imperative of Integration* (Princeton University Press, 2010); Andrew Hacker,

out that in recent years some Native Americans have benefited economically from casinos, but this is only true in a small number of cases.[3]

When an injustice persists, a collective narrative arises that ties past injustices to the present. These past injustices are often seen as causing the injustices of the present. Causality arguments are often hard to prove, but we can make reasonable suppositions. One could argue that the misery of Native Americans was caused by American policies that pushed indigenous peoples aside, shamelessly broke treaties with them, treated them harshly and so on. Yet we don't know what would have happened if Americans treated indigenous peoples with more respect and decency; it is hard to imagine that the traditional indigenous way of life would have survived once whites took to industrialization. It is likely that if indigenous peoples had been treated with more respect, they would have had more control (not complete control) of the transformative process they encountered, and they would have wrestled with modernity from a position of cultural coherence and not decimation. This almost surely would mean that their position today would be much different and better. Many indigenous peoples are suffering in many ways, and it seems likely that if the colonialists had treated them better, they would be better off today. Tying past injustices to current injustices, however, does not say how things would have been different. What we can say is that there is a clear and strong

Two Nations: Black and White, Separate, Hostile, Unequal (New York: Touchstone, 2003). On the large number of African Americans in the criminal justice system, see David Cole, "Can Our Shameful Prisons be Reformed?," *The New York Review of Books* 56, no. 18 (2009), www.nybooks.com/articles/ archives/2009/nov/19/can-our-shameful-prisons-be-reformed/ (accessed January 5, 2010). On the well-being of Native Americans on a variety of measures, economic and non-economic, see David E. Wilkins, *American Indian Politics and the American Political System* (Lanham, MD: Rowman & Littlefield Publishers, 2007). On one insidious affliction, the large rates of alcohol abuse among Native Americans, see Melissa Walls *et al.*, "Early-Onset Alcohol Use Among Native American Youth: Examining Female Caretaker Influence," *Journal of Marriage and Family* 69, no. 2 (2007): 451–64.

[3] "Despite recent economic growth partly due to casino gaming, per capita income for Native Americans living on reservations in 1999 was $7,846, compared with $14,267 for Indians living off reservations and compared with $21,587 for the average U.S. citizen." Terry L. Anderson and Dominic P. Parker, "Sovereignty, Credible Commitments, and Economic Prosperity on American Indian Reservations," *The Journal of Law and Economics* 51, no. 41 (2008): 641–66.

connection between the past injustice and the current injustice, even if we cannot say what the course of history would have been without the injustice.

What is important is that it is reasonable to see a connection between past injustice and present injustice; and it is this connection that makes collective narratives or collective memory important. Collective narratives of suffering and oppression can arise quickly – how long must an injustice persist before it becomes enduring? There is no clear-cut answer to this issue, but clearly the injustice must last more than one generation, and then it must seem that the lives of the children of those who suffered from the radical injustice will not get better anytime soon. If the lives of immigrants are better than those of their parents, we should be cautious about calling the injustice enduring, since the injustice may continue to lessen over time. Sometimes, radical injustices persist so they become enduring; this may be the case in Tibet, where the Chinese have for several decades suppressed Tibetan culture with varying degrees of intensity. It is certainly plausible that this injustice will become enduring, if it has not become so already.

Collective memory, or what I prefer to call collective narrative, is one important element in turning a past injustice into an enduring injustice. The term collective memory is widely used, but it is unclear how a collective can share a memory of an historical event that no one alive today has witnessed. Jews do not have a memory of the Exodus, nor can Black Americans recall slavery or the Cherokee remember the Trail of Tears.[4] I am skeptical about the idea that a group can acquire memories, but people can and do identify with a collective past. People are story-telling and story-living animals. Collective narratives are important because they shape our identities, individual and collective: "Acquiring a group's memories and thereby identifying with its collective past is part of the process of acquiring any

---

[4] Jeff Olick, who shares my concern about the term collective memory, suggests instead the term "social memory studies," which is rather awkward. I prefer the term collective narrative – narratives tie the past to the present, and look upon the future, and help tie the group together. Like Olick, I do not want to make too much of a semantic distinction, since I think the intent of those that use the term collective memory is close enough to the idea of collective narrative, and so I will use both terms, as the former is widely used. Jeffrey K. Olick, *The Politics of Regret: On Collective Memory and Historical Responsibility* (New York: Routledge, 2007), 34.

social identity."[5] Belonging to a group situates people in the world. It gives a point of reference, and a point of pride (and perhaps a point of shame) for group members. It helps tell group members who they are and who they are not. People belong to many groups, as liberals often point out. One feature of collective narratives (or memory) is that those people who feel part of a collective narrative, who feel that this is their narrative, are part of the group. To the extent that some groups do not have collective narratives, they cannot suffer an enduring injustice. When members of a group see themselves as an intergenerational community, tied together by a collective narrative that focuses in part on injustices they have faced, it is likely to create an identity that will be maintained over time.

Just because a collective narrative encapsulates an enduring injustice does not automatically translate into an injustice that demands remedy. Peoples can wrongly use a collective narrative to make demands upon others, even if there is no current injustice. Judgments have to be made about which historical injustices are enduring, and which have ended; these judgments have to be made politically and through negotiations. There is a difference between memory and history, and judgments have to be made to see if the memory bears a resemblance to the history.[6] One worry here is that collective memory becomes a badge of identity, that in the words of Walter Benn Michaels, "a history that is learned can be learned by anyone (and can belong to anyone who learns it); a history that is remembered can only be remembered by those who first experienced it."[7] Michaels's point is that collective narrative morphs into experience; that if an event is part of a group's collective narrative it is part of their experience.

This is one danger of an argument that relies on collective narrative; if people feel a memory is part of their actual living experience it becomes hard to challenge. Yet not all collective memories match the

[5] Eviatar Zerubavel, *Time Maps: Collective Memory and the Social Shape of the Past* (University of Chicago Press, 2003), 3. See too Rogers M. Smith, *Stories of Peoplehood: The Politics and Morals of Political Membership* (Cambridge University Press, 2003).

[6] On this distinction, see Melissa Williams, *Voice, Trust and Memory: Marginalized Groups and the Failings of Liberal Representation* (Princeton University Press, 1998).

[7] Walter Benn Michaels, "'You Who Never Was There': Slavery and the New Historicism, Deconstruction and the Holocaust," *Narrative* 4, no. 1 (1996), 7.

historical record. Dominant and subordinate groups have collective narratives, and both may be misleading. The felt experience of a group may differ from an impartial examination of the group; some groups may feel danger when little or none exists. We cannot be expected to honor a group's narrative regardless of what the group pronounces it to be. Collective narratives can be used and misused for political purposes. These differences cannot easily be adjudicated, and certainly not without context. History and collective narrative will not always readily mesh with each other.

Overall, though, the issue of the truthfulness of a collective narrative is not tantamount to the judgment about whether a group is currently the victim of injustice. If most in a political community agree that a group is a victim of an injustice, it will probably not be difficult to agree if the group's history encapsulates injustice. If this is the case, the accuracy of some historical details may not be particularly important. I am not suggesting that historical accuracy is unimportant, and some particular historical claims may be significant. If a group argues that a certain piece of land is sacred to them, there ought to be some historical basis to the claim. If the concern is a general one – how can the Tatars return to their historical homeland, for example – then specific smaller claims become less important. My argument here is that it is often the general outline of a collective narrative that matters more than particular aspects of it.

I can now answer some issues dangling from the last chapter, as differences emerge between the cases of African and Native Americans on the one hand and women and workers on the other. One issue is whether women and workers have collective narratives like African and Native Americans (and the Crimean Tatars or Indian Muslims, and others), which they may have. Some women work toward creating an intergenerational collective narrative, but the identity of women crosses many other identities – ethnic, racial, and national. This is true for many identities, but for victims of enduring injustice, it is typically that group's identity that trumps other identities. If that were not the case, then the weight of the enduring injustice would not be strongly felt. Moreover, women have made more economic progress since the 1960s than have African and Native Americans, and while women still lag behind men, it is also the case that there is reason to believe that the gap may close; more women attend college than men, for example, and the payoff from that will take some time to see.[8] As I write, more women are employed in the US workplace than men, and some people think that women's skills will serve them well as the economy changes, while some traditional male occupations will become less important. In other words, there is hope that the story of progress for women still holds.

Are workers victims of injustice? Some certainly are, but others may not be; if their wages, benefits, and working hours are reasonable, then it may be hard to call them victims of injustice. Further, if they are victims of injustice, it is not clear if they view themselves as an intergenerational group with a collective narrative. Class lines are often permeable. To some degree, then, to call a group a victim of enduring injustice is to render a judgment that the group has a collective narrative that dominates other narratives, and has been a victim of an injustice in the past, and that there is a good reason to think that the group will continue to feel the effects of the injustice without some change of course. This is a perception, a guess, based on the past and present. But it is also a rendering of the possibilities of liberalism, and the meaning of injustice. Explaining this will help deepen the idea of enduring injustice, and further explain why women and workers are rarely considered victims of past injustice who need redress today.

3.2 A failure of liberalism

Many forms of injustice are remedied with the protection of individual rights and a fair system of distributive or liberal justice (which I defined in Chapter 1). It may take some time for the injustice to disappear with these remedies, but in time it often does. The Huguenots suffered terrible injustices in France a few centuries back. The Huguenots recovered from their losses: having similar views about property and economy to the Catholics, they were able to integrate themselves in the European states that accepted them, and in France as well, once a policy of toleration and then eventually a policy of protecting individual rights and equality was established. In many cases, liberal states emerged slowly, with the barriers of discrimination gradually lifted. English Catholics, Chinese Americans, German Americans, Japanese Canadians, among others, have all become well

---

[8] See the slightly hyperbolic Hanna Rosin, "The End of Men," *Atlantic Magazine*, www.theatlantic.com/magazine/archive/2010/07/the-end-of-men/8135 (accessed July 29, 2010).

integrated into their societies as discrimination against them has
faded, just as the narrative of progress suggested they would.

What unites most cases of enduring injustice, however, is a *failure* of
liberalism. The injustice from the past has not been remedied; it
continues today in some form, and it seems that without a change in
policies, it will continue into the future. A better defense of individual
rights, and a modest or moderate redistribution of wealth will often
not solve the enduring injustice (though sometimes these things will
help). To some degree, these may be the solutions to those workers
who live in poverty; or better regulation of the workplace may be the
solution for other problems that workers face. In other words, our
historical experience gives us reason to believe that the welfare state
can solve certain kinds of injustices, and so they will most likely not
count as historical injustices. This is why workers may be victims of
past injustice, but not enduring injustice.

When an injustice endures in a liberal democracy it is often because
the tools of liberal theory cannot easily rectify the injustice. A failure
of liberal practice is sometimes to blame, but even in these cases
secondary issues arise that are hard for liberal justice to solve (mistrust
is the example I explain below). This is why it is hard to have hope
for the future in cases of enduring injustice; the past and present do
not give the victims of the injustice much hope for the future. What
is needed is a different course, but liberalism is not able to offer
that. When the liberal story of progress has failed some peoples, the
injustice endures, and the solution is often opaque.[9] In what follows,
I examine three ways in which enduring injustice challenges liberal
justice, involving sacred land, the limits of liberal toleration, and
mistrust.

Exile and sacred land

The limits of redistribution of wealth are readily seen in the arguments
of the skeptics. In a comment that represents much of the skeptics'
view, Richard Vernon argues that: "Restitutive claims would at least
be very much less compelling in a distributively just world."[10] In many

---

[9] Duncan Ivison very briefly suggests a similar argument. See Ivison,
Postcolonial Liberalism (Cambridge University Press, 2002), 48.
[10] Richard Vernon, "Against Restitution," *Political Studies* 51, no. 3 (2003), 552.

cases distributive justice can rectify injustice. Yet the assumption behind Vernon's argument – that redistributive justice, along with protection of individual rights, can always or mostly put an end to an enduring injustice – is flawed. David Lyons argues that to compensate for the injustice they have faced, Native Americans have "a valid claim to a fair share of its [the US] resources as well as to social and economic opportunities."[11] Similarly, Jeremy Waldron talks about tribal *owners* of land, wondering if they might have sold it if it wasn't wrongly taken from them. His examples include his Aunt's inheritance, and a stolen car.[12] Lost land, on this view, can be compensated for with either money or different land. What can be lost can be replaced: this is certainly true for money and cars. Waldron does say that his argument may not apply to cases "where the dispossessed subject is a tribe or a community, rather than an individual, where the holding of which it has been dispossessed is particularly important for its sense of identity as a community," but this is a startling caveat, since the main subject of Waldron's essay are tribes (indigenous peoples) whose identity is very much tied to land. Waldron's brief qualification is overwhelmed by the rest of the argument, which is devoted to showing that the land claims of indigenous peoples have faded over time. (Or his caveat undermines his argument, but then why advance the argument in the first place?) Waldron is clear in his conclusion that the main subject of his essay is indigenous peoples: "It is important that defenders of aboriginal claims face up to the possibility of the supersession of historic injustice. Even if this particular thesis about supersession is mistaken, some account has to be given of the impact on aboriginal claims and on the reparation of generations-old injustices on the demographic and ecological changes that have taken place."[13] Waldron's focus on land is followed by many skeptics, who also concentrate on land in their arguments, and see it as a commodity.[14]

I have already mentioned several arguments that discuss the welfare of the victims of enduring injustice; these arguments are all couched in

[11] David Lyons, "The New Indian Claims and Original Rights to Land," *Social Theory and Practice* 4, no. 3 (1977), 268.

[12] Jeremy Waldron, "Superseding Historic Injustice," *Ethics* 103, no. 4 (1992), 20.

[13] *Ibid.*, 27.   [14] See particularly Lyons, "The New Indian Claims."

the contemporary liberal language of the redistribution of wealth, as are arguments for reparations.[15] The redistribution of wealth would help in some cases of enduring injustice, but it is also the case that its usefulness is limited in others. When a radical injustice was inflicted upon a group, its attachments broken, or severely harmed, its people scattered or killed, or its sacred places invaded, monetary compensation and protection of individual rights will do little to repair the injustice. In many cases of enduring injustice the way of life led by the groups was disrupted some time ago, and the harm of this disruption is still felt in some way. A longing is often felt – a longing to return to one's ancestral home or to return to an old way of life. These longings often remain because many of the descendants of the victims feel ill at ease in the world today. Their culture, their way of life, has been broken, and they remain unable to fit into a new culture or to fully repair their own. In other cases, like with indigenous peoples, there is often little sense of voluntary agreement about the way their life is constructed. Many of their ancestors, and those currently living, had little aspiration to integrate into the larger culture. They resent their subjugation and the constraints on their way of life; they resent the way their traditions have been disrupted by outsiders while having little say in the matter.

The importance of the past and collective narrative is readily seen when land is at issue. Certain land is sacred for many peoples. Hills, stones, and mountains are sometimes sacred ground to indigenous peoples, like Ayers Rock in Australia or the Black Hills in the US. The Black Hills are considered sacred to the Lakota Sioux; special ceremonies are performed there. The US federal government assured the Sioux rights to the land in 1850s by treaty. After gold was found there the US broke the treaty to seize the land. This land was, and still is, mined. The Sioux eventually sued, and won in the US Supreme Court, which found the treaties giving the land away to be fraudulent. The Sioux were awarded compensation ($700 million today, including

---

[15] Farid Abdel-Nour, "National Responsibility," *Political Theory* 31, no. 5 (2003): 693–719; Bernard Boxill, "A Lockean Argument for Black Reparations," *The Journal of Ethics* 7, no. 1 (2003): 63–91; Andrew I. Cohen, "Compensation for Historic Injustices: Completing the Boxill and Sher Argument," *Philosophy and Public Affairs* 37, no. 1 (2009): 81–102; George Sher, "Transgenerational Compensation," *Philosophy and Public Affairs* 37, no. 1 (2009): 181–200.

interest), but not the return of the land.[16] The Sioux have refused to accept the money, as they maintain that this sacred land cannot be bought.

Indigenous peoples are not the only peoples that look at land as something other than a commodity. Israel, after all, is often called the Holy Land. During the wars in Yugoslavia after the fall of the Berlin Wall some commentators suggested that the Serbs looked upon Kosovo as "their Jerusalem." Christians have ancient and illustrious monasteries and churches not only in Israel, but also in Lebanon, Syria, and Turkey. Some Hindus look at India as holy ground, and India contains rivers holy to Hindus.[17] The government of Saudi Arabia looks at itself as the guardian of certain holy Muslim sites. Sometimes what is sacred is a parcel of land, but at other times the group wants to live on the sacred land; until that happens, they feel they are in exile. The Crimean Tatars want to return to their land. This normal sounding sentence, however, is pregnant with moral implications, since many of the people who want to return never lived in the Crimea. They look at the Crimea as their ancestral homeland. It is part of their collective narrative that stretches from the past to the present and peers into the future. If one thinks that the Ukraine should have an immigration policy that privileges Tartars (the Crimea is in the Ukraine), then one must think that the past, and the collective narrative of the Tatars, has moral significance.

What I want to suggest is that sometimes the past has moral weight. One can argue that the past just was – history is history, not a normative matter. It can certainly inform us about how we arrived at our world today, but it does not tell us how matters ought to be. This is an implicit idea in the arguments of those skeptical of the idea of historical injustice; we use today's standards of justice to determine what wrongs should be remedied, and we remedy them according to that standard. This is the case when the issue is distributive justice – if some people are below some distribution

---

[16] US Supreme Court, *United States* v. *Sioux Nation of Indians*, 448 US (1980): 371 (accessed November 20, 2006).

[17] Aileen Yoo, "Kosovo: the Jerusalem of Serbia," www.washingtonpost.com/wp-srv/inatl/longterm/balkans/overview/kosovo.htm; William Dalrymple, *From the Holy Mountain: a Journey Among the Christians of the Middle East* (New York: Henry Holt, 1998); Gavin Flood, *An Introduction to Hinduism* (Cambridge University Press, 1996), 212–14.

"W," then they should receive compensation. How they came to be below "W," may not matter at all.

But some wrongs are only understandable if we take the past into account, and when we think of ways to overcome the injustice, the past will usually help inform the remedy. The idea of sacred land only makes sense if the idea of collective narrative and historical attachments have meaning. The Black Hills are sacred to the Lakota Sioux because their spiritual history is tied to the hills. One Lakota Sioux explained: "All of our origin stories go back to this place. We have a spiritual connection to the Black Hills that can't be sold. I don't think I could face the Creator with an open heart if I ever took money for it."[18] If the Lakota had no collective narrative, the Blacks Hills would be just another place, and there would be little problem for them to sell it for money. History does tell us how the injustice came to be; but it also points to the remedy. A focus on contemporary justice that says the history of an injustice is unimportant, that says what matters are injustices today and not their history, cannot account for the importance of the Black Hills to the Lakota. History will have little or no moral weight when the focus is on distributive justice and individual rights, but history and collective narrative play an important role when we turn to the issue of sacred land.

Similarly, history has moral weight when it comes to exile and the desire to return. The Tatar claim that they live in exile only makes sense by taking the past into account. An account of liberal justice would ask if the Tatars receive unequal treatment where they live, or if their rights are violated. These important questions focus on injustice today and do not capture the injustice of exile or of separation from a sacred place. The Tatar homeland is kept alive in exile through stories, paintings, and in other symbolic ways.[19] Exile is not only a loss for those expelled, but it is often a loss for their children, as the collective narrative in which they live places them elsewhere. Some children may find their new homes sufficient; perhaps they can establish a new narrative (and identity) where they live. If they do not, however, then

---

[18] www.sacredland.org/historical_sites_pages/black_hills.html. *United States* v. *Sioux Nation of Indians*, 448 US 371 (1980) (accessed November 20, 2006). See also F. Pommersheim, "The Black Hills Case: On the Cusp of History," *Wicazo Sa Review* 4, no. 1 (1988): 18–23.

[19] Greta Lynn Uehling, *Beyond Memory: The Crimean Tatars' Deportation and Return* (New York: Palgrave Macmillan, 2004).

once again an injustice is enduring. The home that is yearned for will often then be the ancestral one: what other home can be longed for? The Tatars want to return so they can maintain their nation; they want to return so they can be at home in the world. In the contemporary world, national identities live through institutions – universities, schools, media, professional organizations, government bureaucracies, and so on. When a nation lives together, and its numbers are large enough to maintain these sorts of institutions, it can better secure its national identity.[20]

Taking away land is only one way to severely disrupt a group's collective narrative. The US did not just take away considerable amounts of tribal land; it often pursued policies that aimed to destroy tribal structures, and "Europeanize" the Sioux and other tribes. Many tribes used their property communally. The Dawes Act in the late nineteenth century forced most tribes to divide their communal land into individual plots, which was part of a policy to try to make Indians like white citizens.[21] This policy ended in 1934, only to begin again with the unfortunately named Termination policy in the 1950s, which strove to break up ("terminate") indigenous tribes by ending their communal control of land, giving plots of land to some individuals, while others were given money and encouraged to move to urban areas. Like the Dawes Act, Termination was widely considered a failure (though it took the US government less time to realize this the second time around), partly because the cultural structure of some tribes was destroyed.[22] But owning property, learning English, going

---

[20] See generally Ernest Gellner, *Nations and Nationalism* (Ithaca, NY: Cornell University Press, 1983); Benedict Anderson, *Imagined Communities: Reflections on the Origins and Spread of Nationalism*, 2nd edn. (London: Verso, 1991); Will Kymlicka, *Multicultural Citizenship: A Liberal Theory of Minority Rights* (Oxford University Press, 1993). My emphasis here is on identity, not culture. For the importance of this distinction, see Margaret Moore, *The Ethics of Nationalism* (Oxford University Press, 2001), ch. 3.

[21] Stuart Banner, *How the Indians Lost Their Land: Law and Power on the Frontier* (Cambridge, MA: Belknap Press of Harvard University Press, 2005), ch. 8; Linda S. Parker, *Native American Estate: The Struggle Over Indian and Hawaiian Lands* (Honolulu: University of Hawaii Press, 1989), ch. 3; Frederick E. Hoxie, *A Final Promise: The Campaign to Assimilate the Indians, 1880–1920* (Lincoln, NE: University of Nebraska Press, 1984).

[22] Francis Paul Prucha, *The Great Father: The United States Government and the American Indians*, abridged edn. (Lincoln: University of Nebraska Press, 1986), 344.

to school, and learning how to farm did not turn Native Americans into liberal and white women and men. A similar story can be told in Canada, with the now infamous government White Paper of 1969 recommending the end of official recognition of Canadian tribes, and the assimilation of First Nations into the Canadian people, which was rejected.[23] The collective narrative of many indigenous peoples was drastically altered, but it has not fully merged with the dominant culture, and there is little reason to think that it will do so anytime soon.

Sacred practice

A second limit on the ability of liberal justice to end enduring injustice is when the unfolding of liberal rights is of limited help to undo an injustice. Liberal toleration plays a large role in the liberal story of progress: from toleration to individual rights, liberalism can be read as a story of freedom unfolding for more and more people. Yet what is little noticed is how much of a Protestant story this is, and how the role of rights is limited in other contexts.[24] The role of Protestantism within liberalism can readily be seen in Rawls. Rawls argues that one mark of the unreasonable is that they "insist that their beliefs alone are true." What people need to do, Rawls maintains, is to realize the impossibility of reaching agreement on the "truth of comprehensive doctrines." The key question of political liberalism, according to Rawls, is: "How is society even possible between those of different faiths?"[25] Protestantism, or at least certain prominent versions of it, assumes religion to be more about conscience and belief than practice. With religion viewed as a matter of conscience by liberals, religion became a private matter, and then it became easy to tolerate. People could leave their religion if they chose; religions became voluntary

---

[23] A critical exploration of the White Paper, along with a reprint of it, can be found in Dale Turner, *This is Not a Peace Pipe: Towards a Critical Indigenous Philosophy* (University of Toronto Press, 2006).

[24] I expand upon this argument in Jeff Spinner-Halev, "Hinduism, Christianity, and Liberal Religious Toleration," *Political Theory* 33, no. 1 (2005): 28–57. See also S. N. Balagangadhara and Jakob De Roover, "The Secular State and Religious Conflict: Liberal Neutrality and the Indian Case of Pluralism," *Journal of Political Philosophy* 15, no. 1 (2007): 67–92.

[25] John Rawls, *Political Liberalism* (New York: Columbia University Press, 1993), xxiv, 61, 63.

associations, soon to be joined by many other kinds of voluntary (and private) associations. The liberal conception of public and private has its origins in the (eventual) Protestant conception of privatized religion.

Though some Protestant religions have sanctioned discrimination (and other illiberal matters), it was relatively easy for Protestantism to eventually cohere with liberal principles, with its focus on individual conscience. The idea that every person should determine for her- or himself how to worship, that idea that the individual should follow her conscience in religious matters, fits in well with the idea of individual rights. The Protestant emphasis on the individual does not make every church a liberal one but Protestantism makes it easy to put religion in the private sphere, since it is an individual matter. As an individual matter, individuals can join or leave religions as they choose, which alleviates the problem of non-liberal churches. The Church of Latter Day Saints (LDS or Mormons) officially discriminated against Black Americans for much of its history, preventing any from becoming priests. The head of the Mormon Church had a revelation and reversed this view in 1978. He was almost certainly responding to social pressures to do so, but it is doubtful that the US government would have passed a law insisting upon equality within the LDS church. Nor was it crucial that the US government do so: with many churches in the US the fact that one practiced racial discrimination had limited social consequences.

This model of religion as a matter of belief with individual conscience and mobility at its center, does not, however, fit Hinduism well. The issue of whether a religion is true or not, which Rawls takes to be a key issue for liberalism, is not a concern for Hinduism: to most Hindus "the question of 'truth' in tradition does not even make sense."[26] Hinduism, lacking a creed or central tenets of faith, is concerned with stories about deities and with rituals and practices, many of which are social, and allows for exit only with great difficulty. What I mean by social rituals and practices is that they are practiced with others, be they family members or community members. Not every ritual is social – some rituals, like giving offerings to deities, can and are practiced both socially and in solitude.

---

[26] Balagangadhara and De Roover, "The Secular State and Religious Conflict," 75.

Hindu ritual orders life; it regulates social relations, birth, marriage, and death. But Hinduism is also concerned with legitimizing hierarchical social relationships and mollifying deities, not with faith or belief.[27]

Around the time of its independence, the Indian Parliament discussed the issue of outlawing discrimination within temples. Making such discrimination illegal clearly violates religious freedom and toleration. If Western liberal countries tolerated churches that discriminated, why couldn't India do the same with Hindu temples? Nehru and others argued that discrimination against Dalits (Untouchables) was a backwards practice that was also against liberal and democratic principles. Liberalism, however, does not usually insist that churches act "progressively," only privately.

It is this split between faith and practice – or the relative unimportance of the former – that makes the idea of religious toleration an awkward fit with respect to Hinduism. The Christian allows his beliefs to determine his Church, but it makes little sense to say the same thing about Hindus. There are Hindu temples, but there are no congregations or formal services; caste Hindus (those who are not untouchables) attend a temple when they like. Liberal justice assumes that religious toleration can be readily granted to all, since religion is a matter of conscience and so readily privatized. If a religion demanded a hierarchy that one disliked, one could join another religion. The possibility of exit will often put pressure on the Church to respond to the wishes of its members.[28]

The classic liberal response to a Hindu Dalit who is angered by his inability to enter the inner sanctum of a Hindu temple is to simply join another church that does not discriminate. In India, though, before laws outlawing discrimination in temples (and, in many places, even after these laws passed), almost every Hindu temple practiced discrimination. Many rulers and wealthy people in India traditionally built and then endowed temples, usually with either jewels or land, and then turned them over to the Trustees. (Even some idols within temples are endowed.) The Trustees, who often bequeath their positions to their descendants, then used the endowments to run

[27] Frits Staal, *Rules Without Meaning: Ritual, Mantras, and the Human Sciences* (New York: Peter Lang, 1989); Duncan J. Derrett, *Religion, Law and the State in India* (New Delhi: Oxford University Press, 1999), 58.

[28] Albert O. Hirschman, *Exit, Voice, and Loyalty; Responses to Decline in Firms, Organizations, and States* (Cambridge, MA: Harvard University Press, 1970).

the temples. The endowments enjoyed by Hindu temples mean that a Hindu leaving his religion has no financial consequences for Hinduism, since there is no religious hierarchy that needs financial support from its members. It also means temple discrimination persists even in the face of the law outlawing it, partly because of inefficiencies of the Indian state, but also because it is hard to police thousands of temples.

Perhaps if one does not like being a Dalit, one can convert to a different religion, yet caste usually follows Hindus, even when they convert to the religions that are furthest from them, Christianity or Islam.[29] (Hinduism is closer to Jainism, Sikhism, and Buddhism; and in fact under Indian law these religions are considered to be Hindu.) Making exit even more unattractive is that Hindu Dalits are eligible for affirmative action, but those who convert are not supposed to be (though they are sometimes in practice), even though they often face discrimination for being a Dalit after conversion. Moreover, India is a Hindu-dominated country, with non-Hindus often facing discrimination. A Dalit converting to Islam or Christianity may then face even more discrimination than as a Dalit and as a non-Hindu, making exit unattractive for many (though some do convert).

Donald Smith – who wrote the still dominant work on India, religion, and secularism in 1963 and understood quite well the differences between Protestantism and Hinduism – argued in good liberal fashion that the secular state should not interfere with religious matters. Religious reform, he declared, "should never be the motive behind state legislation." Yet Smith wanted some reforms of Hinduism, and agreed with a few of the reforms already instituted by the state. He justified them by arguing that religious reforms by the state are valid only if they are the incidental result of the "state's protection of the public in cases where religious practices clearly tend to injure human beings physically or morally, where religious institutions grossly misuse offerings and endowments made by the public, or where social institutions connected with religion violate basic human rights."[30]

---

[29] Imtiaz Ahmad, *Caste and Social Stratification among Muslims in India*, 2nd edn. (New Delhi: Manohar, 1978); Donald Eugene Smith, *India as a Secular State* (Princeton University Press, 1963), 325.

[30] Smith, *India as a Secular State*, 233. See the criticism of Smith on this and other grounds in Marc Galanter, "Secularism, East and West," in Rajeev Bhargava, ed., *Secularism and Its Critics* (Oxford University Press, 1998), 234–67.

Smith's argument is woefully cramped by his attempt to justify India's reforms of Hinduism within a liberal framework. It is quite hard to argue that these changes were made without intending religious reform. Smith's idea that a religion can be reformed because it morally injures others is simply too vague, since one could argue that many religious practices morally injure others.

This leaves the injustice of caste to endure, however. When religious discrimination is pervasive throughout society, and exit is difficult, liberal toleration runs up against liberal equality. The many strands of Christianity, propelled by the idea that religion is a matter of belief, allow people to escape a religion they dislike. But this is not the case for Hinduism, which is nearly impossible to walk away from in India. The issue is that discrimination against Dalits and lower-caste Hindus is not limited to just religious practice, but pervades much of life in India. The state can outlaw discrimination in public places, as it has, but the power of Hinduism within India means these laws have limited effectiveness, and will probably be limited until and unless discrimination within Hinduism is confronted in a meaningful way. Here the analogy – or the dis-analogy – between Mormons and Hindus is instructive. People can leave the Mormon Church with little harm in the US. And while one might say this is not the case in Utah, one can leave Utah relatively easy. Or one could stay: forty percent of Utah is non-Mormon, with that percentage expected to rise.[31]

With exit difficult if not impossible, with discrimination within Hinduism readily seeping out to civil society and the public sphere, liberal toleration clearly allows considerable injustice to endure. The caste system is not caused by liberal toleration, but toleration makes it hard for liberalism to have the tools to undo the damage that the caste system causes. Without departing from ideals of liberal justice in some ways, the caste system will remain an enduring injustice.

Mistrust and history

A third issue that is hard for liberal justice to tackle is the issue of mistrust. Some enduring injustices are in part a failure of liberal practice, though these often overlap with a disruption in collective

---

[31] Associated Press, "Records: Percentage of Mormons in Utah Declines," www.azcentral.com/news/articles/2008/11/20/20081120fewer-mormons1120-ON.html (accessed July 30, 2010).

narrative. A group may feel the sting of discrimination and subordin-
ation through time, and the liberal state may be unable or unwilling to
ensure equal treatment. This failure of liberal practice means that
justice probably cannot be achieved even if the state redoubles its
efforts at redistributing wealth, because the failure of liberal practice
almost always raises a secondary issue that liberal justice is hard
pressed to solve: the victimized group will often mistrust the government and perhaps liberal democratic theory as well, and for good
reason. Enduring injustice will often result in a group having little
trust for its government; this argument is well articulated by Melissa
Williams (and many advocates of remedying past injustice), so I will
not belabor the point.[32] This mistrust is historically based. These
groups mistrust the government for what it has done in the past, and
because they have little reason to think that the present and future will
be that much different. The Turkish government from its inception in
the early 1920s denied that minorities lived within its borders. The
Kurds in Turkey faced various prohibitions and discrimination; they
were, at various times, prohibited from speaking Kurdish in schools or
from having Kurdish-speaking media. The war that the Turkish
government waged against the PKK (the Kurdistan Worker's Party,
which fought for a Kurdish state) from 1984 to 1999 was often heavy
handed, and resulted in many civilian Kurdish casualties, and many
internal refugees. While some of these restrictions were recently lifted,
the mistrust that many Kurds feel toward the Turkish government is
deep-seated.[33] The reasons for this mistrust are passed down from one
generation to the next; so the mistrust is not just engendered by bad
treatment now, but because this mistreatment fits in a narrative that
many heard when they were children, and then experienced as adults
(and perhaps, of course, as children as well).

Many Black Americans are suspicious of government attempts to
ensure that children receive routine vaccinations, because of their

---

[32] Williams, *Voice, Trust and Memory*. Janna Thompson discusses trust
extensively in Part I of Thompson, *Taking Responsibility for the Past:
Reparation and Historical Injustice* (Cambridge: Polity, 2002); Ivison discusses
trust in Ivison, *Postcolonial Liberalism*; while Burke A. Hendrix discusses it
very briefly in Hendrix, "Memory in Native American Land Claims," *Political
Theory* 33, no. 6 (2005): 774–75.

[33] Dilek Kurban *et al.*, "Overcoming a Legacy of Mistrust: Towards
Reconciliation Between the State and the Displaced" (Geneva: IDMC, 2006).

memories of the infamous Tuskegee experiment, where Black men
with syphilis had treatment withheld by the US government in order
for researchers to follow the course of the disease (which they did even
after penicillin, an effective treatment, became widely available). Similarly, the Tuskegee experiment has apparently led many Blacks to
believe that AIDS is actually a plot devised by the US government to
harm the Black population. In this case, the mistrust makes it harder
for the government to help citizens who often need the most help. Leif
Wenar points out that in cases of enduring injustice (though he does
not use the term), the possibility of future moral relations between the
victims of the injustice and the dominant group in the society is
damaged.[34] This damage can be repaired only by understanding how
the past affects victims' attitudes toward their government today.

The medical mistrust that many Black Americans feel about the US
government is but one variety of mistrust they have. The history of
oppression – one consequence of which is lack of trust – is what links
the past to the present and perhaps the future and is one element that
ties people into a group. Liberal individuality fails people when
members of a group are continually mistreated by a government
because of their group membership. When Blacks see that it is only
members of their group who are wrongly used for a government
medical experiment, and when this is but one instance of being treated
unfairly by the government (or when the government fails to protect
them when they are mistreated by others), they understandably do not
trust the government to act in their best interests. History matters here
because justifiable mistrust is not the consequence of one or two
mistakes by a government – random mistakes are to be expected –
but are a result of repeated mistreatments over time of members of the
same group. The history of the mistreatment leads to the current
mistrust. This history makes group membership matter (there may
be other reasons why group membership matters as well), since group
members understand that it was (and sometimes still is) their group

---

[34] Wenar does not use the term enduring injustice, but I believe it captures much of
his argument about reparations, which is that reparations are considered for
groups that are doing badly now by a principle of justice and have suffered in
the past from injustice. Leif Wenar, "Reparations for the Future," *Journal of
Social Philosophy* 37, no. 3 (2006), 396–405. See too Margaret Walker's
important argument in *Moral Repair: Reconstructing Moral Relations After
Wrongdoing* (Cambridge University Press, 2006), ch. 3.

that is marked out for ill treatment. This is how a collective narrative helps to make an historical injustice an enduring one. If the group in question had no memories of past injustices, the current ones might be ascribed to bad luck or readily reparable mistakes. But if the injustices of today are part of a pattern that extends into the past, they will be less excusable. The stories of past injustices that are passed down will make the current injustices part of a long pattern that will explain a group's mistrust of the government. The identification that one has with one's ancestors is often deepened by patterns of ill-treatment. Here too, however, it is important to note that mistrust has the most moral weight in cases of enduring, not historical, injustice. When the injustice is enduring, then those in power ought to ask what can be done to help restore the trust of the oppressed. The history and memory of the enduring injustice fuels the current mistrust. The advocates of ending enduring injustice do not point out incisively enough that this lack of trust, when justified, is an obstacle to overcome when devising ways to end the enduring injustice. The skeptics might say that focusing on contemporary justice may ameliorate or end the mistrust, but this is not always the case. This memory will cast a pall today; efforts by the government to pursue liberal justice will often be treated with suspicion by victims of the enduring injustice. The collective narrative and history of mistreatment and mistrust means that it may not be enough to treat Black Americans today with justice; it may also mean working to repair a relationship that is wounded.[35]

The failure of liberalism and the resulting mistrust that indigenous peoples have toward the US and Canadian (and many other) governments means that better enforcement of individual rights may in fact cause more resentment and harm than justice (which is true for some other, if not most, indigenous peoples in Western countries). Indigenous peoples today would become quite suspicious if Western governments said that they must intervene in indigenous communities in order to protect the individual rights of the groups' members. The sudden concern of these governments for the welfare of those it has abused for centuries would not be seen as sincere. Liberal justice cannot simply be applied to Native Americans. Treating Native Americans on reservations as individual citizens of the US government

[35] Walker, *Moral Repair.*

will do little to end the enduring injustice they face. One issue that must be faced is that the history of the relationship between Western governments and indigenous peoples puts the justice of the authority of those governments into question. Many Native Americans understandably do not trust the US government to protect them very well, though it is not only trust at issue: the liberal emphasis on the individual has not resulted in Native American well-being. In Canada, where the issues with indigenous peoples are similar to those in the US, John Borrows explains this in the voice of the Trickster, a First Nations character. When faced with former Prime Minister Trudeau's idea of treating all Canadians citizens as individuals and as equals, the Trickster comments: "This is interesting, he thinks, that once you devastate a people, and make them unequal, you then promise equality. Is this justice, he wonders?"[36] The rhetorical force of this question only makes sense if one assumes that collective history and narrative are meaningful. If liberalism meant disaster for the group in question and its members, then the kind of justice applied needs to be considered carefully. When trying to determine how to move forward, the mistrust felt should be accounted for, along with the non-Western modes of life that some indigenous peoples adhere to.

One could argue that liberal theory cannot be blamed for all events that have occurred under liberal regimes. Slavery of African Americans, for example, can readily be called non-liberal or anti-liberal, even though it took place within a (partially) liberal state. Caste pre-dates liberalism by centuries. Liberal democratic theory is a theory, and it cannot be held accountable for all practices within a state. To blame liberalism for the violations of its own principles, at least in these cases, seems unfair. Moreover, one advantage of liberal democracy (or democracies generally) is its capacity to expose non-liberal practices within liberal regimes, or to point out harmful practices, even if they are compatible with liberalism. The ability of citizens to associate, to form groups and organize, to vote, and the benefits of a free press means that public opinion has some effect in democracies. We can say, for example, that one of the unfortunate effects of industrialization that was not foreseen in the nineteenth century is tremendous harm to the environment. There has surely been greater attention to

---

[36] John Borrows, "Re-Living the Present: Title, Treaties, and the Trickster in British Columbia," *BC Studies* 120 (1998), 104.

environmental issues in the last few years. If problems arise within liberal democracies, they can be diagnosed and corrected.

Yet to its victims, the changes within liberalism may seem rather hollow. There is little question that liberalism and imperialism were tied together. This connection may not be inherent within liberalism, but it is undoubtedly part of the history of liberal practice; and there is reason to think it was tied together in theory as well.[37] We are always saddled with a history that we did not make. Furthermore, the challenge that enduring injustices pose is that it is hard to see how they can be easily fixed; and certainly there is reason to be skeptical as to whether liberalism has the tools to fix these injustices. Some enduring injustices certainly occurred as violations of liberal practice; others occurred in non-liberal regimes. Neither liberal theory nor liberal practice can be blamed for the exile of the Tatars. The problem for liberal justice is that enduring injustices are often rooted in a failure or a silence of liberalism; that liberal democracy offers us the ability to see these failures is important, but to look to liberalism as a solution to its own shortcomings is simply too tall an order.

3.3 Responsibility

Most arguments about enduring injustice emphasize the continuity of governments, but if other examples beyond Native and African Americans are used the problems with this emphasis becomes apparent. Nearly every argument about enduring injustice assumes either explicitly or implicitly that the progeny of the victims and perpetrators of the injustice live in the same community as their ancestors, and they want people alive today to take responsibility for injustices that have their origins in the past. The responsibility for the past argument assumes that the state under which a past injustice was committed still exists. The path of history is rarely straight and narrow, however, and it is not surprising that many enduring injustices originate in states that no longer exist, or have left the scene of the crime. The French

---

[37] Uday Singh Mehta, *Liberalism and Empire: A Study in Nineteenth-Century British Liberal Thought* (University of Chicago Press, 1999); Jennifer Pitts, *A Turn to Empire: The Rise of Imperial Liberalism in Britain and France* (Princeton University Press, 2005); James Tully, *Public Philosophy in a New Key: Vol. 2, Imperialism and Civic Freedom* (Cambridge University Press, 2008).

and Spanish committed their share of injustices in North America but left centuries ago. The Romans kicked most of the Jews out of Palestine, but the Roman Empire is long gone. More recently, the Soviet Union committed many injustices but it no longer exists. Stalin expelled the Tatars and several other peoples to Soviet Asia[38] and many now want to return to the home of their ancestors. One might say, as Thompson and Chandran Kukathas do, that if the communities that committed the injustices disappear, then there is no agent responsible to help fix the injustice, and there is nothing to be done.[39] One might think that the skeptics would use this argument – the number of governmental changes through time is one more reason to focus on current injustices, regardless of their historical roots. Why, however, should the vagaries of history be an excuse to allow an enduring injustice to fester?

What constitutes a sufficient government change to leave responsibility behind is also hard to determine. The Japanese government was not completely abolished after the Second World War, but it was radically transformed. Is the Japanese government today responsible for the Japanese government's actions in the 1930s and 1940s? The Turkish government is clearly different from the Ottoman Empire that reigned during the Armenian genocide, though clearly there is some connection between some of the people in power in the Empire's waning years (the "Young Turks"), and those of the Turkish government that arose a few years later. Is the Ottoman Empire the same as the Turkish Republic? The issue of continuation is hard to determine in Latin America, where the forms of government change with some frequency; Venezuela has had twenty-four different constitutions since 1811; Columbia has had twelve, and there have been thirteen in Peru.[40] While constitutions and governments change, they often look

---

[38] A description of these deportations can be found in J. Otto Pohl, "Stalin's Genocide Against Repressed Peoples," *Journal of Genocide Research* 2, no. 2 (2000): 267–93. Stalin expelled eight peoples: the Chechens (who returned later), the Ingushi, the Karachai, the Balkars, the Kamyks, the Volga Germans, the Meshketian Turks, and the Tatars.

[39] Thompson, *Taking Responsibility for the Past*, 76; Chandran Kukathas, "Responsibility for the Past: How to Shift the Burden," *Politics, Philosophy and Economics* 2, no. 2 (2003): 165–90.

[40] Jonathan Hartlyn and Arturo Valenzuela, "Democracy in Latin America Since 1930," in Leslie Bethel, ed., *Latin America: Politics and Society Since 1930* (Cambridge University Press, 1998), 3–66.

the same in the eyes of the indigenous peoples there.[41] The argument for responsibility opens up hard questions about whether the new regime is really a continuation of the old regime or not. Why should relief of an enduring injustice hang on the answer, however, particularly when in many cases the answer will be opaque?

A related argument suggests that those who gained from a past injustice are responsible to make redress; their gains are ill-gotten and so they should make amends.[42] The symmetry between unjust acquisition and responsibility is attractive, but not all enduring injustices caused economic gain. It's not clear that the Ottoman Empire (or Turkey) gained economically from the Armenian genocide, or that the expulsion of the Tatars from the Crimea was economically beneficial. In other cases, it may simply be impossible to determine the economic gains or losses. It also may be the case that the ancestors of both the perpetrators and victims gained economically from the enduring injustice. Descendants of Black American slaves are, as a group, better off economically than the average African. Economic gain, however, is not the real issue. If African American slaves were found to have contributed little to the overall American economy, would that make slavery any less just? The radical injustice of slavery, of snatching people away from their families in Africa, of sending them on a journey to the US where many were killed, of selling people to others who had complete control of them – these radical injustices remain apart from whatever economic gain was made from slaves. Why should repairing the injustice turn on whether the perpetrator gained economically from the injustice?

Justice does not mean that people or communities take responsibility for the past, but rather that political communities take responsibility for the present and future. Injustices that occurred in the past cannot be undone, as the skeptics claim. Political communities can

---

[41] Some recent Latin American governments have in fact taken strides to be more attentive to the needs of indigenous peoples. See Deborah J. Yashar, *Contesting Citizenship in Latin America: The Rise of Indigenous Movements and the Postliberal Challenge* (Cambridge University Press, 2005).

[42] Variations of this argument include Kukathas, "Responsibility for the Past," 184; Robert Sparrow, "History and Collective Responsibility," *Australasian Journal of Philosophy* 78, no. 3 (2000), 355; Thomas McCarthy, "Coming to Terms With Our Past, Part II: On the Morality and Politics of Reparations for Slavery," *Political Theory* 32, no. 6 (2004), 758; Daniel Butt, "On Benefiting From Injustice," *Canadian Journal of Philosophy* 37, no. 1 (2007): 129–52.

and should work to undo current injustices. A political community may not be responsible for an enduring injustice, in either its history or its present form, but it still may have a responsibility to help end the injustice. History may help us better understand the form of an injustice and its possible remedy; history may also bring peoples together in ways that both sides dislike or resent, but the world and its injustices rarely work neatly.

We ought to relax (though not sever) the connection between causality and responsibility that is commonly assumed in historical injustice arguments. Here I loosely follow David Miller's argument on responsibility. Miller argues that there are four principles for deciding who is responsible to alleviate a wrong: those who are causally responsible, those morally responsible, the people who have the capacity to do so, and those who share a moral or political community with those who have suffered the wrong.[43] Miller proposes a connection theory: we should fix responsibility on the agent who is connected to the one suffering in some way; if several agents are connected, we will choose the agent with the strongest connection to the sufferer or we can divide up the responsibility among those with a connection. Miller argues that one principle of responsibility is not enough, since doing so will too readily leave no one responsible for alleviating some harms. This of course is exactly what is wrong with the arguments of the advocates of repairing past injustice, which leaves some enduring injustice without an agent that is responsible to repair the injustice.

Instead of repeating Miller's argument, I want to emphasize the general idea that responsibility is not necessarily tied to causality. When terrible natural disasters hit, countries that are able to give aid to the victims often feel responsible to do so, even though no one caused the disaster. While one might think that this is different from an injustice, since there is no causal agent when there is a natural disaster, this is misleading. The poor are often victims of natural disasters more than are the wealthy because the poor have less protection from these disasters. In the US, for example, mobile homes are more prone to being badly damaged during natural disasters than the

---

[43] David Miller, "Distributing Responsibilities," *Journal of Political Philosophy* 9, no. 4 (2001): 453–71. Miller argues that one might be causally responsible for an event without being morally responsible: if I accidentally trip and then knock you down, I am causally but not morally responsible for your fall.

houses of wealthier citizens.[44] Flood walls are often constructed where the wealthy live, leaving the poor more vulnerable when waters rise. So even if natural disasters have no causal agent, their consequences are often heavily influenced by government policies. Even where there is a more obvious causal agent, others often feel responsible to help victims. Host countries often take in refugees, even though they may not be responsible for their plight. Many people argue that wealthy countries owe aid to poorer countries, even beyond any responsibility the wealthy countries may have for the situation of poorer countries. I bring up these examples to show that responsibility and causality are not always so intertwined in everyday and philosophical thinking, and there is no reason why we should presume this to be the normal model, as the advocates of repairing past injustice do.

Instead of first finding the responsible party for an enduring injustice, I suggest we first look to see who is best able to repair the injustice. Sometimes, these two views will overlap. If trust is to be rebuilt between African Americans and the US government, then the latter has some work to do; the argument from responsibility will also argue that the US government must work to remedy enduring injustices suffered by African Americans. Still, it is worth noting that while the advocates emphasize the importance of the government's continuity through time in cases of historical injustice, what governments often ought to do is show that it is very much *not* like its predecessors. Robust acknowledgement of enduring injustices – through museums, monuments, and so on – is one way to show that the government is committed to a new path. One problem with flying the Confederate flag over government buildings is that this suggests there is not much of a break with the racial injustice of the past. What Black Americans rightly want are signs from their government that it is no longer committed to the racist policies of the past; one way to do this is to show a break with previous governments. In the case of Native Americans, the combination of competing conceptions of land and mistrust may justify granting or sustaining tribal autonomy.

I will not offer a general theory of responsibility here, since there is no a priori way to decide who is responsible for repairing enduring

[44] Ted Steinberg, *Acts of God: The Unnatural History of Natural Disaster in America* (Oxford University Press: New York, 2006); Piers Blaikie *et al.*, *At Risk: Natural Hazards, People's Vulnerability and Disasters* (New York: Routledge, 2003).

injustices, and a typology like Miller's can only point us in the right direction when we have a specific case at hand. The general point I want to make is that looking for a causal agent is not always needed or fruitful when thinking about responsibility to work to end the injustice.

A liberal political community has a responsibility to try to repair or end injustices within its midst. Few, if any, communities will be able to successfully end all injustices, and many will have to prioritize which they will tackle first. There is no way to say a priori that enduring injustices should be at the top of the priority list, when trying to repair an enduring injustice means using up resources. (When resources are not an issue, then it is hard to see what principled reason could be given for not attempting to repair the injustice; politics is another matter.) Yet I do want to argue that there is a prima facie reason to put enduring injustices toward the top of the list of problems that a political community should try to confront. There may be reasons to override this priority, but they ought to be very good reasons. Enduring injustices leave their victims frustrated, and with little hope for the future. A decent political community does not, and cannot, promise everyone that they will lead fulfilling lives, but a decent society should give all of its members this possibility. An enduring injustice is a stain on the body politic, one that calls into question its commitment to decency, if not justice. To shunt pockets of people aside, to allow the injustice to fester, to allow this set of people to feel ill at ease in the world, alien to the political community is certainly indecent. While a liberal focus on individual rights and economic distribution may sometimes allow for this indecency to persist (though sometimes parts or all of an enduring injustice will violate liberal dictates), a liberal community should also be a decent one. It should provide citizens with the hope that their lives will not be awash with injustice, and that matters can get better. This means, certainly, tying liberalism to progress once again, but this knot must be a loose one: liberalism should no longer be certain of progress, but it should nonetheless offer hope to victims of enduring injustice.

Apologies are relational; remorse does not have to be relational.

4 | *Apology and acknowledgement*

Why should apologies come at the end?

Explain + raise an objection to... critically discuss whether...

Accompanying the argume[...] arguments for apologizing [...] proclaims, "The Age of A[...] proliferating. I mentioned [...] are more. The universities [...] using slave labor earlier in [...] Jewish and foreign lawyers [...] French doctor's organizatio[...] French police union (thoug[...] John Paul II apologized ove[...] committed by the church.[2] [...] failing to enact anti-lynchin[...] 2009 the California Parliame[...] against Chinese Americans in[...] the twentieth centuries. The list goes on, as government apologies have become increasingly common.

Most arguments advocating apology maintain that if the dominant community apologizes to victims of past (and sometimes current) injustices, all will be well – or at least we will be on the road toward transformation and healing. These arguments are another version of the exceptions to progress view I examined in Chapter 2; apologies are given for the exceptions, with the expectation that the apology will then usher in an era where the exception is no longer. Most of the arguments for apologies are for what I call enduring injustices, though this is rarely if ever stated. Politicians sometimes slip in apologies for past injustices – like the apology to Chinese Americans for discrimination that they or their ancestors faced – but these apologies are rarely

[1] Mark Gibney *et al.*, eds., *The Age of Apology: Facing Up to the Past* (Philadelphia: University of Pennsylvania Press, 2008).
[2] http://en.wikipedia.org/wiki/Apologies_by_Pope_John_Paul_II (accessed 23 July, 2009).

85

noticed. In the cases of enduring injustice, apologies are often thought
to restore justice, though what that means exactly is vague. Apology
advocates impute considerable power to apologies, but I cast doubt on
their power in this chapter. One important problem with the arguments for apologies is that they do not present a theory of apology. As
Michael Freeman notes: "Apologies seem theory free."[3] A theory of
apology would help us to determine when apologies are appropriate,
and here apology advocates share a problem with those who want to
repair historical injustice: for which past misdeeds should democratic
governments apologize today?

In this chapter I aim to show that most arguments for apology
promise too much, and I will argue that the hoped for results of a
government apology for past injustices will come forth only some of
the time. Instead of a theory of apology, apology advocates present an
argument on the functions of apologies. One key problem is that most
of these functions work for individual apologies; apology advocates
often effortlessly transpose these functions from the individual to the
group, though the analogy between people and groups is never
defended, and is fraught with difficulties. I will argue below that issues
of sincerity and regret are much easier to determine in individuals than
in groups. The transposition to groups often undermines the meaning
of group apologies, and makes them easily subject to political calcu-
lation or manipulation. I will also argue that apologies for injustices
that are *enduring* are almost by definition suspect – to apologize for
present behavior is, at best, rather odd. Many apology advocates
argue that apologies and transformation of the behavior should march
hand in hand, but this is clearly much more easily said than done. On
the other hand, apologizing for past injustices means apologizing is
fraught with another set of difficulties, as I have already argued, it is
hard to make those of today's generation responsible for events that
occurred before their birth.

I will argue that a process of acknowledging the enduring injustice is
usually more important than apology, though this process may lead to
the appropriate conditions for an apology. My term "acknowledging"
is meant to convey the idea that this is an ongoing process, but I will
often use the term "acknowledgement" because it is a more felicitous

---

[3] Michael Freeman, "Historical Injustice and Liberal Political Theory," in Gibney
et al., eds., 50.

term. My argument is not meant to oppose all government apologies for enduring injustices, but my aim here is to de-emphasize apology. Government apologies, as they are currently defended, are too easy to give, and often do not accomplish enough. Acknowledgement promises less than apology, making fewer claims about the future, and its narrative of progress is muted. But this modesty is an advantage. Acknowledgement is a process, not a moment in time. I should note that I am not against all swift government apologies; nothing I argue here suggests that governments should not apologize for imprisoning the wrong person or accidentally shooting down an airplane. My focus here is on enduring injustices, though I will briefly note that acknowledgement and apologies work differently in some other kinds of cases.

One might suggest that my argument for acknowledgement is simply a form of apology. But if one thinks that enduring injustices are very hard to solve, then apologies for them ought to be rare, and can only really be effectual after a long process of acknowledgement, and attempts to move beyond the injustice. I do not think this is impossible; I suggest a case where this seems to have happened at the end of the chapter. But I do think genuine apologies for enduring injustices should in fact be rare. It is also the case that in some instances of enduring injustice, there is no entity that can in fact apologize. The apology literature assumes an intact political community – that the political community today is recognizably the inheritor of the community that committed the injustice. (It is obviously questionable that an intact political community can apologize for past events.) I will work with this assumption in the first part of this chapter, and assume there are few advocates for apology in other cases, like the expulsion of the Tatars from the Crimea. In the latter part of the chapter, where I turn to acknowledgement, I relax this assumption and show how acknowledgement can work across borders and between communities.

Still, some of what apology advocates aim for is similar to what I hope acknowledgement can accomplish: a real understanding of the injustice and a real attempt to overcome it. Yet I also want to place acknowledgement in the larger context of how political communities can acknowledge the enduring injustice, which I begin in this chapter and continue through the next two. Acknowledgement and apology also lie outside the usual liberal framework of justice, since they are not about rights or the redistribution of wealth. Those who want to deny the importance of the past for normative issues today cannot explain why the ancestors of the perpetrators of injustice so often deny or suppress the unjust actions of their ancestors or of previous governments so vigorously. Calls to ignore past injustices disregard the close link between collective narrative and identity for many, including the ancestors of both perpetrators and victims. Ignoring injustices of the past may be better than denying them, but to the ancestors of the victims both are harmful affronts to their dignity. The example of sacred space, which I explore toward the end of this chapter, illustrates one important way in which acknowledgement also lies outside the liberal framework.

4.1 The persistence paradox

While apology advocates describe the function of corporate apologies, they rarely present an argument about which injustices deserve an apology. There are countless historical wrongs: Which demand an apology and which do not? Few accounts of apology directly speak to this issue. Mark Gibney and Erik Roxstrom argue that one problem with former British Prime Minister Tony Blair's apology for England's role in the Irish Potato Famine is that "there was no attempt to place the event within the broader context of British colonial rule more generally."[4] Of course, the British committed many injustices during the colonial period, and Gibney and Roxstrom do say "this does not mean that the British Prime Minister (or the Queen) needs to be stomping all around the Commonwealth with an encyclopedia of British wrongs."[5] What it does mean, though, is unclear. Gibney and Roxstrom argue that what is needed is "some attempt at placing events into a historical context."[6] This is surely right, but it sounds like very sensible advice about how to write a textbook or construct a museum exhibit. Its connection to an apology is opaque. Do Gibney

---

[4] Mark Gibney and Erik Roxstrom, "The Status of State Apologies," *Human Rights Quarterly* 23, no. 4 (2001), 933. In an email correspondence, Gibney wrote: "I don't think 'events' demand an apology. Also, what I disagreed with was Queen Elizabeth going around the world issuing individual apologies to individual states. Rather, I would much prefer a more general discussion and treatment of 'colonial' practices quite generally, and certainly not country by country."

[5] Gibney and Roxstrom, "State Apologies," 933.   [6] *Ibid.*

and Roxstrom mean that one apology to the Irish set in the proper historical context is enough for all British colonial misdeeds, or do all apologies for British colonialism need such context? The former seems insufficient: it seems doubtful that the people in Uganda or India will be satisfied with an apology for colonialism made to the Irish, even if set in the correct historical context (which would surely set off many debates). Gibney and Roxstrom cannot intend the latter, since they have excused the Queen from having to trot all around the former British Empire, apologizing for past injustices. This leaves us with a basic question unanswered that haunts the literature on historical injustice as well: Which events demand an apology and which do not?

Most scholarly arguments about apologies do focus on enduring injustices, though some do discuss apologies for the Holocaust, and governments have apologized for some historical injustices that are not enduring. I will, however, focus on apologies for enduring injustices here, which are prominent enough in the apology literature. A fundamental problem with apologies for enduring injustices is their paradoxical quality, for injustices that are both past and current. Apologies are normally given for past and current behavior. It is odd to apologize for behavior that is ongoing, and has little chance of changing. Yet enduring injustices are continuing injustices; an apology for an enduring injustice is an apology for a current injustice. What good is an apology if remedies for the injustice are not forthcoming? One rejoinder to this argument is that apologies and remedies could be concurrent; an apology could be part of a program to undo the effects of the injustice that has endured from the past to the present. This would mean, however, not merely arguing for an apology, but arguing that an apology is only appropriate when accompanied by a set of appropriate policies.

Some apology advocates argue for something close to this, that apologies are meant to transform relations between the oppressors and the oppressed. Advocates of apologies proclaim that past state practice is "negated by the apology"; that apologies by the American government will "enable Americans to use their conflictual past as a site upon which to build a new or reinvigorated vision of the future"; that national apologies will allow societies to "move on in a cleansed way" and that they add "to the sum of justice in the world"; apologies can "reconstitute relations between communities ripped apart by conflict." In Australia an apology to Aborigines "provides a means for Australia to explicitly shift its political culture."[7]

Unlike many arguments about historical injustice, many arguments for apologies often explicitly tie the past and future together. These arguments often suggest that the injustice is not merely in the past, but is ongoing. What apology advocates hope or assume is that the apology will help set the stage for a change in the future. Apologies, in the eyes of their advocates, are meant to change the trajectory of the future and of the injustice, to put matters back on the road of progress, and to help the political community achieve justice. They argue that government apologies are not merely about the past, but also about the future. To give a sincere apology is not just to be sorry about a past event, but to try to ensure that such injustices do not occur again.

This imputes considerable power to apology, but why will apologies have such power? Apologies may have considerable power between two people, but when it comes to enduring injustice it is hard to see their power. How the apology will, by itself, be so transformative is left unclear. One argument suggests that government apologies can shift the "normative framework" as to how people perceive an enduring injustice and its victims, but few apology advocates point to actual government apologies that have been transformative.[8] It is hard to see how apologies would be so transformative. Apology advocates often write as if apologies will cause a culture shift among the members of a political community, but culture shifts, or large changes in a community's normative framework, take time – many years, and sometimes decades. It might be meaningful if apologies came toward the end, or in the middle, of a change in a community's normative framework, if one could detect this change as it was occurring.

---

[7] *Ibid.*, 935; Brian A. Weiner, *Sins of the Parents: The Politics of National Apologies in the United States* (Philadelphia: Temple University Press, 2005), 172; Julie Fette, "The Apology Moment: Vichy Memories in 1990s France," in Elazar Barkan and Alexander Karn, eds., *Taking Wrongs Seriously: Apologies and Reconciliation* (Stanford University Press, 2006), 277; Michael R. Marrus, "Official Apologies and the Quest for Historical Justice," *Journal of Human Rights* 6, no. 1 (2007): 75–105; Elazar Barkan and Alexander Karn, "Group Apology as Ethical Imperative," in Barkan and Karn, eds., *Taking Wrongs Seriously*, 9; Danielle Celermajer, "The Apology in Australia: Re-Covenanting the National Imaginary," in Barkan and Karn, eds., *Taking Wrongs Seriously*, 176.

[8] Celermajer, *Sins of the Nation*, 240.

The best transformative argument is given by Danielle Celermajer. She (or others) might respond to my argument by saying they are describing how political communities should respond to past injustices, not how they actually do so. Even if many government apologies are not transformative, they ought to be so. Celermajer recognizes that many political apologies fall short of the normative standards that she sets. She notes early in her book that many political apologies aim at distancing the current nation from the people that committed the injustice.[9] Toward the end of the book, however, where she focuses on the Australian case, she argues that the apology given by the Australian Prime Minister to Aborigines shows "that political communities become enrolled in apologies because they contribute to future orientated projects of political reconstitution."[10] While Celermajer's statement is declarative, it is not clear that this is what many apologies are doing. One might argue that apologies *should* contribute to projects of political reconstitution, and it may be that many people hope or plan to be part of such a reconstitutive project. Yet this is a hard project to undertake; this hardly means it is not worth doing, but it does mean that an apology can at best be only part of this project. But since this project is such a difficult undertaking, it is better that an apology come at the end of a process of political reconstitution, not at the beginning, where it may simply be a false promise.

Celermajer argues that an apology for a past injustice is not just an admission of failure to live up to an ethical principle, but is a "performative declaration of a new commitment, a new covenant [for the nation] for *now* and into the future.[11] Drawing on J. L. Austin, she argues that a political apology is not just speech, but also an act; it is performative speech. A political apology can both acknowledge the identity of those who did the wrong and establish for themselves a new normative identity, which establishes a vantage point from which the wrong can be condemned: our nation committed terrible injustices, but we will now reconstitute ourselves so that we can distance ourselves from that wrong because we are now different.[12] The apology does not merely usher in a transformative process; it is part of that process. The

[9] This is an important theme in Danielle Celermajer, *The Sins of the Nation and the Ritual of Apologies* (Cambridge University Press, 2009), ch. 1.
[10] *Ibid.*, 172.   [11] *Ibid.*, 247. Italics in the original.   [12] *Ibid.*, 198.

apology is not just words, but an act that will help transform relations and will help the political community to reconstitute itself.

One danger of apology is that the government giving the apology may think they are done with the issue once the apology is granted. If apologies are performative speech, if apologies are transformative acts, then why do more than utter the apology? Yet enduring injustices may last for decades or centuries, while apologies are but a moment in time. This very asymmetry should cause us to wonder about apology's power. A political apology might begin a process of political trans-formation, but it is hard to know if the words of apology are mean-ingful if the right kind of action does not follow the words. Celermajer wants apologies to help shift the normative framework, to help citi-zens recognize how their political community was complicit in inflict-ing and perpetuating an injustice, and how that injustice persists. If an apology begins this normative shift, then Celermajer's argument that apologies are not just words but action can make sense. Yet what happens if this normative shift does not occur? And what would this normative shift mean? Celermajer notes that many government apolo-gies for past injustices are accompanied by comments saying how the current political community is actually quite different from the com-munity that performed the injustices. Some apologies given to victims are also made to the nation that committed the injustices, the idea being that the nation was wrongly hijacked by some group or ideol-ogy, or mistakenly strayed from its true identity.[13] In other words, many if not most of the apologies discussed by Celermajer do not intend to be transformative, but intend to apologize to victims of historical injustice while preserving the nation's sense that it is a just political community. Many apologies then aim to be restorative, not transformative. Celermajer is critical of restorative apologies; she think that apologies for past (or enduring) injustices ought to be transformative. But she argues not just that government apologies can be transformative, but that the act of apology itself *is* transforma-tive, which clearly is not true on her account. Still, the idea of trans-formation is appealing, and my argument is not against the possibility of a transformative apology. But I am skeptical that apologies for enduring injustice will always or nearly always be transformative;

---

[13] *Ibid.*, 16–26. See also Craig Blatz *et al.*, "Government Apologies for Historical Injustices," *Political Psychology* 30, no. 2 (2009): 219–41.

and I am skeptical that an apology should come at the start of this process of transformation, instead of at the end. Indeed, one cannot with much certainty give an apology at the beginning of the transformative process, since one cannot be sure that the transformation will occur. In some cases, apologies are simply inappropriate.

4.2 Regret

Sincerity and regret are closely related when the topic is apology, but I will separate them out here. Sincerity, which I discuss in the next section, is future orientated, and is meant to change current and future behavior; regret is backward-looking. Apologies are meaningful when they express regret – they express sorrow that the incident took place, and wished it had not happened. I mean by regret that it also reflects an attitude of remorse, as many apology advocates suggest.[14] The statement that some politicians make when certain actions turn out to be mistaken, "I regret that mistakes were made," does not necessarily reflect remorse. An apology made without remorse is not particularly meaningful. A remorseful apology happens (or should happen) with accidents and mistakes. When someone is falsely imprisoned, a remorseful apology is appropriate, since the criminal justice system aims to imprison the guilty and not the innocent. When an army wrongly kills civilians, an apology is appropriate. People rightly apologize for mistakes that hurt others, and governments should often do the same.

Not all apologies need to mean that one wishes one could change the offending deed. If I do something that makes you feel bad – say I argue against your position in a faculty meeting – I may feel sorry that our disagreement upset you, but I may not be sorry about the position I take on the issue. I do not regret much at all; or perhaps I regret some of the pointed language I used. Perhaps I could have said the same thing in a different, less biting, manner. But I do not regret the meaning of what I said, and given the chance again, I would make

---

[14] Jean-Marc Coicaud and Jibecke Jonsson, "Elements of a Road Map for a Politics of Apology," in Mark Gibney *et al.*, eds., *The Age of Apology: Facing Up to the Past* (Philadelphia: University of Pennsylvania Press, 2008), 77–91; Kathleen Gill, "The Moral Functions of an Apology," *The Philosophical Forum* 31, no. 1 (2000): 11–27; Trudy Govier and Wilhelm Verwoerd, "The Promise and Pitfalls of Apology," *Journal of Social Philosophy* 33, no. 1 (2002): 67–82.

the same kind of arguments. This kind of apology is understandably not what most people have in mind when they call for apologies for historical injustices – the problem is not that the US government hurt the feelings of Native Americans or Black Americans, or that Christians hurt the feelings of those (including many Orthodox Christians) during the sacking of Constantinople. The problem is that injustices occurred; an expression of regret means that the apologizer wished the event had not happened. But do we – most members of the Western states – regret all the injustices of the past?

There are undoubtedly many historical injustices committed in Western democracies that their citizens find appalling. We can point to particular (and many) massacres, tortures, and so on that many find shameful as part of their national history. When it comes to indigenous peoples, for example, the list of injustices is depressingly long: what conquistadors, colonists, and imperialists did to the people they found is often nearly unbearable to read about. That land changed hands between indigenous peoples and Europeans was rarely a result of cultural misunderstandings. Rather, treaties were made and understood, and then broken by the US and Canadian governments because they wanted land they previously agreed was owned by a particular tribe.[15] Sometimes, treaties were not made, and land simply taken. In other words, the US (and many other countries in the Americas, Australia, and New Zealand) imposed its will on weaker peoples in ways that contradicted its own understanding of property, treaties, and morality because of greed. In the process it killed many people or expelled them from their land.

It seems doubtful that Western governments would agree to such actions today. While some governments do engage in massacres and mass expulsion, few liberal democracies today do so directly. When Native Americans or Black Americans want an apology (and not all do), they want an admission that the injustices done to them were wrong and should not have happened; regret means that if we had a time machine we would go back in time, and prevent the injustices that occurred to these groups. The advocates of apology want government apologies to be regretful in this sense, that we would do things much differently in the past if that were possible. Advocates argue that

---

[15] Stuart Banner, *How the Indians Lost Their Land: Law and Power on the Frontier* (Cambridge, MA: Belknap Press of Harvard University Press, 2005).

apologies should express an "attitude of regret and a feeling of remorse"; group apologies are a way of "expressing moral regret."[16] A few years ago, the Assistant Secretary for Indian Affairs under President Bill Clinton, Kevin Gover, did apologize to Native American nations for the past wrongs inflicted upon them by the federal Indian policy as implemented by the Bureau of Indian Affairs. (This was not an official government apology; Gover said he made it on behalf of the BIA.) Gover mentioned many injustices, including the policies of forbidding the speaking of Indian languages and the practice of traditional religious activities, along with the "ethnic cleansing that befell the western tribes." Gover then said "we desperately wish that we could change this history, but of course we cannot."[17] This is a clear statement of regret.

[handwritten margin note: Not an official gov't apology]

If Gover meant that we wish we could change history so the tribes would not have been pushed off their land, then the statement is one that few Americans would endorse (though for Gover, as a member of the Pawnee nation, the matter is different). We non-Native Americans in the US can think that certain events were unnecessarily cruel – massacres of Indians were certainly not needed, most expulsions were done in a cruel manner. There are certainly specific unjust acts that Americans today can feel particularly bad about.

Can we apologize for our ancestors – or previous generations of Americans and American governments – for being so greedy and so cruel to Native Americans? Certainly, the US government could have kept more of its treaties than it did, and agreed to allow tribes to keep more land than the government allowed them to do. And of course, the United States could have certainly dominated the land it currently occupies without being as cruel as it was to many tribes. The American government could apologize for excessive greed and cruelty; it could apologize for the Trail of Tears. Yet even apologies like these would certainly be circumscribed. The general outline of the story that white colonists and later the US government set about to squeeze the Indians into ever smaller plots of land, in order to get land for non-native Americans so they could pursue a life of farming and industrialization, is one that it is hard for Americans to regret. David Lyons

---

[16] Gill, "Moral Functions," 12; Govier and Verwoerd, "The Promise and Pitfalls of Apology," 69.

[17] Kevin Gover, "Remarks of Kevin Gover," www.tahtonka.com/apology.html (accessed June 29, 2011).

argues that the Lockean proviso invoked by Robert Nozick means that Native Americans would have had to share their land with the Europeans that came across the ocean.[18] Lyons does not excuse the way Native Americans were expelled from their land, but he does argue that the need Europeans had for more space, and the considerable land used by the relatively small population of Native Americans, does suggest that justice means the latter should have shared their land with Europeans. If we Americans (and one could say the same about Canadians, Mexicans, Central and South Americans, Australians, and New Zealanders) could change the general course of history, would we (non-native peoples) change it?

An apology that says that we apologize for previous governments having taken too much land, and of having used too much force, might not be seen as particularly sincere. One might say, as Janna Thompson does, that we can be sorry for the good things we now possess that are the result of injustice.[19] We could say that we would have certainly preferred our existence as Americans (or Canadians, or Mexicans, or New Zealanders and so on) to come into being without doing an injustice to indigenous peoples. Yet how meaningful this could be is unclear. We (non-native Americans) like our way of life, which is incompatible with the traditional Native American life. It is not just that we live on this land, but that most of us live in a certain way, as part of a Western, industrial way of life, with a story that we tell about ourselves. Part of the American identity is its history – of conquering the frontier, of building the railroad to connect the West with the rest of the country, of the small farmer working against considerable odds; of eventually, the US becoming a very wealthy country, with very productive farmland and with great industrial cities. The idea that the land should be productive, that industrialization is connected to progress, is part of the Western narrative. When Locke argued that one acre of cultivated land was worth more than a hundred acres uncultivated by the Indians, he was expressing a widespread view toward the land and exactly how it ought to be used.[20] The Native

[18] David Lyons, "The New Indian Claims and Original Rights to Land," *Social Theory and Practice* 4, no. 3 (1977): 249–71.

[19] Janna Thompson, "The Apology Paradox," *The Philosophical Quarterly* 50, no. 201 (2000): 470–75.

[20] John Locke, *The Second Treatise of Government* (Indianapolis: Hackett, 1980 [1689]), ch. 5. A good criticism of Locke on the issue of indigenous peoples and

American narratives – the great Buffalo hunts, the fights with other tribes that were part of the warrior cultures of the Plains Indians, along with others – cannot co-exist with the non-native American narrative, not simultaneously.[21] This narrative is not just a story, of course, but in part a story that constitutes the Americans' identity. The narrative that Mill and Marx tell about progress has not been completely achieved, but their ideas about the connection between civilization and industrialization has tremendous credence in the West; it is, to a large degree, our story. Even if there are many aspects of this story that we dislike, it is hard for most of us to distance ourselves from our general way of life. This does not mean that we must condone everything done by Western governments; we may think that we should become better stewards of the land, that we should drastically change our diet, that our lifestyle is too orientated toward material goods and comforts. But unless we Americans repudiate the way we live, the American story is one that is incompatible with leaving the Native Americans alone, or even treating them justly.

If we were sorry that our gains were made at the expense of others, we could make modest amends now, which many of us are reluctant to do. Many of the Lakota Sioux are willing to accept a compromise on the Black Hills, getting back about one-fifth of it, which would mean not displacing anyone. This bill, however, died in Congress, in part because it was opposed by the South Dakota congressional delegation.[22] Mining continues in the Black Hills, and the idea that wealth is more important than Indian land has strong support in this country. It also puts the contrast between the Indian and industrial views of land in stark relief. To be sure, many Americans (including myself) would back the compromise bill giving back the Lakota some land. Clearly, though, Americans are still split about land disputes with Native Americans, despite our rather awful history in relation to them. Yet, here lies a possibility for an appropriate apology: if the American government were to give part of the Black Hills back, along

---

land is James Tully, *Strange Multiplicity: Constitutionalism in an Age of Diversity* (Cambridge University Press, 1995), 71–78.

[21] For a theoretical exploration on the meaning of the end of the traditional way of life of the Plains Indians, see Jonathan Lear, *Radical Hope: Ethics in the Face of Cultural Devastation* (Cambridge, MA: Harvard University Press, 2006).

[22] www.argusleader.com/specialsections/2001/bighorn/Wednesday feature.shtml (accessed July 15, 2008).

with some compensation, and this package was accepted by the tribe, then an apology by the American government *might* be appropriate. Even this apology is fraught with difficulties, for one must determine what the apology is for. As Nick Smith argues, government apologies are often selective and vague.[23] Would the apology be for the general way in which the Lakota were treated by the US, or just for the treaty violations?

Even if such an apology were given, it would be a rather limited one, not one that is transformative. One might argue that if such a deal were made between the Lakota Sioux and the American government, it might lead to the settlement of more tribal claims, paving the way for more apologies. This is a possibility, but there is no reason to think that one settlement will lead to others. And this one settlement with the Lakota Sioux is out of reach, at least as I write.

We may be sorry that our gain was at the expense of others, we wish it had happened differently, but in the end we are not sorry for our gain. We may feel sorry that our gains came at the tragic expense of Native Americans, but the larger point remains, that the way we live our lives and the traditional life are incompatible with one another. Instead of saying we feel regret and remorse we might say that we have a tragic situation – the triumph of non-native Americans came at a great and unnecessarily terrible cost. The victory of a great liberal democratic nation came at the expense of many Indian tribes. Noting this tragedy, and feeling bad about it, however, is different than wishing for a completely different history, even if many of us do wish the US government had treated the Indians much more honorably than it did, and think that our great expansive land could have been better shared. Can we apologize for a clash that was tragic for some peoples but triumphant for another?

4.3 Sincerity and the problem of agency

In some cases, though, there may be genuine regret for a past injustice. The labor of Black slaves did much to fortify the wealth and power of the United States, but the US would surely have become a great industrial country without slave labor. An apology for slavery could be

---

[23] Nick Smith, *I Was Wrong: The Meanings of Apologies* (Cambridge University Press, 2008), 221–25.

made with real regret. How do we know if the apology is also sincere, in the sense that there is a real desire to change the behavior that allows the injustice to endure? One question we can ask first is whether apologies must be sincere. Nearly every parent of more than one child has instructed their children at one time or another to apologize for hurting the other child; and then comes the kicker: "Say it like you mean it!" Of course, this means the parent is knowingly extracting an insincere apology from the child. Since the child mumbles the apology or resists in other ways, there must be something at stake in this theater. Bill Miller argues that the mumbler resists because this is a ritual of humiliation, in which the "apologizer must humble himself before the person he injured."[24]

This helps to explain why many citizens – and government officials – are reluctant to offer apologies in many cases. When there is a border clash, for instance, and one side takes prisoners from the other, the side with the prisoners often wants the other side to apologize. Apologies often become politically sensitive, but this is more because of the humiliation they entail than any policy change associated with the apology. Citizens will often oppose a government apology if they see it as humiliating. A government apology may undermine their pride in their nation and government, at least temporarily. This is undoubtedly what is behind the first President Bush's blanket refusal to apologize for the US government's actions: "I will never apologize for the United States of America, I don't care what the facts are."[25] This humiliation may make some of the victims feel a little better for a moment or two, but will do little to underscore the underlying issues. This is why apology advocates want a sincere apology. If the apology is going to be part of a change of behavior, then the apology should be sincere. So simply apologizing may achieve little, unless temporarily humiliating a government and nation is considered to be an important success.

Not all apologies need to be humiliating, of course. The deeper problem with the idea of a sincere apology from a government is that it is unclear what it means for a government to be sincere. The power imputed to apology may often be true for individuals. Many advocates of group apologies argue that what is right for individuals is also

---

[24] William Ian Miller, *Faking It* (Cambridge University Press, 2003), 88.
[25] Michael Kinsley, "Essay: Rally Round the Flag, Boys," *Time Magazine*, www. time.com/time/printout/0,8816,968407,00.html (accessed August 2, 2010).

correct for groups and states, but this is a suspect move. It is easier to see sincerity in individuals than in groups. When advocates assume that the apologies given are sincere and "come from the heart," we can wonder if governments have hearts.[26] One might suggest, as Jeffrey Blustein does, that sincerity is possible if the apology is given by an agent with moral standing to do so.[27] Yet this is much more complicated than apology advocates note. The problem, as Nick Smith contends, is that many of their arguments "extend Kantian notions of individual responsibility into a framework for group culpability."[28] Much of Smith's argument is aimed at apologies for recent wrongs; so he argues that group apologies often mask the culpability of particular individuals. Instead of a government official stepping forward to admit that he made certain mistakes, for example, the official says that "we were wrong," or "we made mistakes," so those individuals who actually made the mistakes are shielded from view by the "ether of institutional doublespeak."[29]

It is also unclear who can speak for the group. One obvious answer – elected officials – does not work well when the issue is sincerity. It may be relatively easy to determine if an individual's apology is sincere, but how to determine if a group sincerely apologizes is quite difficult (unless the group is quite small). This issue is apparent in Janna Thompson's criteria for a government apology. She argues for the importance of an agreed-upon ceremony for the apology by the apologizer and the representatives of the victims; the apology should be endorsed by the people of the nation responsible for the wrong; the government should take steps to demonstrate that the history of the injustice is part of the nation's history in schools and in public institutions; and the government should ensure that similar wrongs will no longer occur.[30] It is hard to see how a government could ensure that no similar wrongs will ever occur, but more important for my argument is the difficulty in getting citizens to feel remorse for their government's

---

[26] Govier and Verwoerd, "The Promise and Pitfalls of Apology," 70; Roy Brooks, "The New Patriotism and Apology for Slavery," in Barkan and Karn, eds., *Taking Wrongs Seriously*, 226.

[27] Jeffrey Blustein, *The Moral Demands of Memory* (Cambridge University Press, 2008), 143.

[28] Smith, *The Meanings of Apologies*, 187.   [29] *Ibid.*, 199.

[30] Janna Thompson, "Apology, Justice and Respect," in Gibney *et al.*, eds., *The Age of Apology*, 41–42.

past actions. What if some, or many, citizens do not feel remorse? Incorporating the history of an injustice into a nation-state's narrative in part by teaching the injustice in schools is a way to help citizens understand their political community's history, which may then induce remorse. Some citizens, however, may not feel remorse, pointing out that they cannot sincerely apologize for an action that they had no part in committing. Even if we put these problems aside, Thompson's argument is internally inconsistent. Thompson wants apologies to have the sincere backing of citizens; but a sincere apology must presume a decent understanding of the injustice. Understanding should precede the apology; yet in Thompson's argument, understanding comes *after* the apology. It may be that in some cases, understanding does come after an apology; a government official can apologize without the support of the majority of citizens, and hope that with more education will come understanding for their apology. But even in this case, the apology is not sincere in the way that Thompson intends and hopes it to be.

This problem is highlighted in Jennifer Lind's exploration of apologies between states for past injustices. When some Japanese officials apologized to South Korea for the period it held the latter as a colony (and when its colonial officials often acted brutally), it provoked a backlash from many Japanese citizens, who then worked hard to ensure that school history books presented a sanitized version of Japanese colonialism.[31] They were wrong to do so, of course, but this is not the point I want to make here, which is that it is very hard for groups of millions (or tens of millions) of people to give a sincere apology. One might point out that Germany's apologies for its Nazi past do seem more sincere, and have not provoked the same intense backlash as in Japan. But these apologies came decades after the injustice, one that succeeding governments could distance themselves from – the injustice was past, not enduring. During these decades, the German government acknowledged the past, with the advent of memorials and apologies coming along slowly.[32] Yet even under these conditions – a past, not enduring injustice, a different regime, and the passage of time – there was some backlash, particularly when the

---

[31] Jennifer Lind, *Sorry States: Apologies in International Politics* (Ithaca, NY: Cornell University Press, 2010).
[32] *Ibid.*, Ch. 3.

"New Historians" argued that the emphasis on and lessons taught about Germany's Nazi past were mistaken.[33]

4.4 Time and transformation

Beyond the problem of agency (who is authorized to make a sincere apology?), the intent of the apology is often unclear, further questioning how sincere the apology can be.[34] (This issue is another facet of an issue flagged above: the vagueness of many government apologies.) In the US we could say that most people find racism appalling, and so one might think that an apology for slavery and racism is appropriate. Several state legislatures have in fact apologized for slavery. Here's a passage from the state of Alabama's recent apology for slavery:

WHEREAS, in Alabama, the vestiges of slavery are ever before African-American citizens, from the overt racism of hate groups to the subtle racism encountered when requesting health care, transacting business, buying a home, seeking quality public education and college admission, and enduring pretextual traffic stops and other indignities.[35]

All the subtle racism that the apology calls our attention to still occurs, yet the apology says nothing about ending this racism, except for some platitudes about the "remembrance and teaching about the history of slavery." There is surely something odd about apologizing for ongoing behavior. "I'm sorry for stepping on your toes, I'm certain that it hurts, but I am going to continue to do it," is not much of an apology. This paragraph nearly says the same thing: racism still continues, for which we are sorry. Of course, if "we" were sorry about this – most or all of the citizens of Alabama (and the US) – then much of this behavior would stop. It's hard to see how this apology can mean much, since the resolution says little about stopping racism and its effects. Still, one could respond that the problem is with the construction of this apology; it could be more specific about how to end racism, and there could be parallel legislation to help do so. That

---

[33] *Ibid.*, 134; Peter Baldwin, *Reworking the Past: Hitler, the Holocaust, and the Historians' Debate* (Boston: Beacon Press, 1990).

[34] The opague nature of group apologies is well explored in Smith, *The Meanings of Apologies.*

[35] The text of the apology can be found at http://abamablog.blogspot.com/2007/05/alabama-to-apologize-for-slavery.html (accessed August 2, 2010).

some apologies are vague does not mean that all government apologies must be constructed in this way.

Yet changing racism takes more than an apology. Leaving aside the controversy surrounding the amount and effects of racism in the US today, the process of eradicating racism in a society, or changing US foreign policy, or of changing a political culture all must occur, if they do, as part of a long drawn out process, and not in a moment or two. If someone wants to change US foreign policy toward Turkey, looking to an apology for actions in Guatemala is not the method to do so. If group apologies are to have future effects, then one has to be sure that there is a high level of agreement on the apology and its meaning. Celermajer argues that a political apology need not be emotive like a personal apology; yet it is the case that a political apology must be supported by a large percentage of the populace to have the transformative effects that she wants for a political apology. Actually, it is not just the apology that needs to have support, but on her account, the idea that the nation should be re-imagined and re-covenanted which must be supported by many citizens.

If an apology is supposed to be transformative, or be part of a transformative process, then it must be supported by many if not most citizens. This is a tall order, but not an impossible one. Nations certainly change; American racial attitudes are much different today than a hundred or even fifty years ago. Yet this change took considerable time, while an apology is but a moment. The issue of time is a difficult problem for the idea of a transformative government apology. Images of nations (and nation-states) among members (and citizens) change over time; but these changes are the effect of many processes, struggles, and events, and often occur slowly. Indeed, that Celermajer's argument fits enduring injustice (but not other past injustices) buttresses this point: enduring injustices are difficult to solve, and so it is odd to think that a political apology will readily usher in an era of transformation and reconstruction. Celermajer cites Prime Minister Rudd of Australia's apology to the "lost generation" in February 2008 as an example of this transformation. Rudd apologized first and foremost to the children and their parents of those taken away to be placed with white families, but also generally for the treatment of Aborigines. Celermajer approvingly quotes someone who said a few days after the apology that "I think it's a different country since Wednesday."[36] Yet one can ask

---

[36] Celermajer, *Sins of the Nation*, 212.

if this feeling about the country will persist – once the afterglow of the apology wears off, will there be any serious differences in the country caused by the apology or associated events? One important Aboriginal leader, Noel Pearson, was skeptical, noting that the apology was not accompanied by much in the way of action, and asked: "Which is more sincere: to say 'we will not apologise to the Stolen Generations and we won't pay compensation', or 'we will apologise but we won't pay compensation'? If this issue is of such importance to the majority of Australians, then surely an appropriate fraction of the $30 billion tax cuts could be committed to compensation."[37]

Putting aside the issue of compensation, Pearson's point is poignant: an apology by itself will often do very little for the victims of an enduring injustice. What Pearson understandably wants is action that will help Aborigines overcome the enduring injustice. If words are a kind of action, like Celermajer suggests, they are, by themselves, feeble action in cases of enduring injustice. An individual may grant an apology that will be transformative, but it is hard to see how this works when a democratic government apologizes. An apology cannot be a substitute for the process needed to gain the necessary support from a polity's citizens to make the apology sincere. The question then is whether apologies can be part of this process, but then we return to the paradox of apologies: how can they be given before there is any certainty that the people believe in the apology?

Beyond the issue of whether the people of the nation are ready to engage in a transformative project, there is the question of what it actually means for the nation to be transformed. Celermajer discusses the importance of recognition when it comes to Aborigines; she argues, rightly enough, that recognizing Aborigines as equals to whites and as equal members of the Australian polity is crucial to ending the injustice they face. This is only a start to ending the enduring injustice, however. The problem of enduring injustices is that they are so difficult to end; unsurprisingly Celermajer provides few hints about how to end the enduring injustice faced by Aborigines beyond recognition and reconstituting the nation. If apologies are to be transformative, *how* will the mainstream and Aboriginal communities be transformed?

---

[37] Noel Pearson, "Contradictions Cloud the Apology to the Stolen Generations," *The Australian*, www.theaustralian.com.au/news/features/when-words-arent-enough/story-e6frg6z6–1111115528371 (accessed May 28, 2010).

4.5 Acknowledgement

I suggest the best way for political communities to treat enduring injustices is through acknowledgement that may (but need not) lead to an apology. Though the context is different, Jennifer Lind finds that acknowledgement of past injustice is important for former enemies to reconcile, more so than an apology. What paved the way for Germany and France to reconcile after the Second World War was not German apologies – which did come, but not until after reconciliation – but that in its schools and by its government officials Germany (slowly) acknowledged many of the atrocities and injustices of the Second World War.[38] This does not mean that the past was never whitewashed, denied, or forgotten; in the main, however, Nazi atrocities were not discussed much in Germany in the years right after the war, though neither were they denied, except by people on the fringe. The many public commemorations, memorials to Nazi victims, and apologies all came several decades after the war.[39] The French apparently did not need the German people to publicly feel remorse; though vigorous denials of Nazi atrocities would have probably been an obstacle to reconciliation, as are sometimes Japanese denials or whitewashing of past colonial atrocities.[40] Of course, matters between states are different than those of a state and a group within it, but the international case does highlight the possibility that acknowledgement is more important than apology, and that it is often important for acknowledgement to precede apology.

Many advocates of apologies elide acknowledgement with apology; they see acknowledgement as part of what an apology does.[41] Apology presumes acknowledgement: an apology requires acknowledgement that some harm was done to a particular community.[42] But

---

[38] Lind, *Sorry States*, ch. 3.

[39] Karen E. Till, *The New Berlin: Memory, Politics, Place* (Minneapolis: University of Minnesota Press, 2005).

[40] Lind, *Sorry States*, ch. 2.

[41] Govier and Verwoerd, "The Promise and Pitfalls of Apology"; Melissa Nobles, *The Politics of Official Apologies* (Cambridge University Press, 2008); Rebecca Tsosie, "The Bia's Apology to Native Americans: An Essay on Collective Memory and Collective Conscience," in Barkan and Karn, eds., *Taking Wrongs Seriously*, 185–212; Marrus, "Official Apologies."

[42] Nicholas Tavuchis, *Mea Culpa: A Sociology of Apology and Reconciliation* (Stanford University Press, 1991), 19.

I think it is best to distinguish between the two. The past can be acknowledged without an apology. Acknowledgement will have some similar effects as apology, but there are important differences, and acknowledgement properly done is not merely a subset of apology. My aim is not to suggest that apologies are never suitable for an enduring injustice, but to move away from the idea that apologies can be particularly meaningful by themselves, or that apologies will start a process of transformation. I will argue that apologies are rarely necessary, and only occasionally appropriate.

Acknowledgement will certainly not fix matters quickly, but it avoids many of the problems that plague apologies. Acknowledgement does not have to be sincere or express regret, take responsibility for the past or present the illusion that matters will turn around quickly. Acknowledgement is not emotive like apologies are, and so the roles of sincerity and regret do not come into play. Acknowledgement does not need to come from the heart, nor does it raise the question of whether a polity can apologize for deeds that happened decades ago by and to people who are dead. Since apologies are a moment in time, they can readily allow people to think that once an apology is given, the matter at hand is over. This is often the case when one person apologizes to another, assuming forgiveness is forthcoming. This idea is also implicit in some of the arguments that advocate government apologies, which is why they expect apologies to have transformative effects. This lack of transformation, however, may not prevent some people from thinking the issue is over since an apology has been given. Acknowledgement, in contrast, is a process, not a moment in time, and can occur in different kinds of settings. Acknowledgement can better avoid looking at the past and present in a dichotomous way, as seeing groups as good or bad.

If the intent behind a sincere apology is to take a past injustice and its contemporary effects seriously, then what is needed are ways to commemorate past injustices; to educate the populace about them; and to seek ways to overcome the injustice. None of this is easy to do, which is why an apology for ongoing injustices is often not particularly meaningful. There is no assurance that acknowledgement will lead to the end of an enduring injustice. Like apology, acknowledgement is not a magic elixir that can move a political community on a different path. Acknowledgement promises less than apologies, and so better recognizes the difficulty in ending the enduring injustice.

Acknowledgement will often come in uneven ways. One could say that democratic states should ideally acknowledge past injustices and work to rectify them, including offering an apology if that is appropriate. Yet ideally, the injustice would never have occurred in the first place; or if it did, it would have been rectified quickly; and if that was not possible, then it should have been rectified slowly. In many ways, the ideas animating apology continue in this vein of ideal theory, that ideally states would issue transformative apologies that would quickly and decisively alter the course of the injustice, and move all parts of the political community on the path toward justice.

Yet if this path is blocked, or difficult to take, what is the alternative? The dominant political community has lived with the enduring injustice for quite some time, and so it clearly feels no urgency to try to rectify the injustice. I want to suggest that acknowledgement can mean two things. First, that liberal theorists recognize how the history of an injustice may affect how we think of liberal justice in some cases of enduring injustice. Of course, this has implications for the policies of liberal democracies as well. I take up this kind of acknowledgement in the next two chapters. The second meaning of acknowledgement is for governments and citizens to begin or continue on a path of living up to their own ideals of treating members of their political community with decent concern and respect.

What I hope acknowledgement can do is help pave the way towards overcoming the enduring injustice. Acknowledgement aims to push the political community toward recognizing the enduring injustice, while understanding the difficulties in solving the injustice. Moreover, acknowledgement is a political process; acknowledging an enduring injustice requires a political coalition that will push the political community toward recognizing the injustice. There is an issue of political power at play here; political communities do not often give up power or resources without some pressure to do so. But I write with the idea that liberal democracies will often respond, in some way, to moral pressure that redounds to their ideals; that when it is pointed out, sometimes forcefully, to a liberal democracy how it is failing an ideal like equality it might be moved to action. Or rather, that parts of the liberal democracy may be moved to action, perhaps in fits and starts, sometimes with half steps, and sometimes with fuller steps. Transformation, if it happens, will often take place slowly.

Examples of a process of acknowledgement of an enduring injustice can be found in the US and Canada. Both Canada and the US have given more power to native peoples over the last two decades.[43] In Canada, the province of Nunavet was created in 1999, giving Inuit considerable power in the province. In the mid-1990s, the Canadian government announced a new policy toward Aboriginal peoples designed to "ensure that Aboriginal peoples have greater control over their lives."[44] In the US, the decision to allow Indian tribes to open up casinos was a move toward respecting indigenous autonomy. These moves have taken place after considerable changes in portrayals of indigenous peoples in the schools and textbooks.[45] In 2007 the US Congress passed a law requiring "the Secretary of the Treasury to mint and issue coins in commemoration of Native Americans and the important contributions made by Indian tribes to the development of the United States and the history of the United States, and for other purposes."[46] One can find similar processes of acknowledgement in Australia and New Zealand. These processes of acknowledgement are, for the most part, just that: a process that is not complete (with one important exception, which I note at the end of this chapter). Another possible process of acknowledgement is in Turkey, where there is some hope that the cultural oppression of the Kurds will be acknowledged, as Turkey has given more freedom to speaking Kurdish in schools and in the media in recent years, which may lead to more freedom generally for the Kurds (or these new policies may be reversed, only time will tell).[47]

One might think that acknowledgement is simply a first step toward apology, or that the idea behind it is something like apology, just less so. Acknowledgement may lead to an apology, but it need not do so.

---

[43] Samuel V. Laselva, "Aboriginal Self-Government and the Foundations of Canadian Nationhood," *BC Studies* 120 (1998): 41–54.

[44] Ronald Irwin, "The Government of Canada's Approach to Implementation of the Inherent Right and the Negotiation of Aboriginal Self-Government," www.aadnc-aandc.gc.ca/eng/1100100031843 (accessed August 8, 2010).

[45] For changes in how American historians have portrayed Native Americans see R. David Edmunds, "Native Americans, New Voices: American Indian History, 1895–1995," *The American Historical Review* 100, no. 3 (1995): 717–40.

[46] Public Law 110–82 110th Congress, www.usmint.gov/mint_programs/nativeamerican/Legislation.pdf (accessed August 2, 2010).

[47] Thomas Hammarberg, *Human Rights Report: Turkey* (Strasbourg: Commissioner for Human Rights of the Council of Europe, 2009).

There is certainly overlap between acknowledgement and apology, but the differences are important. Unlike apologies, acknowledgement does not presume anyone is responsible for the past, but acknowledgement does presume responsibility for the present and future. This has a decided advantage, since it allows acknowledgement to recognize injustices that take place across borders; it does not insist that the injustice takes place within the same political community.

Acknowledgement might, over time, lead to a transformation within the political community, but this is a possibility, not something that is an inherent part of the process of acknowledgement. There are two reasons to be skeptical of transformation in some cases of enduring injustice. First, in many cases it is clear what the injustice is, but what justice would mean is unclear. Indigenous peoples suffer from injustice, but what would justice mean for them? I will argue in the next two chapters that what justice means in some cases is hard to determine, if not simply elusive. Second, in some cases of enduring injustice, what is needed is a process of compromise and negotiation. One example of this is the Tatars: what is needed is a negotiated process that will allow some Tatars to return to the Crimea over time. An apology is not what is needed to facilitate this process, though acknowledgement by the Ukraine of the enduring injustice is needed.

In some cases, acknowledgement may lead to new "normative framework" – or perhaps to a new a set of practices. When the dominant community in the US accepted Blacks as equal to whites, was a new normative framework established, or an old one finally fulfilled? The Civil Rights Movement was certainly transformative – it transformed many practices, and the normative framework of some Americans. It was also a process, one that took years or decades, depending on how one marks the movement. (The Civil Rights Movement clearly took place from the early 1950s to the late 1960s, yet many events occurred prior to the 1950s that laid the groundwork for the more pointed Civil Rights actions in the 1950s.) An apology for slavery and segregation in the 1950s would not have made a lot of sense, given the state of racial discrimination at the time.

Was the Civil Rights Movement transformative? It clearly was in many ways. Certainly the achievement of legal equality among all citizens in the US is a real and important, and transforming, achievement. Yet this transformation was also disappointing, as the interest now in enduring injustice attests; if this transformation was so successful, there would be little talk about reparations to Black Americans today. The direction and pace of change for overcoming enduring injustices are not predictable, which is why the transformative language of apology and new normative frameworks is misleading. It can readily promise a false hope that will often lead to disappointment.

Another advantage of acknowledgement is that it can avoid dichotomizing groups into good and bad, as apologies are apt to do. The implicit narrative encapsulated in most arguments about apology remains within the fold of progress. The idea of apology for a past injustice fits neatly into a modified version of progress; progress uplifted many, but not all. Those that benefited from progress should apologize to those left behind, make amends, and with the injustice over, progress can proceed. The underside to this is a simple romantic narrative of oppression. The oppressors did terrible things to the oppressed, who deserved to be treated better (which is certainly the case). Yet this history is a dichotomous one, with no shades of gray. It is plausible enough to think that the US government was mostly the bad oppressor and Native Americans the victims. Yet it is also the case that Native Americans were (and are) not all good. Most were patriarchal cultures; some were also warrior cultures, where male warriors gained honor and glory by killing warriors from other tribes. The urge to have former colonial states apologize for colonialism, and perhaps build museums to display the evils of colonialism (of which there are many) can easily leave us with the lesson that matters in the former colonial world would have been fine but for the intervention of colonialism. Yet there is little reason to believe this is the case. Many pre-colonial states were not peaceful egalitarian communities. India, for example, was not a peaceful democratic community before the Europeans arrived. Women, lower castes, and untouchables rarely lived in liberated conditions before colonialism; depending on the princely state, either Hindus or Muslims may have been subordinate. Some Indian rulers were benevolent, and many were malevolent. Apologies, the desire to categorize groups into good and bad, can too easily romanticize the victim, making it harder to criticize the group. Colonialism was bad, but the world would not be a rosy place if it had never occurred.

Romantic narratives of the past do not help us understand how complicated the solutions sometimes will be to an enduring injustice. A romanticized oppressed group is hard to criticize; beating a group when it is down is certainly unseemly, and a history that presents groups in terms of oppressed and oppressor makes it even harder to criticize. I am not suggesting that criticizing the oppressed is an inherent good, but some possible solutions to many enduring injustices involve trade-offs, involving different goods and rights that liberal democracies value. A process of acknowledging the past has the advantage over apology of being more nuanced, and allowing for more negotiation over the possible solutions to the enduring injustice. Acknowledgement can also allow the dominant group to be recognized for any good that it brought, if that is the case. Movement away from dividing groups into two categories – good/bad – allows us to see the past and future in ways that allow us to negotiate a better future, instead of being in a situation where one group simply makes demands on the other.

An example of how acknowledgement can also avoid romanticizing the victim, as apologies do, is a well-designed museum or textbook. Museums can explain the way of life of Native Americans and their interactions with white Americans in all its complexity. It can explain the warrior culture of the Plains tribes; it can show how white Americans lied to and cheated the Indians. It can discuss the range of attitudes that white and Native Americans had (and have) toward each other. It can invite the audience to examine both cultures, their faults and their strengths. I am not suggesting that all museums need to be evenhanded, or that every museum needs to show the complexity of all cultures. Museums about the Holocaust or African-American slavery need not investigate the divisions and fault-lines within Jewish or African American communities. Yet the museum can show how some people were led to commit atrocities and how some Germans and Americans opposed the Holocaust and slavery (as many did). Without defending British imperialism, a museum about British colonialism can show how the British attempted to outlaw the practice of sati (widow burning) in India. There is much to fault British missionaries with, but the caste system of Hinduism is hardly something to celebrate. Some apology advocates do mention museums in their work, but a well done museum need not paint the interlocutors in black and white, as apologies often do.

My argument for acknowledgement means that textbooks ought to pay important attention to enduring injustices, as apology advocates would certainly suggest. It also means acknowledging shared space, and not merely through official pronouncements designed for foreign media consumption, but through the educational system where it might have real impact on the political community's attitudes. Symbolic acknowledgement can be important – street signs, proclamations by the national or lower legislatures – but in cases of enduring injustice these are matters of secondary importance (except if signs or city names are changed to insult a group, to show how the dominant community does not care about the injustice or even if it revels in the enduring injustice.)[48]

My argument here suggests that it is a mistake to ask political communities to take responsibility for actions that precede the lives of all or nearly all if its members. Apologies are rarely transformative, nor should we expect that they will be so. Further, many government apologies will be vague and obscure. Of course, one can insist that government apologies be meaningful, an idea I return to in the conclusion. While my argument here is skeptical of the efficacy and meaning of many government apologies, I do want to emphasize that some of the consequences that the apologies advocates argue for overlap with the goals of the acknowledgement. My argument against most government apologies is not an argument against learning about the past, or aspiring to transform the political community. As Celermajer argues about apology, acknowledgement can give recognition to a group that has been ignored or not treated with decent respect. Acknowledgement – in textbooks, museums, street signs, national holidays – can be a way of saying that this group is an important part of the political community. They were ignored or misrecognized in the past, and now the political community corrects that mistake with recognition. Or it is possible that some parts of the political community can do so: acknowledgement will often come in fits and starts, and one museum in one place does not mean that a state has acknowledged an enduring injustice. Yet one museum may inspire others; changes in curricula in one place may spur changes in other places.

None of this means the path to acknowledgement is assured; I do not want to assume that progress will be made in cases of enduring injustice. Yet I want to argue for acknowledgement as a normative

[48] Jacob Levy, *The Multiculturalism of Fear* (Oxford University Press, 2000), 28–29.

value, and to argue that this acknowledging is something the political community should aspire to do. Once acknowledgement seeps in, the idea is that suggestions on how to overcome the enduring injustice do not seem as strange as they once did. Ultimately the goal is for members of the dominant political community to acknowledge that the injustice is enduring, and that something different should be done to overcome the injustice. Acknowledgement is at the beginning of a process of overcoming an enduring injustice; an apology, if appropriate, comes at the end of the process.

4.6 Shared space

Injustices that occurred in the past cannot be undone, as the skeptics claim. Political communities can and should work to undo current injustices, however. A political community may not be responsible for an enduring injustice, in either its history or its present form, but it still may have a responsibility to help end the injustice. The political community that is able to help remedy the enduring injustice needs to acknowledge its ability to do so, and then work to realize this ability. Determining who is responsible for the injustice is beside the point, since that does not necessarily tell us who is responsible for ending the injustice.

Symbolic forms of acknowledgement may be important, but surely more than symbolism (which apologies can often become) is needed to overcome enduring injustices, which will often be the case when land is at issue. To make this argument I want to build upon the basic model of political responsibility: that members of a political community have a responsibility toward one another. I assume this model, rather than defend it, since all those involved in the historical injustice debate do so. I want to expand this model in one small but important way, and argue that political responsibility reaches out, at least, to those who share space. Those who inhabit a political community share space, which often defines the community. A space can be shared, however, by people who do not concurrently occupy it. The descendants of a community who once lived in a place, but were expelled or mostly killed, have some claim to that space too. They are not members of the political community that occupy that land now, and so are outside most of the current arguments on enduring injustice and apology, but the injustice that led to their expulsion

[margin handwritten note: who is responsible ≠ who is responsible for ending injustice]

should not mean that they have absolutely no claim to the land they formerly occupied. Such a denial equates might with right; it means the injustice is enshrined in political exile. If a political community aspires to be fair, it would be unfair and morally arbitrary to argue that the descendants of those who were expelled or victims of massacres or genocide have no claims to the land, particularly if the injustice is enduring. It should acknowledge that the space it now inhabits is in some way shared by others. This sharing does not mean that the descendants of the enduring injustice have a claim to live on the space; but it does mean that what is done with this space is done with these descendants and their view of this land in mind.

The argument that with time the injustice fades assumes that the people who have moved into the land (and their descendants) have their lives intertwined with the space that they now inhabit. As time passes, their lives are evermore part of this space, and to expel them would be an injustice. The attachment of the current residents to the land, however, does not mean that the ancestors of the people who were expelled no longer have their lives intertwined with that space. The collective narrative of a people may center upon the land from which they were expelled, or the horrors of the past may mean a terrible memory tied to a particular space that they do not want or are unable to forget.

One claim about land focuses on return, which is kept alive when the ancestors of those expelled do not feel at home in what they consider to be an alien land. The collective narrative of at least some significant portion of the group leads them to long to go back home. The injustice of expulsion that their ancestors suffered some time ago still haunts their lives; the injustice endures. Yet there is no agent today who claims responsibility for this expulsion and can apologize for it. Neither the Russians nor the Ukrainians owe the Tatars an apology; what the Russians living in the Crimea and the Ukrainian government owe the Tatars is an acknowledgement of their claim to the Crimea and to facilitate the return of those that aspire to do so in ways that are fair to all concerned. The Russians in the Crimea may complain that it is too morally arbitrary to give them the responsibility of helping to repair the enduring injustice suffered by the Tatars. Yet the fact that the Russians live in the Crimea is also morally arbitrary: they can hardly claim that they deserve to live there, since they or their recent ancestors were allowed to move there following Stalin's expulsion of the Tatars. Indeed, where people live is usually a matter of luck, accident, or fortune (or perhaps misfortune or bad luck). People do not control where their ancestors moved to, and few control the visa policies of states, the wars that may have engulfed a region, and so on. However people may have made it to a land, their lives often have become interwoven with it; and when this happens they have some claim to that land. Sometimes those expelled (or their descendants) will learn to make their way in their new land, but when this does not happen their claim to the ancestral land should be respected in some fashion.

Acknowledging the exile of the Tatars means facilitating their return to the Crimea. Return does not mean reclaiming their ancestral houses, or that all Tatars can return. These houses have been occupied now for quite some time, and expelling their current occupiers would create a new set of injustices. Neither can it mean, however, that the current occupiers simply ignore the pleas of the Tatars. Exile causes (at least) two injustices. One is the particular injustice suffered by every expelled Tatar family; the other is the joint injustice of losing one's homeland. The former set of injustices will rarely be reversed. There may certainly be particular cases of Tatar families buying their ancestral home, but clearly not many will be able to do so. Enduring injustices are group matters. Individual families can certainly suffer over generations, but the project of reclaiming individual homes will certainly lead to more injustices, if coercion is involved. Buying one's ancestral home on the open market does not raise any issues of justice; the government confiscating the home clearly does. The enduring injustice must be solved as a group injustice, even if individuals and families are harmed.

The injustice to individual Tatars and families was their forcible eviction from their homes. An unjust eviction from one's home is an injustice, but not a challenge to liberalism or even an enduring injustice. It is, rather, more properly thought of as a crime. The collective eviction of a people, however, poses a more fundamental challenge to liberalism and begs for a group solution. The injustice to the Tatars as a people is their exile from their ancestral homeland, and so overcoming it means facilitating their return in a general way, in ways that do not cause another injustice. The Ukrainian government can work to facilitate the return of the Tatars who want to do so, without forcibly displacing the current residents. The Tatars can be given the opportunity to buy land (and perhaps be given the funds to do so) in their ancestral homeland without much trouble. Burke Hendrix suggests that indigenous peoples be given the right of first refusal when their former lands come up for sale, which are the settlements the New Zealand government and several indigenous tribes have agreed upon; this suggestion can be used for the Tatar as well.[49] The government too should help facilitate the Tatar integration into Crimean life. None of this means that all Tatars will be able to return to the Crimea. The return of many Tatars does not mean that the radical injustice they suffered is erased or reversed, but it may mean that it can be overcome.

A second land claim is about sacred space. Serbians should have access to their holy places in an independent Kosovo (if this occurs); Muslims should have access to the Dome of the Rock in Jerusalem. I will explain this argument by looking at places of cruelty that have special meaning to the ancestors of the victims since it is so intimately tied to their history, but where return is either not wanted or is impossible. Bloodied places where terrible events took place – mass killings or destruction – are akin to sacred space. The idea of commemorating the dead is not unusual; that's what graves do, and most states have memorials to their war dead. There is no reason, however, that there should be memorials to their dead only. Auschwitz is under Polish sovereignty, but the Polish government ought not to feel free to do what it will with Auschwitz. It instead has an obligation, to the victims' descendants at the least, to maintain Auschwitz as a memorial and museum, even though Germans ran Auschwitz. Many people would rightly be appalled if the Polish government sold Auschwitz to someone who razed the place, and then built an amusement park on it. They would be appalled because the Polish government would be violating that space and the memories it holds; it would be in particular a violation of Jewish memory. The museum and memorial signify not only the event, but the place as well. Memorials can have meaning to all people, but they have special significance to the ancestors of the victims, since that place has a special place in their collective narrative. It may become a place of pilgrimage, part of the people's way of

[49] Burke A. Hendrix, *Ownership, Authority, and Self-Determination: Moral Principles and Indigenous Rights Claims* (Pennsylvania State University Press, 2008), 49.

tracing their past, and of understanding who they are. The idea that states do not have complete control of their territory is in fact something that nearly every state has agreed to, since to date 178 states have signed the World Heritage Convention. Once a place is designated a World Heritage site, it "belong[s] to all the peoples of the world, irrespective of the territory on which they are located"; the signatories express "a shared commitment to preserving our legacy for future generations."[50]

The Holocaust is a radical, not enduring, injustice but I use it to illustrate the principle of shared space. When space is shared between different political communities because of the vagaries of history, the appropriate response is not to search for the party responsible for the expulsion or mass killing to offer an apology, but rather for the political community that occupies the space to acknowledge the claims of the other political community on the same space. Memorials on bloodied space are also, importantly, a way for the people who keep the memorial to keep their distance from what happened. A terrible event happened in this place, the memorial symbolically states, but the political community that maintains this place does so to remind us that what happened here will not happen again; the political community maintains the memorial in part to show that it too mourns what happened. The memorial acknowledges the importance of that space to the victimized group; it treats that space as sacred to them.

4.7 A place for apology

What if an apology is politically efficacious, however? It may not have to be sincere or transformative to have good effects. What if, for example, an Israeli government apology for expelling some Palestinians in the Israeli War of Independence was the one issue left in peace negotiations between the two governments? One might question the sincerity of the apology, and of course it would not be made with a sense of real regret, but if it facilitates a peace agreement, one would be hard pressed to argue against an apology in this case, and I will not do so here. What if, however, a particular group – say, Chinese

[50] UNESCO, "World Heritage," http://whc.unesco.org/en/about/ (accessed August 8, 2010).

Americans – are pressing for a government apology, why not give one? The cost is quite low, particularly if there is accompanying language that insists that the apology should not be construed as an invitation for reparations. If such an apology would please a particular group, it seems rather mean-spirited to say no. Of course, an apology in this case is really about the past, and so does not need to work in tandem with transformation. One might go further, and ask why not give apologies to victims of enduring injustice as well, even if they will not usher in or be accompanied by transformative policies.

I have suggested some reasons why apologies without meaningful action are not a good idea in cases of enduring injustice: they are bound to be seen as insincere, and will disappoint at least some of the intended audience of the apology. Apologies for past (not enduring) injustices will not suffer from these problems, but then we need to have some criteria to determine which past injustices should receive an apology and which not, which no one has yet presented. Of course, politicians do not need a theory to reach consistency; they can just do away with consistency. The danger that some groups receiving an apology will anger other groups may simply be something that some politicians will care little about. In some cases, doing so may simply not be that big a deal, a mistake perhaps, but one that registers rather low on the Richter scale. At other times, however, other groups may object: why did one group receive an apology, but not them? Mexican Americans may rightly be angered that Chinese Americans in California received an apology but not them. Of course, governments can freely grant apologies, like the main character in Jay Rainer's novel *Eating Crow*, who becomes for a time the chief apologist for the UN's Office of Apology, trotting off to many places around the world to apologize for any number of injustices, rendering all the apologies meaningless.[51]

None of this means that apologies can never be meaningful, just that meaningful government apologies are (and will be) rare. If an apology is granted to an intergenerational group that suffers from an enduring injustice, if the apology is part of a package of legislation that works toward ending the injustice, and which enjoys considerable public support, then it may be appropriate. In these circumstances, the importance of the apology is limited; what matter equally, or more,

[51] Jay Rayner, *Eating Crow* (New York: Simon & Schuster, 2004).

are the actions that accompany the apology. Still, apologies have symbolic meaning, and it may bring the process of acknowledging and overcoming the injustice to a close. My argument is not that apologies are never useful, but that in the limited cases when they are useful, they should come toward the end of the process of acknowledgement, where they might be sincere, not at the beginning.

One set of cases where an apology may be appropriate is in New Zealand, where the government is trying to settle with different Maori tribes. The government is recognizing some land claims, and offered financial compensation for past injustices. When coming to an agreement with the tribe, the Queen apologized for past unjust actions committed by the government. Not all tribes have settled, but some have, and the government is attempting to negotiate with all of them. The apologies that are forthcoming are part of a good faith settlement. That the Queen is apologizing, rather than the New Zealand people, makes the issue of sincerity easier to determine.[52] Still, there could be times when a government can apologize sincerely, with the backing of many of its citizens. This apology will be most meaningful, however, when accompanied by actions that not only genuinely try to end the enduring injustice, but also seem to have some success in doing so.

---

[52] Information about these treaties, including the apologies, can be found at www.ots.govt.nz/.

5 | *Legitimacy and the cast of history*

The specter of history rarely haunts liberals as much as it should. Eighteenth- and nineteenth-century liberals wanted to learn from history, but they wanted to begin anew, to begin a new historical trajectory. Yet now recent history in many of the Western democracies is a liberal history, so to ignore history is to ignore the practices of liberal governments – or to ignore the practices often implemented in the name of liberalism. My argument about history and memory in the previous chapters has focused on understanding enduring injustices: many can only be understood by taking the collective narrative of the victims into account, and their solutions need to be historically informed. Here I turn from the collective narratives of the victims of enduring injustice to the history of liberal states, which matters in important ways. This argument is implicit in my previous discussion of mistrust, an issue I return to here. I argue that acknowledging the history of the practices of liberal states that have caused or contributed to enduring injustices complicates the idea of implementing liberal justice in some historically oppressed communities because it questions the legitimacy of the liberal state.

I begin this chapter with a brief discussion of non-ideal theory, which is the framework for the political arguments I put forth in this and the ensuing chapters. I then turn to what I call a detour from liberal justice. In some cases, the history of an enduring injustice suggests that a temporary deviation from liberal principles is needed to ensure the realization of liberal justice. I then show how the history of an enduring injustice will sometimes question the legitimacy of the state's authority over the group, at least in a partial way. Many of the arguments that insist that these groups protect the individual rights of their members work within a framework of liberal justice and progress that ignores the history of enduring injustices; these arguments wrongly assume the justice and legitimacy of the liberal state in cases of enduring injustice. Taking that history into account, I argue, questions the authority of the liberal state to impose its view of justice on historically oppressed groups. For some groups, this means that they ought to have autonomy. This is another and important way of acknowledging the enduring injustice; not just through museums and symbolic ways, but in the policies of the state, some of which I suggest in the ensuing two chapters. My argument about legitimacy grants some autonomy to certain oppressed groups, but this does not mean that oppressed communities can have whatever rules their leaders choose. The worry that some groups may use their autonomy to undermine equality or the rights of some members is a critical one; I take this important issue into consideration when I present an account of what makes group autonomy legitimate.

5.1 Nonideal theory

Liberal theory often takes the form of what is called ideal theory: we establish what a just society looks like, we determine the rules of justice, and this gives us the goal that we need to move toward as we travel from injustice toward justice. Nonideal theory helps us to see how we might actually achieve the goal of justice. John Rawls argues that nonideal theory looks for courses of action that are "morally permissible, and politically possible as well as likely to be effective."[1] In an ideal society, we may assume that all citizens receive a good education. But in our society, we may have to figure out how all citizens receive such an education. Ideal theory tells us the goal, but we may have to look elsewhere to determine how to reach that goal.

There are times, however, when ideal theory may be an obstacle to a better society. Elizabeth Anderson argues that sometimes ideal theory can obscure the route out of injustice.[2] The move from nonideal practice to the ideal may mean not following ideal principles of justice. A colorblind society may be ideal, but that does not mean that society should demand that all of its institutions implement colorblind strategies right now. Anderson argues that starting with nonideal theory means using ideals as hypotheses, to be tested to see if they end or curb the injustice: "We test the ideals by putting them into practice and

---

[1] John Rawls, *The Law of Peoples* (Cambridge, MA: Harvard University Press, 1999), 89.
[2] Elizabeth Anderson, *The Imperative of Integration* (Princeton University Press, 2010), 3–11.

seeing whether they solve the problems for which they were devised . . . and offer a way of life that people find superior to what they had before."[3] If a state's institutions are colorblind in congruence with liberal theory, but this does nothing to alleviate the racism and oppression faced by Black Americans (or makes matters worse), then these institutions might have to rethink their colorblindness, at least for a time.

Anderson's characterization of nonideal theory is useful, and is something I draw upon. Yet a tragic liberalism sometimes puts more distance between justice and injustice than Anderson's nonideal theory, and argues that sometimes a theory of justice does not give us a goal to strive for, at least not right now. In the Rawlsian account of ideal theory, nonideal theory is a transition to an ideal society; and good nonideal policies are not aimed at just one injustice, but are part of an integrated goal of eliminating all injustices.[4] This means that nonideal theory does not aim at second best, unless second best is part of a transition to the ideal.[5] One can imagine a second-best nonideal state that is its own end, that is not a transition to first best; but for Rawls, this is a goal to avoid. Nonideal theory should aim to help reach the ideal society.

There are two ways in which Rawlsian nonideal theory can be unhelpful. First, taking injustice seriously means sometimes accepting the idea that an injustice stands on it own, not as the opposite of justice, and not as something that justice can overcome. When someone's rights are unjustly usurped, the solution is often the protection of these rights; the injustice shows us how justice should be protected. Yet some injustices are simply outside the purview of liberal justice, as in the example of the injustice of exile. It is not as if there is another, readily accessible view of justice we can draw upon in this case. Even though there are arguments about the importance of national self-determination, which can help us determine that exile is unjust in fact, that does not make return obviously just. If other people now live on the land, then the matter of return is hardly simple; nor is it clear what the just solution is in this kind of situation. In other words,

---

[3] *Ibid.*, 6.

[4] My account of Rawlsian nonideal theory is heavily indebted to A. John Simmons, "Ideal and Non-Ideal Theory," *Philosophy and Public Affairs* 38, no. 1 (2010): 5–36.

[5] *Ibid.*, 25.

for some injustices, there is no ideal justice that we can strive for. The solution will surely have to be a result of negotiation and compromise. One might say that the ideal solution is for both peoples to live in their homelands; and if that is not possible, then nonideal theory points us to a compromise that is second best and tries to balance the just claims of each side in a fair way. This is probably the best that can be done in this kind of situation. This does not mean we need to make great revisions in the idea of Rawlsian nonideal theory, which may be quite applicable in other cases. That the ideal cannot be posited in the abstract, but is a result of negotiation and compromise, is an addendum to ideal theory, a note that sometimes the ideal is not possible.

Yet in some other cases, different versions of justice will have to be balanced against one another. Rawlsian justice is an integrated whole, and nonideal theory aims to help reach a fully just society. Part of my argument in the next two chapters, however, is that procedural and substantive justice may tug in different directions. How and by whom a decision is made is often a matter of justice; and the substance of the decision is also often a matter of justice. In these cases, ideal theory does not necessarily give us a single goal to strive to reach. Ideally, of course, legitimate authority and procedures will lead to an ideal version of justice. But there will be times when these two kinds of justice will pull in different directions, as I hope to show toward the end of this chapter. Rawls mostly discusses substantive principles of justice; he assumes that liberal regimes have complete legitimate authority. It is this assumption that I question in much of this chapter.

5.2 A detour from liberal justice

It is possible, and often worth trying, to take a temporary detour from liberal justice in order to sustain liberal justice in the longer term.[6] Mistrust may be a reason to detour from the usual contours of liberal justice; once action is taken to reverse the mistrust that a group has toward a government, then liberal justice may be restored. Affirmative action is the classic liberal detour, about which I will only comment briefly. One important justification for affirmative action is that it is

---

[6] A good but critical discussion of the idea of detour from liberal principles is Juliet Hooker, *Race and the Politics of Solidarity* (Oxford University Press, 2009), ch. 2.

supposed to help members of some groups overcome discrimination. Once that goal is achieved, affirmative action ought to end. The Roma (gypsies) have very high unemployment rates, face deep-seated prejudice, police abuse, low rates of education, and tremendous poverty. The problems that the Roma face in many European countries may need more than the typical liberal remedies, including affirmative action, to correct.[7] Many special measures may need to be taken to give the Roma something close to equal opportunity and to have their individual rights protected, measures that may be needed for many years. There are of course many arguments about affirmative action, and there is not just one justification for it (for example, some arguments for affirmative action focus on the importance of diversity), but instead of repeating the arguments of this rather large literature, I want to turn to a different kind of case where a temporary detour from liberal principles may be justified.[8]

In Chapter 3 I discussed some of the challenges that Hinduism poses for liberalism, and some of the changes that the Indian state made within Hinduism to help better realize social and political equality. One might argue that changes within Indian Hinduism were necessary to pave the way for liberalism. Some changes were made to Hinduism in the name of liberalism by the Indian state and its predecessor, the British Raj. The British outlawed the practice of sati (widow burning), which mostly faded away in India. In many parts of India, there was a tradition of dedicating to Hindu temples young women (the devadasi) who were often considered to be married to the Gods (sometimes at a young age), who danced and sang in the temples and in religious processions. This tradition degenerated by the nineteenth century, and some of the women ended up working for the temple's trustees

[7] Angus Bancroft, *Roma and Gypsy – Travellers in Europe: Modernity, Race, Space and Exclusion* (Aldershot: Ashgate Publishing, 2005); Ivan Szelenyi and Janos Ladanyi, *Patterns of Exclusion: Constructing Gypsy Ethnicity and the Making of an Underclass in Transitional Societies of Europe* (Boulder, CO: East European Monographs, 2006); Nidhi Trehan and Nando Sigona, *Romani Politics in Contemporary Europe: Poverty, Ethnic Mobilization, and the Neo-Liberal Order* (Basingstoke: Palgrave Macmillan, 2010).

[8] Arguments for affirmative action include Kwame Anthony Appiah and Amy Gutmann, *Color Conscious* (Princeton University Press, 1998); William G. Bowen and Derek Bok, *The Shape of the River* (Princeton University Press, 2000); Anderson, *Integration*; Ronald Dworkin, *Sovereign Virtue: The Theory and Practice of Equality* (Cambridge, MA: Harvard University Press, 2002). Anderson discusses several different justifications for affirmative action.

as prostitutes. Animal sacrifices were also common at Hindu temples. These last two practices particularly offended Hindu reformers, who led the mostly successful charge to ban them in pre-independence India.[9] The laws outlawing the devadasi and animal sacrifices are rather dubious from a liberal point of view. The practice of devadasi may have degenerated into prostitution, but that makes the case for reform not abolition (assuming prostitution is against liberal principles).[10] One can outlaw prostitution without making dancing illegal. There may be a case for regulating animal sacrifices to prevent cruelty to them, but this too does not mean outlawing animal sacrifices altogether.

One might argue that these changes to Hinduism are in accord with liberalism, because liberalism is a transformative political theory, that is not only about protecting individual rights, but about creating a political community that contains the right kinds of attitudes and institutions to support a culture of equality, autonomy, and mutual respect.[11] There is much to this, to be sure, but liberalism cannot ensure that citizens embody these liberal values. It can certainly teach and encourage these values in schools and through political culture, and it can have laws and policies that mitigate against discrimination in the name of equality. Yet liberalism will not always be successful when it faces deeply rooted attitudes and behaviors, and it has traditionally been reluctant to interfere with the rules of religion; when it does, it usually does so controversially (unless physical harm is an issue).

One justification for detouring from liberal principles can be found in civic republicanism, which in its recent incarnation focuses on domination instead of individual rights.[12] Civic republicans are

---

[9] Kay K. Jordan, "Devadasi Reform: Driving the Priestesses Or the Prostitutes Out of Hindu Temples?," in Robert Baird, ed., *Religion and Law in Independent India* (New Delhi: Manohar, 1993), 257–78. For an interesting argument on religious animal sacrifices see Paula Casal, "Is Multiculturalism Bad for Animals?," *Journal of Political Philosophy* 11, no. 1 (2003): 1–22.

[10] A liberal argument against prostitution is Peter de Marneffe, *Liberalism and Prostitution* (New York: Oxford University Press, 2009).

[11] Stephen Macedo, "Transformative Constitutionalism and the Case of Religion: Defending the Moderate Hegemony of Liberalism," *Political Theory* 26, no. 1 (1998), 56.

[12] A good explanation of civic republicanism is Philip Pettit, *Republicanism: A Theory of Freedom and Government* (Oxford University Press, 1999).

interested in the freedom and equality of all citizens; with citizenship as their primary focus, they are less interested in protecting the private sphere than are liberals. Civic republicans suggest that key obstacles to non-domination – to social and political equality and liberty – ought to be combatted. The focus of civic republicanism is the individual, but if a group of people is dominated, then the sources of that domination should be dismantled or in some way prevented from dominating members of the group. Great disparities of wealth may cause domination; and so large concentrations of wealth may have to be dismantled to secure the notion of freedom that most republicans advance. If dismantling church or temple power is necessary to dismantle patterns of domination and unequal citizenship, then civic republicans would usually favor doing so.

The idea of non-domination is different from liberal rights; one's rights can be intact and yet be dominated by others. If the rights of lower caste members and Dalits were not violated in India (they clearly are too often) they still might face arbitrary power from upper caste members in ways that sustain domination. While some may argue that deep-seated domination does in fact violate liberalism, since it is hard to see how such domination can co-exist with social and even political equality, civic republicans will usually have fewer qualms about reaching into the private sphere than will liberals. The idea of domination is a straightforward way to describe the harm of large group-based discrimination within civil society; this is not a harm perpetuated by the state, but by many members of society. Liberals face the tug between the importance of equality and the importance of protecting the private sphere when facing this kind of domination.

The departures from liberal justice taken by the Indian state are not justified because of past discrimination or oppression; the detour is justified because of the pervasive current discrimination and oppression, because of the domination that Dalits and lower caste citizens are subjected to by some members of the upper castes. The detour is needed because history suggests the discrimination and oppression have deep-seated, and that the usual tools of religious toleration and liberty (and perhaps redistribution of wealth) will not produce equality. In the case of Dalits, it is hard to see how the injustice they have endured will fade without strong state action aimed at combating the discrimination they face.

When the history of the injustice strongly suggests that the usual liberal methods will not undo the injustice, then other means ought to be considered. This is another method of acknowledgement: it means the political community acknowledges that the injustice is enduring, and that it may have to reach beyond liberal solutions to try to overcome the enduring injustice. Affirmative action is one possible option, but the Indian case shows that other options may be available, depending on the case at hand. What exactly are the right measures to take cannot be determined without knowing the particulars of the case. I have suggested in the Indian case that liberalism's traditional respect for religion as mostly a private matter may have to be bent in order to overcome the enduring injustice.

Another possible detour from liberal justice is the redistribution of land. Land ownership in some Latin American countries is quite skewed, with many having little land and others holding vast amounts. Liberalism may be ambiguous when it comes to the redistribution of land. The disparities of wealth and land ownership in Latin America certainly undermine the conditions for liberal equality and liberty. Yet liberal principles of property ownership suggest that confiscating land in the name of equality is suspect – though some also read Locke's labor theory of value as justifying confiscating land from owners if the current occupants ignore the land, and others mix their labor with the land.[13] The land ownership disparities did not arise from the differences in the hard work of various citizens, but largely from property ownership patterns established by the colonial powers. Unsurprisingly, the groups with the least amount of land tend to be indigenous or Black.[14] Yet liberalism has little to say about what to do if the origins of property distribution are unfair. In this kind of situation, the idea of domination provides a more straightforward way of explaining why huge disparities in wealth and land ownership ought to be changed rather than liberal equality.

Another kind of detour, though one that may have fewer implications for political institutions than the others I have suggested here, is the idea of group solidarity. It would clearly be a mistake to think

[13] Wendy Wolford, "Land Reform in the Time of Neoliberalism: A Many-Splendored Thing," *Antipode* 39, no. 3 (2007): 550–70.
[14] William C. Thiesenhusen, *Broken Promises: Agrarian Reform and the Latin American Campesino* (Boulder, CO: Westview Press, 1995), 12.

that the state will by itself work to undo an enduring injustice. The state will have to be prodded and pushed to do so. If African Americans are to reach equality with others in the US, there will continue to be a political struggle, one that should not be exclusively African American, but one in which African Americans play a prominent role. This means that there is an important role for Black solidarity, or what Tommie Shelby calls pragmatic Black nationalism, in achieving liberal goals. Shelby argues for a pluralistic Black nationalism, which is a nationalism not valued for its intrinsic worth, but for pragmatic ends: antiracism, equal educational and employment opportunity, tolerance for group differences, and substantive racial equality.[15] These are all (or can readily be interpreted as) liberal goals; when they are achieved – which Shelby notes will take some time – then the case for Black solidarity or pragmatic Black nationalism recedes. Few of liberalism's dictates oppose a group of people gathering together to press for political reform, but Shelby's notion of Black solidarity goes beyond condoning the idea of voluntary associations. The political goals of Black solidarity often mesh with the ideals of liberal democracy, but along the way Black solidarity may lead to (or push for) certain kinds of racial pride, symbolic and substantive ways of recognizing African Americans (Black History Month, African American Studies Programs, and so on), and for a long-term political strategy that coalesces around an ascriptive identity. Some liberals may (and some do) object to the idea that Black Americans should achieve recognition as Black Americans (as opposed to individuals who are American and Black), but this solidarity is certainly justified under conditions of enduring injustice. As the injustice fades, then the solidarity of African Americans may weaken, though liberalism certainly allows people to identify with particular groups.[16] In the meantime, group solidarity of some oppressed groups with exclusive membership may be a detour from the spirit of liberalism.

---

[15] Tommie Shelby, *We Who Are Dark: The Philosophical Foundations of Black Solidarity* (Cambridge, MA: Harvard University Press, 2007), 246–47.

[16] I argue that when the oppression of a group fades, the bonds of the group weaken in modern liberal societies, in Jeff Spinner, *The Boundaries of Citizenship: Race, Ethnicity and Nationality in the Liberal State* (Baltimore: Johns Hopkins University Press, 1994).

5.3 Legitimacy and reform

Unfortunately, there is no assurance that a detour from liberal justice, even one couched in the language of civic republicanism, will work; my argument is that they are often worth trying. For much of the remainder of this book I will leave aside the detour cases from liberal justice, and focus on what I take to be the harder cases, where the endpoint may not be liberal justice at all. A basic virtue of liberalism is its insistence that the rights of individuals be protected, that all are treated with equal (or as I will argue below, decent) regard. Yet when a liberal state fails in this basic task, it does not have full legitimacy over the ignored – or victimized – group. This is another way in which the history of an enduring injustice matters, as it calls the authority of the liberal state into question, or at least partial question. Ideal theory assumes the moral authority of the liberal state is legitimate, but I argue here that this assumption is sometimes mistaken. The moral weight of the past sometimes matters – it is the history of liberal states acting unjustly that should lead us to question, in a partial way, their legitimacy today.

Civic republicanism does not fare any better here. One might ask why domination cannot simply be used to explain the relationship of indigenous peoples to Western governments. It is certainly true that tribes in the New World (and other places as well) are dominated. But while the idea of domination looks at groups, it does so only in a pragmatic way;[17] its focus on the individual gives it limited use when it comes to enduring injustice. When Frank Lovett uses civic republicanism to look at cultural accommodation, he is clear that though he uses the term "group" in his argument, "the idea of cultural group performs no actual work in the argument."[18] Group is just a shorthand for a collection of individuals who share a social practice. If tribes have inegalitarian rules with unequal rights, for example, then civic republicans would focus on the rights violations within these communities as much as state domination of the tribe. Like many versions of liberalism, civic republicanism is usually blind to history. Lovett, for example, gives little credence to enduring injustice or the illegitimacy of the state.[19]

---

[17] Pettit, *Republicanism*, 143–46.

[18] Frank Lovett, "Cultural Accommodation and Domination," *Political Theory* 38, no. 2 (2010), 258.

[19] Lovett does grant that one might delay outlawing a social practice that contributed to domination for pragmatic reasons. He argues that it is possible,

Traditional liberal arguments about legitimacy focus on consent: if a people consent to a government then it is legitimate, and the people are then obligated to obey it. Since few people actually do consent to their government, consent theorists resort to tacit consent as the vehicle on which to rest legitimacy and obligation. Yet as Hume argued, tacit consent leaves people with too stark a choice: agree to a government that has been imposed on them or leave. Those least able to leave, the poor, are the people that have the least reason to consent to their government. It is certainly likely that the victims of enduring injustice are among the least likely to consent to the government. Besides Hume, others have persuasively argued that the search for legitimacy should look elsewhere.[20] The best arguments for legitimacy focus on individual rights, and how citizens are treated and heard, and I follow their lead here.[21]

These recent liberal arguments about legitimacy focus on rights and equal concern for all citizens. Political authority, it is commonly argued, is justified when it upholds individual rights, and when the state shows equal regard for all citizens. While I discuss three authors

---

    if one places too many traditional social practices under direct or indirect burdens, that it may provoke a conservative reaction, undermining efforts to reduce domination. So one might need to be strategic about outlawing or putting pressure on certain dominating practices. *Ibid.*, 257–59.

[20] David Hume, "Of the Original Contract," in *Essays: Moral, Political and Literary*, ed. Eugene Miller (Indianapolis: Liberty Classics, 1985 [1742]); see too the beginning of Buchanan's essay, which succinctly summarizes the main criticisms of consent theory, Allen Buchanan, "Political Legitimacy and Democracy," *Ethics* 112, no. 4 (2002): 689–719; for a historically based critique, see Don Herzog, *Happy Slaves: A Critique of Consent Theory* (University of Chicago Press, 1989).

[21] Working within the framework of what I will describe as the standard view of liberal legitimacy, I ignore philosophical anarchism. A. J. Simmons prominently argues that while consent is important to political legitimacy, tacit consent will not do; what is needed is actual consent from the citizens for a government to be legitimate. Since this actual consent is not forthcoming for most or all citizens, most governments are then illegitimate. Simmons's philosophical anarchism does not mean people are free to disobey the law, since Simmons is a philosophical anarchist, not a political anarchist. A. J. Simmons, *Moral Principles and Political Obligations* (Princeton University Press, 1979). For specific criticisms of Simmons, see Anna Stilz, *Liberal Loyalty: Freedom, Obligation, and the State* (Princeton University Press, 2009); Jeremy Waldron, "Special Ties and Natural Duties," *Philosophy and Public Affairs* 22, no. 1 (1993): 3–30. One important attempt to resurrect consent theory is David M. Estlund, *Democratic Authority: A Philosophical Framework* (Princeton University Press, 2009).

here, this is a widespread (though not universal) view.[22] This will seem intuitively obvious to most liberals, but I want to show how this argument becomes ambivalent when it comes to enduring injustice. There are different ways in which scholars come to this view, but the core of these arguments is similar: that liberalism is a theory that shows concern for all of its citizens. The arguments that I examine later in this chapter when I turn to cases of enduring injustice have a similar structure, basing political legitimacy on the protection of individual rights.

Constructing her argument with an interpretation of Rousseau and Kant, Anna Stilz contends that a state is legitimate if it adheres to several conditions. The state should protect the minimal integrity and freedom of movement of everyone's body; each person has a sphere of negative freedom in which he or she can pursue his or her own ends; there is a set of minimal economic conditions that must be in place; there must be equality before the law; and citizens must have some concern for all other citizens.[23] Thomas Christiano argues that a just society advances the interests of all persons in the society and advances the interests equally. A person has a right to participate in the shaping of the world she shares with others; since people have equal interests, they should have equal voice in the governing authority. A state is legitimate, according to Christiano, as long it upholds equality.[24] Allen Buchanan expresses a liberal view of legitimacy based on rights: a wielder of political power is legitimate "if and only if it (a) does a credible job of protecting at least the most basic human rights of all those over whom it wields power, (b) provides this protection through processes, policies, and actions that themselves respect the most basic human rights, and (c) is not a usurper (i.e., does not come to wield political power by wrongly deposing a legitimate wielder of political power)." Buchanan argues that these principles incorporate the "Robust Natural Duty of Justice," which is a

---

[22] Ronald Dworkin argues that "no government is legitimate that does not show equal concern for the fate of all those citizens over whom it claims dominion." Ronald Dworkin, *Sovereign Virtue: The Theory and Practice of Equality* (Cambridge, MA: Harvard University Press, 2002), 1. See too Waldron, "Special Ties."

[23] Stilz, *Liberal Loyalty*, 92–94.

[24] Thomas Christiano, *The Constitution of Equality: Democratic Authority and Its Limits* (Oxford University Press, 2008), 12.

duty to help ensure that all persons have access to just institutions. This duty rests on one factual and one moral premise: "The factual premise is that ensuring that all persons are treated with equal regard requires just institutions and, more particularly, institutions that protect their basic human rights. The moral premise is that equal regard for persons requires helping to ensure that their rights are respected."[25]

The easy way to examine how this argument applies in some cases of enduring injustice is to look at condition (c): that the wielder of political authority did not wrongly depose a legitimate political power. Certainly many indigenous peoples argue exactly this, that their political authority was wrongly usurped. I will not repeat those arguments here, since it seems rather hard to argue that whites legitimately deposed indigenous governments. Yet I do not want to rest on this argument for two reasons: first, I want to press on the legitimacy argument to see how it works in other cases of enduring injustice, where the issue of the origins of the governing authority is not germane and second, because I do not want to blithely toss aside the injunction that legitimate governments respect basic human rights and show equal concern for all citizens. In other words, to say that some governments unjustly usurped the authority of others does not say what makes for a legitimate government. As David Copp reminds us, nearly all governments began in "some combination of events that includes a share of skullduggery, or worse."[26] An account of legitimate government will rely to a large degree on what the government does now and has done in the recent past.

What unites the different versions of liberal legitimacy that I have presented here is their interest that all citizens be treated with equal regard, and that they all have an equal voice in the political authority. This is put concisely in the factual premise that Buchanan presents: "that all persons are treated with equal regard requires just institutions." What if, however, certain groups of people are marked out and not treated with equal regard, and this unequal treatment persists? Christiano discusses "persistent minorities," and argues that the inability to treat them with equal regard undermines the legitimacy

---

[25] Buchanan, "Political Legitimacy and Democracy," 704.
[26] David Copp, "The Idea of a Legitimate State," *Philosophy and Public Affairs* 28, no. 1 (1999), 3.

of the state. A persistent minority "almost never has its way in the process of collective decision-making," which makes it hard for their members to provide a corrective to the cognitive bias of the majority. A minority of people will not be able to make the larger world in which they live a home for themselves. Since their interests are being neglected by the democratic process, they will have reason to think they are not being treated as equals, which Christiano argues is unjust.[27]

Anna Stilz similarly argues that one criterion for legitimacy is that citizens must generally be concerned with all their compatriots when they govern, and not just a subset. If the majority in government routinely ignores the concerns of a religious, ethnic, or racial group, then it acts illegitimately over the minority. So even if the composition of the majority shifts, but some group persists in the minority, and its concerns are disregarded, then one of the basic functions of democracy – the government looking out for the basic interests of all citizens – is not working. Citizens ought to be able to trust that their interests will be taken into account in basic legislation concerning rights and duties.[28] Yet this does not happen in many cases of enduring injustice, putting the legitimacy of many liberal states in question.

These legitimacy arguments argue that persistent minorities are not treated justly, yet they do not say what should be done when persistent minorities do exist. It is too simple to declare a state that is unjust as illegitimate, since no state is fully just. A legitimate state does allow for citizens to press their vision of justice (within limits), though it does not assure them success. A legitimate state may contain glaring injustices within it; but if all citizens are treated with equal regard and their interests taken into account, these glaring injustices would not persist, though doubtless other injustices would. Even by distinguishing justice from legitimacy, however, persistent minorities raise troubling questions; the presence of persistent minorities does not necessarily make a state illegitimate, but it does raise the possibility of partial legitimacy. This idea may be implicit in the liberal arguments about legitimacy, but it is rarely teased out, much less discussed.

A government can be partially legitimate in two ways. A government is legitimate if it protects the rights of its citizens (or those who should be citizens) and treats them with equal regard.

---

[27] Christiano, *Constitution of Equality*, 296–97.
[28] Stilz, *Liberal Loyalty*, 94–95.

A government is partially legitimate if it treats most of its citizens with equal regard, but does not do so with a group of citizens who are marked out and continually not treated with equal regard. Most members of the US (and Australia and Canada and Israel and India and so on) view their government as legitimate, and with good reason. Their rights are protected and they are treated reasonably well. This idea is encompassed in the idea of enduring injustice: most citizens are treated with equal (or at least decent) regard by their government, only some are not.

If there is a continual denial of rights over a certain group of people, then the legitimacy of the regime over at least that group is doubtful. (I assume here that a group that is denied rights is also not treated with equal regard.) The US government did not exercise legitimate authority over slaves, and it did not exercise legitimate authority over African Americans during the Jim Crow years. In some cases of enduring injustice, then, when the original forces of oppression are still set in place, the government cannot be seen as fully legitimate from a liberal democratic perspective. In this way, a government is partially legitimate because its authority is legitimate over most citizens, but not all. If one thought that with time the government would extend an equal concern over all of its citizens, then no action may be needed, as its legitimacy would extend over time. In cases of enduring injustice, however, we do not have these expectations, and so the state's legitimacy remains partial.

A second way a state can be partially legitimate is if it secures the rights of all its citizens, but some are treated with less than decent regard. African Americans (and Native Americans) have what Rawls calls their constitutional essentials secure: they have freedom of speech, conscience, religion, assembly, and association; the right to vote and run for office; the right to due process and judicial fairness (sort of), and so on. Yet it is hard to say that these rights alone secure justice. Tommie Shelby notes that Rawls "correctly maintains that we do not have obligations to submit to unjust institutions, or at least not to institutions that exceed the limits of tolerable injustice." The difficulty, Shelby says, "is ascertaining just where to draw the line beyond which injustice becomes intolerable."[29]

---

[29] Tommie Shelby, "Justice, Deviance, and the Dark Ghetto," *Philosophy and Public Affairs* 35, no. 2 (2007), 145.

The state is partially legitimate when a group of citizens find themselves to be victims of an enduring injustice, even if their formal rights are upheld. Saying this kind of government has partial legitimacy over the victims of enduring injustice preserves the distinction between say, China and the US, while still recognizing that the protection of individual rights is insufficient for justice and legitimacy. The US certainly does a better job than China in protecting individual rights, yet that is not all there is to say about legitimacy. The impoverished in the US may have their rights protected, but Shelby argues that the injustice faced by the urban poor is intolerable, which often understandably translates into their viewing the social order as lacking legitimacy.[30] The urban poor live impoverished lives, lack decent educational opportunities, and are far from having fair and equal opportunity. The urban poor have at least most of their constitutional essentials secure, but Shelby argues that this shows securing basic rights is insufficient for legitimacy: "The problem with using the constitutional essentials as the threshold for tolerable injustice is that it does not ensure genuine conditions of reciprocity for the most disadvantaged in the scheme. Each citizen should be secure in the thought that he or she has equal standing within the scheme of cooperation. This means that the scheme should be organized so that it publicly conveys to each participant that his or her interests are just as important as any other participant's."[31]

Establishing real equal standing for all is difficult, and may be too high a bar to set for legitimacy, one that few states can meet. Yet the core point that Shelby makes is correct: if a group of people lives under conditions of considerable injustice then the fact that their formal rights are more or less secure is insufficient. Shelby's argument that each person's interests be treated equally is similar to the liberal argument that every person be treated with equal regard for a government to be considered legitimate. Even if the standard of equal regard is too high and we lower it to a decent regard of everyone's interest, the legitimacy of a government's actions over victims of enduring injustice still comes into question.

We can say that if the government protects the constitutional essentials of all but does not treat everyone with decent regard, then it is partially illegitimate in a second sense. The US government may have

---

[30] *Ibid.*, 143–51.   [31] *Ibid.*, 148–49.

been partially legitimate in the 1930s since it treated most citizens with decent regard and protected their individual rights, but it also marked out certain groups – Native and Black Americans – and did not treat them with decent regard. My argument for decency and decent regard instead of justice is simply a modest amendment to the liberal argument for equal regard, in order to establish a standard of legitimacy that governments can actually meet, since much of my argument here is about the difficulty in reaching justice. The standard for legitimacy should not be utopian, since that would make all states illegitimate. By a decent society, I follow Avishai Margalit who argues that a decent society's institutions do not humiliate its members.[32] (Margalit contrasts this with a civilized society, where the members do not humiliate one another.) Humiliation is any sort of behavior or condition that constitutes a sound reason for a person to consider his self-respect injured. This is a normative, not a psychological definition – Margalit's emphasis is on the reasons for feeling humiliation. A decent society does not act in ways that give the people under its authority reasons to consider themselves humiliated. Putting people on reservations, and giving them few resources with which to live decently, trying to take away their language, and so on, is certainly not treating people decently. When a group has a standard of living considerably below other citizens, when a third of its men are enmeshed with the criminal justice system, that too is not decent.

The intersection of enduring injustice and the illegitimacy of the government is one place where the history of the injustice matters. That some people are poor or treated indecently is insufficient to show that the authority of the government over them is illegitimate. A government is not necessarily illegitimate, or even partially illegitimate, if some immigrants are not treated with decent regard, particularly if there is a track record of the government treating other immigrants with decent regard. There is no magic number of years that determines when indecent treatment of a group of people makes the government partially illegitimate, but one wants to be confident that the injustice is persisting before an otherwise decent regime is seen as partially illegitimate. When a people is treated indecently for two or

---

[32] Avishai Margalit, *The Decent Society* (Cambridge, MA: Harvard University Press, 1996), ch. 1.

more generations, and with little hope that it will end soon, then one can say that they suffer from an enduring injustice.[33]

When a people lives under unjust or indecent conditions for many years, the idea that the government will correct the situation becomes questionable. Why believe that matters will change now? This is the situation in the case of many indigenous peoples, the ghetto poor, and Indian and Israeli Muslims. Years of bad treatment have undermined the legitimacy of the larger political community over these groups. In some of these cases, like the ghetto poor, there seems little choice but to work with the dominant political community in order to try to improve matters.[34] In the case of African Americans generally (and sometimes other minorities), where group autonomy is nearly impossible, some have argued for special representation rights. Minorities are easily outvoted in a democracy, and depending on the rules for electing representatives, it may be difficult for minority representatives to gain elected office. To ensure that minority interests are represented, some argue that democratic governments ought to take steps to ensure minority representation among elected bodies (which is another way to express the idea of partial legitimacy).[35]

Liberals could argue that the history of the liberal state may have illiberal moments, but for a liberal government to regain its legitimacy it should ensure that individual rights are protected and that all citizens are treated with decent regard. The failures of the past need not lead to failure in the future; the past need not repeat itself, after all. One response to this rejoinder is that the moral authority of the state to tell a group it has oppressed how to act is weak. Understandably, when we hear the collective narrative of indigenous peoples, it is the legitimacy of the liberal state to impose its version of justice that becomes questionable. Recall the Trickster: "This is interesting, he thinks, that once you devastate a people, and make them unequal, you

---

[33] Two generations is a reasonable but somewhat arbitrary number that I defend in Chapter 1.

[34] Shelby argues, however, that the questionable legitimacy of the regime over the ghetto poor should make us understand why some of the ghetto poor break the laws of the regime. Shelby does not condone all lawbreaking, but he is surely right to suggest that many of the ghetto poor will not see good reason to follow some laws of the dominant regime.

[35] Will Kymlicka, *Liberalism, Community and Culture* (Oxford University Press, 1989); Melissa Williams, *Voice, Trust and Memory: Marginalized Groups and the Failings of Liberal Representation* (Princeton University Press, 1998).

then promise equality. Is this justice, he wonders?"[36] When liberal states act cruelly (and illegitimately) and when this cruelty is severe and aimed at a particular group, it doesn't have the legitimacy to simply say now it has changed and it will act benignly from now on.

Increasing the challenge to liberal legitimacy is the way liberalism and injustice have (sometimes) been intertwined. The Western story of progress has been used and misused to scorn or pity many Third World and indigenous peoples as backward and uncivilized. While the Western story of progress has rung true for many peoples, for others it has been a failure; and for others still it has been used to undermine their cultural practices and identity. While there was some protest against the policies toward indigenous peoples heard in liberal states, most everyone agreed that the indigenous way of life was outmoded; while some simply wanted to kill many indigenous peoples and let the rest rot on reservations, others argued that Native Americans could survive by becoming civilized: "by the law of historical progress and the doctrine of social evolution civilized ways were destined to triumph over savagism, Indians would ultimately confront a fateful choice: civilization or extinction."[37] Progressives thought the choice was obvious, and went out to civilize the Indian. The Indian was then seen to be at a "patriarchal stage," and would benefit greatly from the ideas of "individualism, industry and private property."[38]

The liberal regime has often been an oppressive regime to those marked out as different or uncivilized. The idea of civilization need not be racist – one could point out that some indigenous peoples were civilized (urbanized, with a developed agriculture, sophisticated ruling structures, and so on). Yet the idea of civilization was used in racist and unfair ways, which sets up a problem: liberalism promises liberation, yet to some it has been oppressive. I want to add to my contention that the history of an enduring injustice questions the legitimacy of the liberal state over an oppressed group: the enduring injustice often questions the legitimacy of liberal justice itself. One could argue

---

[36] John Borrows, "Re-Living the Present: Title, Treaties, and the Trickster in British Columbia," *BC Studies* 120 (1998), 104. On the issue of legitimacy, see too Dale Turner, *This is Not a Peace Pipe: Towards a Critical Indigenous Philosophy* (University of Toronto Press, 2006).

[37] David Wallace Adams, *Education for Extinction: American Indians and the Boarding School Experience 1875–1928* (University Press of Kansas, 1997), 6.

[38] *Ibid.*, 15.

that liberal oppression is not inherently part of liberalism, that when liberals used the idea of civilization in a hierarchical way that justified thinking some civilizations were less developed, they were departing from liberalism's core commitments. Yet what is important is that liberal thinkers did use liberal ideas in ways to justify liberal societies – the civilized – to either try to absorb or lift up other societies.[39]

Ironically, the idea of civilization is enveloped within the rubric of progress. Just as the idea of progress reveals enduring injustice, it is – in some but not all cases – the cause of radical injustice. The standard nineteenth-century view was that as a state progresses, it became more civilized, an argument that easily justified imperialism. The civilization argument is surely not an inherent part of liberalism – some liberals argued against empire and imperialism – but the argument is compatible with some versions of liberalism, and was propagated by liberals. What is important for my argument is the association of liberalism with the idea of civilization; with the idea that advanced liberal peoples should help the "backward" reach a superior state. Liberals should not run from this history, or try to suggest that this was an aberration. Rather, we should acknowledge the history of liberal imperialism, and recognize its implications, which question the legitimacy of the liberal state over victims of enduring injustice.

That a state is only partially legitimate does not mean that citizens are (morally) free to disobey its laws. All states, even illegitimate ones, have what David Copp calls "morally innocent laws," that ought to be obeyed by all: laws that direct what side of the road one must drive on, laws against murder, fraud, and so on.[40] Yet even laws that seem unfair cannot readily be ignored. Civil disobedience is often a justifiable strategy to protest unjust laws in a partially just state, but civil disobedience is most effective when there are specific and clearly unjust laws to protest about. One injustice faced by Black Americans is the relative lack of access to retail and commercial services,

---

[39] Thomas McCarthy, *Race, Empire, and the Idea of Human Development* (Cambridge University Press, 2009); Jennifer Pitts, *A Turn to Empire: The Rise of Imperial Liberalism in Britain and France* (Princeton University Press, 2005); Uday Singh Mehta, *Liberalism and Empire: A Study in Nineteenth-Century British Liberal Thought* (University of Chicago Press, 1999); James Tully, *Public Philosophy in a New Key: Vol. 2, Imperialism and Civic Freedom* (Cambridge University Press, 2008).

[40] Copp, "Legitimate State," 35.

compared to white Americans.[41] There is no law mandating that businesses do not locate near or in Black American neighborhoods; and it is hard to imagine a law that directs where businesses should open up shop. Many Black Americans prefer to live in neighborhoods that are about half Black and half white, while many white Americans prefer to live in neighborhoods with a more lopsided balance between Blacks and whites. This does not mean that government policies are causally innocent. Government policies certainly influenced racial housing patterns for much of the twentieth century.[42] Still, there are not many laws that can be changed that will ensure fairer housing patterns in the US or redirect the placement of retail and commercial enterprises.

People can still organize protests aimed at corporations and make demands at stockholder meetings, but this is different than organizing in order to change specific laws. Some injustices cannot readily be undone by challenging current laws. There may be reason to demand a different set of laws or policies, but it is in general easier to highlight the immorality of a current law that clearly discriminates than the immorality of an absence of a law.

There may nonetheless be laws that are unfair (or worse) to victims of enduring injustice, and it may be that civil disobedience is justified. But depending on the law, and the attitudes of the state's citizens, it may be hard to trigger their moral outrage. Many citizens in a partially just state, who are treated reasonably well and find the state reasonably responsive to their needs, will have a hard time seeing the gravity of the state's unjust laws, or understand the need for new laws. This is not a moral reason to avoid civil disobedience, since it may be justified whether it is effective or not. (One may be justified to disobey some laws of an authoritarian state, but one might obey for prudential, not principled, reasons.)

The response to partial illegitimacy will clearly depend on the circumstances, and the nature of the illegitimacy. That the illegitimacy is partial clearly makes it harder to come up with clean and neat solutions; revolution is acceptable in a clearly and completely

[41] Amy Helling and D. Sawicki Sawicki, "Race and Residential Accessibility to Shopping and Services," *Housing Policy Debate* 14, no. 1 (2003): 69–101.

[42] Citations to some of the relevant literature can be found in Jeff Spinner-Halev, "The Trouble With Diversity," in Jonathan S. Davies and David L. Imbroscio, eds., *Critical Urban Studies: New Directions* (Albany, NY: SUNY, 2010), 107–20.

illegitimate regime. But revolution is not necessarily justified in a partially legitimate regime; there is no assurance that the potentially new regime will be more legitimate than the current one. If there is enough support for a democratic revolution, then surely there is enough support for lesser steps to repair the enduring injustice. If there is not widespread support for the revolution, then one must worry about what kind of revolution there will be, and what comes afterwards. What is needed, then, is not for the partially legitimate regime to be overturned, but for it to be reformed. This will not be easy, and undoubtedly the victims of the enduring injustice will have to be agents in the push for reform. And liberals need to accept the idea that sometimes reform will be contrary to some liberal principles.

5.4 Group autonomy

One possible response to an enduring injustice may be some form of group autonomy, depending on the circumstances. Many feminists and liberals (and liberal feminists) argue that group autonomy, where groups have legal authority over their members, is too often unfairly and unjustly used to discriminate against women.[43] Many indigenous tribes, for example, control their membership rules, some of which are discriminatory. In many Muslim countries personal laws (marriage, divorce, inheritance) are controlled not by civil, but by religious law; this is the case in India and Israel as well. Some scholars argue that group autonomy often results in the coercion of women by restricting individual autonomy; or it means that women's choices are more restricted than men's choices.

---

[43] Marilyn Friedman, "Women's Rights, Oppressed Minorities, and the Liberal State," in Barbara Arneil *et al.*, *Sexual Justice/Cultural Justice: Critical Perspectives in Political Theory and Practice* (New York: Routledge, 2007), 89–102; Susan Moller Okin, "Feminism and Multiculturalism: Some Tensions," *Ethics* 108, no. 4 (1998): 661–84; Susan Moller Okin, "'Mistresses of Their Own Destiny': Group Rights, Gender, and Realistic Rights of Exit," *Ethics* 112, no. 2 (2002): 205–30; Susan Moller Okin, "Multiculturalism and Feminism: No Simple Question, No Simple Answers," in Avigail Eisenberg and Jeff Spinner-Halev, eds., *Minorities within Minorities: Equality, Rights and Diversity* (Cambridge University Press, 2004), 67–89; Sarah Song, *Justice, Gender, and the Politics of Multiculturalism* (Cambridge University Press, 2007); Ayelet Shachar, *Multicultural Jurisdictions: Cultural Differences and Women's Rights* (Cambridge University Press, 2001).

Yet before we insist that small, oppressed groups conform to liberal norms, we liberals ought to be more mindful of our history and our attempts to "civilize the savages." The attempt to impose liberal justice on some has sometimes led to further oppression, not liberation. Even my use of the term group autonomy may be seen as imperialist: many indigenous tribes argue that they are sovereign nations, and it is not up to the liberal state to grant them something which they already have. I accept this view in part. Sovereignty for many tribes will have to mean something different than sovereignty for most nation-states, since many tribes are too small to fully exercise sovereign powers. I also partly agree with the liberal views of legitimacy, which suggest that no government can claim an inherent right to sovereignty (whether a people can is another issue); governments that act in brutal ways are not legitimate. While I use the term group autonomy in this chapter, that phrase is understood to include sovereignty as well.

The feminist critique assumes a normal model of liberal citizenship: the citizen votes and has certain other rights, and the state then has full authority over the citizen. This model, however, is blind to the possibility of a state oppressing a particular group. When this happens, the assumption of an unmediated relationship between state and citizen that is normally made needs to be questioned. The feminist critique assumes the legitimacy of the liberal state; it ignores the possibility of partial legitimacy, the possibility of a state continually treating a group of people with less than decent respect and regard. A philosophical argument about the importance of rights protection too easily skips a crucial political question: Who enforces these rights?

Most of those who join the feminist critique have an ahistorical view of the liberal state, that the liberal state is charged with upholding liberal values and liberal justice, and that it ought to do so when it can. The legitimacy of who is making the laws is rarely considered; what is considered is whether the law itself is just. The standard assumption is that if a government is committed to upholding individual rights it will do so for all its citizens; and liberals assume that most governments treat their citizens with equal or at least decent regard. This view suggests that the citizen has certain rights, including the right to vote, and the state in turn has legitimate authority over the citizen. One example of this standard assumption is found in the work of Brian Barry, who contends that the model of universal citizenship – that all adults in the political community receive the same rights and protections – is one of the great triumphs of liberalism.[44] Yet this is small comfort to indigenous peoples, whose way of life was destroyed by liberals, and who cannot be expected to gleefully become liberals now. Similarly, Israeli and Indian Muslims – both of whom have state-sanctioned family law practices that discriminate against women – do not look upon the state as a liberator set out to install reforms in their community with their community's interests in mind.

One could try, as does Tom Flanagan, to argue that indigenous peoples have benefited from civilization. But Flanagan's defense is weak, pointing out that indigenous peoples can now read and write, participate in advanced economies, vote, and have grown in population.[45] Of course, the world population has grown dramatically over the last two centuries, so it is unclear how meaningful the last point is. While literacy and voting are important, if one's life is impoverished, disease and alcoholism rampant, and the future bleak, it is hard to see how the triumph of individual rights has been of much benefit for indigenous peoples. Flanagan does say that all is not well with indigenous peoples, but "it is important to grasp that not everything has failed."[46] This is surely a feeble defense of civilization's treatment of indigenous peoples. Despite the triumphs of liberalism, the damage that liberal states have done to indigenous peoples has been considerable, and the intent of the liberal state to now treat indigenous peoples fairly is understandably viewed by many with great suspicion. The legitimacy of most Western states to treat indigenous peoples like other citizens has been greatly undermined by the history of these states.

Martha Nussbaum understands that oppressed groups are not keen to work with newly reformed states to reform themselves. She says that "tribal peoples are few, uninfluential, and bitterly opposed to cooperation with the former oppressor." But she is unimpressed by this bitter opposition. It is hard to understand, Nussbaum says, "how the sad history of a group can provide a philosophical justification for the gross denial of individual rights and liberties to the members of the

[44] Brian M. Barry, *Culture & Equality: An Egalitarian Critique of Multiculturalism* (Cambridge, MA: Harvard University Press, 2001), ch. 2.
[45] Tom Flanagan, *First Nations? Second Thoughts* (Montreal: McGill-Queen's University Press, 2008), 45.
[46] *Ibid.*, 45.

group."[47] This argument, though, misses the point: understanding that the state cannot simply impose reforms on groups does not provide a philosophical justification for denying individual rights. It is instead an argument for an understanding that the history of states and political institutions matter when it comes to the legitimacy of liberal states implementing protection of individual rights. My argument does not aim to justify rights violations. Rather, my argument aims to highlight that there must be an agent to protect individual rights, and the legitimacy of this agent may be an important issue in some cases. The bitter opposition of tribal groups to cooperating with the former oppressor when it comes to reform is understandable and justified. Why are we so confident that we are in fact right that our attempts to bring progress to native peoples will actually succeed? And why do we assume that the legitimacy of *our* state is unquestionable, but then suggest *their* authority, the authority of the tribes – or other victims of enduring injustice – is questionable if they do not accord with our version of justice?

One important reason why liberal justice should not always be imposed on oppressed groups is that the legitimacy of doing so needs first to be examined. There is a second, consequentialist reason to be skeptical of imposing liberal justice, which is that any *effective* change will take the state's legitimacy into account.[48] Attempts to reform oppressed groups may very well backfire. If the effort to secure individual rights is done in an illegitimate manner, then individual rights may end up less secure. In many contexts when change is imposed by an oppressor, either despondency or violence is the reaction. The members of the oppressed group may feel defeated and "not at home" in the culture of the oppressors. Feeling out of place, feeling the lingering effects of discrimination, members of groups that are forced to assimilate often live defeated lives. If the response to attempts to protect the rights of a group's members is dejection, high suicide rates, considerable unemployment, low education rates, and so on, then the attempt to protect rights hasn't been very successful. This is of course not a hypothesis: the attempts to forcibly assimilate groups like

---

[47] Martha C. Nussbaum, *Sex and Social Justice* (Oxford University Press, 1999), 109.

[48] On this point see too Duncan Ivison, *Postcolonial Liberalism* (Cambridge University Press, 2002), 161.

indigenous peoples clearly highlight the harm of forced assimilation with results that are clear, well known and absolutely disastrous.

The history of rights from the point of some may not seem so liberating – here again we see how the history of an injustice may matter. Individual rights may not seem so liberating when they are associated with the oppressor, and it is hard to blame people for not wanting to turn into their oppressor. Liberal rights have been liberating for many – but not for all. This is the case even if their oppressor isn't completely bad. One could respond by saying that insisting that Native Americans, Indian Muslims, and Israeli Muslims respect the rights of their members hardly means that they are turning into their oppressor. But this may be how it looks from the point of view of many in the community. When their community's rules are forcibly changed to look more like the rules of the dominant community, it will often appear to many in the oppressed community that these changes are one aspect of an assimilation program and will often be interpreted as an affront to their identity. Some within the community may object that rights are a good regardless of their origins, an argument with which I am sympathetic. Yet many in the community will often think otherwise, and their objections may be hard to overcome. It's no accident that the Hindu nationalists in India are calling for the end of Muslim family law, just as they claim that India contains only one identity, that of Hinduism.[49]

One argument against giving a community too much power over its members is that doing so can too readily lead to the violations of individual rights. Communities are not monolithic, and when their leaders have considerable power, then oppression of individuals can all too easily occur, unless individual rights are protected. My argument questioning the legitimacy of the liberal state does not mean that any or all rights violations in communities that are victims of enduring injustice should be permitted. The debate between universal modes of justice or more contextual accounts can arise here, since some argue that the Western emphasis on rights may undermine other community goods. Several scholars and indigenous peoples argue that indigenous and liberal conceptions of justice are different, and that it is wrong to assume that the liberal conception

---

[49] Thomas Blom Hansen, *The Saffron Wave: Democracy and Hindu Nationalism in Modern India* (Princeton University Press, 1999).

is superior.[50] Some argue that the decision-making process among indigenous peoples is different than but not inferior to Western democratic models. Whether or not different conceptions of justice lie between indigenous peoples and Western governments, some tribes may very well prefer alternative social, political, and economic arrangements to those dominating liberal states. We can accept this idea without excusing violations of basic rights. If a group were to systematically deny what Henry Shue calls basic rights to its members – the right to physical security and to subsistence – then interference by other states is called for.[51] These basic rights are so fundamental to the enjoyment of human life and their routine violation so shocking "to the moral conscience of mankind" that intervention is called for, and is the minimal standard to which a liberal can adhere.[52] This standard that justifies humanitarian intervention into any state when cruelty is widespread in a polity (though whether that intervention occurs is another issue)[53] certainly fits groups as well. The same kind of practice that would justify humanitarian intervention in a foreign state would justify pressuring or forcing a minority group from stopping such a practice. In practice, however, this situation will rarely arise when it comes to groups within liberal states. These sorts of rights violations do not generally occur within indigenous communities, and rarely within Indian and Israeli Muslim communities. I will suggest in the next chapter a further and significant qualification to my argument about group autonomy, and subject their autonomy (over their rules upon which they have jurisdiction) to a democracy constraint.

[50] Ivison, *Postcolonial Liberalism*; Andrew Sharp, *Justice and the Māori: The Philosophy and Practice of Māori Claims in New Zealand Since the 1970s* (Oxford University Press, 1997); Turner, *This is Not a Peace Pipe*; Alfred Taiaiake, *Peace, Power, Righteousness: An Indigenous Manifesto* (Oxford University Press, 1999).

[51] Henry Shue, *Basic Rights: Subsistence, Affluence and U.S. Foreign Policy*, 2nd edn. (Princeton University Press, 1996).

[52] Michael Walzer, *Just and Unjust Wars: a Moral Argument With Historical Illustrations* (New York: Basic Books, 1977), 107. Walzer defines what is shocking in a way that is more minimal than I do here.

[53] There is the issue of political will, but potential intervening states must consider if their actions will produce more harm than good: will the resistance to their intervention be so fierce that the good of the intervention will be outweighed? See Eric A. Heinze, *Waging Humanitarian War: The Ethics, Law, and Politics of Humanitarian Intervention* (Albany: State University of New York Press, 2010).

It is possible to accept the consequentialist reason (that the consequences of imposing liberal values on groups that are victims of enduring injustice will have ill-effects) and reject the legitimacy reason (or the reverse), but it is important to note that while these two reasons are distinct, they are also frequently related. When groups react to state-imposed changes that appear to be positive with despondency or violence it is often because the state lacked the legitimacy to impose the change. Native Americans think (rightly so) that many changes imposed upon them by the US are illegitimate. It is not always the case that the consequentialist and legitimacy reasons are related, since groups may wrongly feel aggrieved, making the consequences of imposing reform harmful because of this mistaken perception. Nonetheless, when groups react badly to liberal reforms it is often because the state has illegitimately imposed reform on the group. Liberal states lack the "moral authority and legitimacy among indigenous peoples to promote effective change."[54]

My argument about the importance of state legitimacy suggests that when an oppressed group uses its autonomy in a discriminatory way against women it should not simply be forced to stop this discrimination. When a group is oppressed but lacks autonomy the particular problem that is at issue here does not exist, and so I will only briefly address this situation. My argument's implication for oppressed groups that lack autonomy is that they should be *provisionally privileged* when it comes to group autonomy of other kinds of group-differentiated rights.[55] This means that oppressed groups have a better case for group-differentiated rights than non-oppressed groups, everything else being equal. This does not specify what kind of rights should be given nor whether the rights they do receive should be in the form of group autonomy or integrative multiculturalism, since this is too context-dependent to determine in the abstract. The kind of autonomy given to a group will often depend on the kind of group in question. How much oppression the group has suffered might matter, along with the legitimacy of the state over the group, while territorially concentrated groups can typically receive stronger forms of autonomy than geographically dispersed groups; religious groups can control

---

[54] Ivison, *Postcolonial Liberalism*, 161.
[55] The idea of group-differentiated rights is explained in Will Kymlicka, *Multicultural Citizenship: A Liberal Theory of Minority Rights* (Oxford University Press, 1995).

family law but others kinds of groups may have a harder time doing so. Provisionally privileging oppressed groups does not mean that oppressed groups always deserve the rights they currently have, or even that they deserve any rights, but it does mean that barring cases of serious physical harm in the name of a group's culture it is important to consider some form of autonomy for the group.

5.5 Majorities and minorities

Arguments for imposing individual rights too often abstract from the agent who is enforcing the rights. Individual rights are powerful tools, but liberal ideals have often been misused and abused, with this abuse often incorporated into the collective narratives of the victims of enduring injustice. From *their* perspective, liberalism is not a liberating doctrine. From their perspective, liberalism and the liberal state are intertwined; their collective narratives show how the liberal state has oppressed them. The idea of individual rights may appear to be obviously correct in theory, but victims of enduring injustice have not faced only theory; the liberal state, sometimes because of the theory behind it, and sometimes in spite of it, has caused great harm to some peoples. The history of the relationship of the liberal state's victims with the liberal state matters in ways that arguments focusing on constructing models of liberal justice cannot see. How things seem from the abstract lens of liberal justice may not be the same when viewed through the lens of historically oppressed groups. My argument here urges those who use the former lens to take a more historically informed look at victims of enduring injustice. I will fill in my argument by looking at Muslims in Israel and India, and at Native Americans, all the victims of enduring injustice, and groups often discussed in the multiculturalism literature.

In Israel and India much of family or personal law is governed by religious laws, but not all religions are given the same leeway. In both Israel and India the minority religion, Islam, has been subject to less intervention by the state than have the dominant religions, Hinduism and Judaism. Israeli Muslims are oppressed in many ways. They are less educated than Israeli Jews, more likely to be unemployed, make less money than Israeli Jews if they do work, and are largely shut out of important positions in the major political parties. This oppression is long-standing, with little reason to see it changing soon.[56] Indian Muslims too are oppressed, though their oppression may not be as severe as that of Israeli Muslims. Indian Muslims felt like a besieged minority in India at independence, a feeling that continues today.

Shortly after Indian independence, the state did not attempt to undertake any reforms in Islam like it did with Hinduism. There were certainly calls to do so, and there is even a non-binding directive in India's constitution directing the state to establish a uniform civil code and abolish the legal standing of religious personal laws. The classic book on secularism in India confidently predicted in 1963 that in twenty years there would be a uniform civil code.[57] While some people noted the irony of Muslim and Christian legislators voting on the reformation of Hindu law, the Indian Parliament has many more Hindu members than non-Hindu members. If the Indian Parliament was to try to reform Muslim family law, or simply abolish its legal standing, it would be perceived by many Muslims as an intrusion on their community by Hindus.

The infamous Shah Bano case highlighted the importance of Muslim personal law to Muslim identity in India. Shah Bano claimed she was kicked out of her husband's house and she sued him under criminal law for financial support, which mandated financial support for indigent family members. Her husband of forty-four years (who had married another women some years previously) responded by divorcing her, and claimed that under Muslim law he had to give Bano only three months of financial support. The Indian Supreme Court sided with Bano, saying that the criminal code trumps civil law, such as Muslim personal law. The Court argued that despite the divorce, Bano was still owed maintenance until she remarried, whatever Muslim law might say. The Court further declared that the Koran does not put a limit on a period of maintenance for divorced wives, and concluded with a plea for the state to finally develop a uniform civil code.

---

[56] Sherry Lowrance, "Identity, Grievances, and Political Action: Recent Evidence From the Palestinian Community in Israel," *International Political Science Review/ Revue internationale de science politique* 27, no. 2 (2006): 167; Barbara Okun and Dov Friedlander, "Educational Stratification Among Arabs and Jews in Israel: Historical Disadvantage, Discrimination, and Opportunity," *Population Studies* 59, no. 2 (2005): 163–80.

[57] Donald Eugene Smith, *India as a Secular State* (Princeton University Press, 1963), 134, 291.

The reaction of much of the Muslim community was swift and angry, with large demonstrations all over the country protesting the decision. Given a recent history of riots against Muslims, the Hindu destruction of the Babri Masjid, a centuries old mosque (that resulted in riots all over India, killing at least two thousand people), and the Sikh-Hindu tensions in North India in the mid-1980s, many Muslims viewed the Shah Bano decision as part of a pattern to assimilate Muslims and others within the larger Hindu culture.[58] That the Supreme Court also decided to interpret the Koran in its decision only added to the anger of many Muslims. The Shah Bano decision and the destruction of the Babri Masjid are the "two most important land-marks in the recent history of the Indian followers of Islam."[59] Now a third can be added, the pogrom at Gujarat, where over two thousand Muslims were killed and many more injured and raped by Hindus, with support from the state.[60] The importance of these three decisions in furthering Muslim distrust of the Hindu majority can scarcely be exaggerated.

The Muslim community is not monolithic, and while nearly all Muslims condemned the destruction of the Babri Masjid, some Muslims supported the Shah Bano decision, and some Muslim women's organizations voiced their support. The opposition, however, was vociferous and succeeded in persuading the Indian Parliament to pass legislation to reverse the Shah Bano decision and restore the traditional role of Muslim family law.[61] The few Muslim politicians who favored the Shah Bano decision quickly lost power. A critic of the reversal of the Shah Bano decision laments that the "renewed feminist

---

[58] Kativa R. Khory, "The Shah Bano Case: Some Political Implications," in Robert D. Baird, ed., *Religion and Law in Independent India* (New Delhi: Manohar Publishers, 1993), 121–38; see also Hansen, *The Saffron Wave*. On Muslim personal law see Tahir Mahmood, *Personal Laws in Crisis* (New Delhi: Metropolitan Book Co., 1986); Rina Verma Williams, *Postcolonial Politics and Personal Laws: Colonial Legal Legacies and the Indian State* (New Delhi: Oxford University Press, 2006).

[59] Niraja Gopal Jayal, *Democracy and the State* (New Delhi: Oxford University Press, 1999), 103.

[60] I briefly described the pogrom in Chapter 1. A more detailed description can be found in Martha C. Nussbaum, *The Clash Within: Democracy, Religious Violence, and India's Future* (Cambridge, MA: Harvard University Press, 2009).

[61] The new law allows Muslims at the time of marriage to elect to use the criminal code to adjudicate disputes between spouses instead of family law, but few Muslim couples choose this option.

debate on a Uniform Civil Code may also be traced to this case which demonstrated conclusively that claims to gender justice or women's rights had poor prospects when pitted against claims to rights of religious community."[62] Another critic of the decision argues that "although most Muslims in India seemed to oppose a uniform civil code, many might have supported some specific reforms of Muslim personal law," if they were reformed within the framework of Islam.[63] But this of course is another way of saying that how the decision to reform is made is as important as the substance of reform.

At first, Martha Nussbaum dismissed the importance of Muslim personal law to Muslim identity in the face of oppression, stating that the insistence of some Muslims to reverse the Shah Bano decision meant that they "were haggling over how not to be required to pay a destitute woman $18 per month."[64] Nussbaum also suggested that Muslims are politically empowered, noting that Muslim political parties formed an important part of the governing coalition in India after the 1996 election. However, she backpedaled when the BJP, the Hindu nationalist party, rose to power. Under these circumstances, Nussbaum concedes in parentheses, "Islamic courts should therefore probably be protected, though also urged to reform."[65] This parenthetical comment is left hanging, but in more recent comments Nussbaum is more understanding of the besieged feeling of the Indian Muslim community. Now she does recognize that the call to change Muslim personal law is threatening, and that external reform should wait until a climate of respect and support for the Muslim community emerges, which she admits may be a long time coming.[66] Still, Nussbaum's comments here are purely pragmatic. While I do think the pragmatic argument matters, Nussbaum has an uncontested view of the state, and never questions the state's legitimacy to interfere in the affairs of oppressed, cultural groups: she is concerned only with the effects of doing so.

---

[62] Jayal, *Democracy and the State*, 103.

[63] Williams, *Postcolonial Politics and Personal Laws*, 145.

[64] Nussbaum, *Sex and Social Justice*, 105. This statement is hyperbolic not only because Nussbaum understands that issues of identity, not just money, were at stake in the case, but because $18 a month is quite a sum to some Indians.

[65] *Ibid.*, 109.

[66] Martha C. Nussbaum, *Women and Human Development: the Capabilities Approach* (Cambridge University Press, 2000), ch. 3.

The extensive reform of Hindu law has not been replicated in Jewish law in Israel, but the Israeli state has intruded more on Jewish law than on Muslim law. Jewish law is mostly restricted to matters of marriage and divorce, while Muslim law in Israel also covers issues of dowries, some issues concerning second marriage, adoption, and other matters. The Israeli state has occasionally tried to change Islamic law, but with the partial exception of outlawing polygamy, these interventions have been ignored by the Muslim community, even when Muslim religious leaders share the goals of Israeli reforms.[67] Unsurprisingly, the Muslim community doesn't want a Jewish legislature that is seen as an oppressor reforming its laws. Israeli Muslims would undoubtedly protest vigorously and violently if a Parliament of mostly Jews decided to change or abolish Muslim family law. Since much of the Muslim community's life is controlled by Israeli Jews, they would find abhorrent the idea that Jewish legislators almost surely would interfere with one of the few areas that they do control. Who is changing the laws – who controls the state – matters when intervening in a community's long-standing rules. Here again we see how the history of an enduring injustice can matter: the historical relationship between the victims of enduring injustice and the state helps us to understand why imposing reform on the victims is of dubious efficacy and questionable legitimacy.

This explains why Egypt has been able to change Muslim personal law with little protest. As in India and Israel, personal laws in Egypt are guided by religious law, but these laws were recently changed to allow for both men and women to leave a marriage if they wish; they also mandate that men give financial support to their ex-wives (and if they cannot or somehow manage to avoid doing so, the state will give divorced women financial support). There was considerable anger in the Egyptian Muslim community about the old discriminatory rules of divorce, and they pressed the mostly Muslim legislature to change these rules. These changes in the laws were made with the assent of

---

[67] Martin Edelman, *Courts, Politics, and Culture in Israel* (Charlottesville: University Press of Virginia, 1994), 80. There are many personal laws in Israel: besides Muslim and Jewish laws, there are personal laws for the Druze (an offshoot of Islam), the Bahai, and ten different Christian communities. For simplicity's sake, I will only discuss Muslims here. Polygamy is still practiced among Israeli Bedouins.

some Muslim clergy.[68] There is a large difference, of course, between a mostly Muslim legislature and a mostly Jewish legislature changing Muslim law. Muslims will more readily accept the former changing their personal laws than the latter.

A similar if more stark dynamic occurs with Native Americans. In a well-known case, the daughter of a Santa Clara Pueblo tribal member was denied tribal membership because her father was not a tribal member. In a discriminatory fashion, however, the tribe did accept children of male tribal members who had offspring with non-members. Julia Martinez and her daughter Audrey sued the tribe, but the US Supreme Court ruled that it did not have jurisdiction in the matter, since matters of tribal membership were up to the tribe to decide. Ayelet Shachar complains that the court left Audrey *"without legal remedy."*[69] This is the view that the state's relationship with all its citizens is unmediated by the oppression of a particular group: the US, in Shachar's views, has the legitimate right to change Native American law. But Native Americans have been trampled upon by other Americans for centuries, often without legal remedy. Any legal remedy they may have had was to appeal to the US Supreme Court. This court, the "court of the conquerors," as Will Kymlicka notes, has "historically legitimated the dispossession of Indian lands and the forcible resettlement of Indian peoples."[70] The moral authority of the US to tell Native Americans how to run their own affairs is rather weak. After centuries of abusing Native Americans, why does Shachar now assume the US will act fairly toward them?

---

[68] Susan Sachs, "Egypt's Women Win Equal Rights to Divorce," *New York Times* (2000), 1.

[69] Ayelet Shachar, "Group Identity and Women's Rights in Family Law: The Perils of Multicultural Accommodation," *Journal of Political Philosophy* 6, no. 3 (1998), 303. Shachar's emphasis. See also Shachar, *Multicultural Jurisdictions*. For a more in-depth criticism of Shachar see Jeff Spinner-Halev, "Feminism, Multiculturalism, Oppression, and the State," *Ethics* 112, no. 1 (2001): 84–113, and Jeff Spinner-Halev, "Liberalism and Religion: Against Congruence," *Theoretical Inquiries in Law* 9, no. 2 (2008): 554–72.

[70] Will Kymlicka, "An Update From the Multiculturalism Wars: Comments on Shachar and Spinner-Halev," in Steve Lukes and Christian Joppke, eds., *Multicultural Questions* (Oxford: Oxford University Press, 1999), 118. Here oppression is what moves Kymlicka's argument, but this argument cannot support the group autonomy that he argues other national minorities should have.

Not all liberal feminists mean to ignore the history of oppression suffered by some groups at the hands of the liberal state. A more nuanced approach is presented by Sarah Song, who in an argument that parallels my own, argues that the history of oppression of a group presents a more robust case for group autonomy (or group-differentiated rights) than arguments grounded in self-respect.[71] Song also argues that one way to address historical injustice is to restore collective self-government rights for tribes, yet she also says, in an argument consistent with the standard liberal view of legitimacy, that Aboriginal sovereignty (like any sovereignty) must be justified and consistent with the basic rights of its members.[72] Unlike Shachar, Song does not assume that Western governments must safeguard the individual rights of indigenous citizens. What Song argues for is limited government, and there are different routes to that end. Song points out that Western governments are limited; some are restricted through the Bill of Rights and judicial review (and in Europe, by supranational courts). Song suggests similar institutional restraints are appropriate for tribes – constitutional constraints or an international tribunal.[73]

The strength of Song's argument is that she is willing to allow different mechanisms to protect individual rights, and she insists that all political authority be limited by one of these mechanisms. Yet Song also seems less interested in how these restraints are imposed than in ensuring that they are imposed. Song notes that in the Martinez case, the family saw themselves as members of two political communities and they appealed to the larger one to ensure that their equal civic status would be recognized within the minority community. Deferring to tribal sovereignty, the US Supreme Court "failed to uphold the civic equality of a particular class of Santa Clara women and their children."[74] Song is willing to allow the US to be the mechanism that limits tribal authority if there is no other mechanism available. From the point of view of the tribe, however, this seems once again to be the imperialist US intervening in tribal affairs. That the US can claim to be the superior authority because it has a better ability to protect individual rights seems to be working in line with its imperialist history.

---

[71] Song, *Justice, Gender,* 59. I address the argument that connects group-differentiated rights to self-respect in the next chapter. See also Jeff Spinner-Halev and Elizabeth Theiss-Morse, "National Identity and Self-Esteem," *Perspectives on Politics* 1, no. 3 (2003): 515–32.

[72] Song, *Justice, Gender,* 76, 117.   [73] *Ibid.,* 61.   [74] *Ibid.,* 120.

Nahshon Perez also says he wants to hold on to liberal justice that pays attention to history and to the importance of group identity. However, liberal justice trumps all: "While a healthy level of suspicion is definitely needed when dealing with majority justice, if after meticulous scrutiny of the law proposed, we recognize it as just, the identity of the source of the law has no importance whatsoever."[75] Well, who is the we here? This sentence is begging the question: Who is scrutinizing the law, who is recognizing the law as just (or not)? Similarly, when Song says that all political authority is limited, the question becomes, Who is doing the limiting? In the case of Native Americans, Song clearly wants the US Supreme Court to be the limiting authority, in the absence of any other. But why does the court of the oppressors have legitimate authority over Native Americans?[76]

Nussbaum's concerns for individual rights and particularly women's rights lead her to argue that there is no reason to give tribal men power over women "if we concluded [as we have] that women should have guarantees of equal protection in our nation generally."[77] Nussbaum's argument, though, is also question begging: Who is included in "our nation?" Many Native Americans don't think of themselves as part of our nation (the United States), and given the historical record it's hard to think of reasons why they or we should think otherwise. Certainly Nussbaum offers none. She simply assumes that all citizens are alike, and the state has full authority over them. Susan Okin's concern for discrimination with indigenous peoples also leads her to assume an unmediated relationship between the American state and Native Americans. She begins one of her essays by noting: "Until the past few decades, minority groups – immigrants as well as indigenous peoples – were typically expected to assimilate into majority

---

[75] Nahshon Perez, "Should Multiculturalists Oppress the Oppressed?," *Critical Review of International Social and Political Philosophy* 5, no. 3 (2002), 61.

[76] Similarly, Duncan Ivison, who is sympathetic to claims for indigenous sovereignty, argues that indigenous self-government claims are justified but when "membership rules adversely affect the basic capabilities or interests of vulnerable members," then matters are a little different. There should be attempts to persuade the group to change its rules, or if not then an appeal to an agreed upon authority should be made. This is better than giving the dominant state the authority to establish rules for the oppressed community, but it still begs the question: Why must oppressed groups have an authority that reviews their membership rules, but not states, including oppressive states? Ivison, *Postcolonial Liberalism*, 157.

[77] Nussbaum, *Sex and Social Justice*, 109.

cultures."[78] Okin's language here is telling and strikingly ahistorical: it suggests that indigenous peoples, like immigrants, are one among many minority groups in the US. But indigenous peoples are not like immigrants over whom the state's authority is undisputed and legitimate. Okin never considers the history of oppression that indigenous peoples face or that the larger political community might want to take into account the idea that they are not just another minority group poised to assimilate into the liberal Western world. Okin notes that indigenous groups were expected to assimilate, but she never says that these expectations turned into disastrous policies; she leaves hanging the possibility that the idea of assimilation – the normative goal of civilizing the native – was a good one.

There is no understanding in the liberal/feminist argument that the ideas of liberalism and civilization are not seen as a solution to the problems faced by many historically oppressed groups within liberal societies, but are often seen as part of the problem. These arguments are often ahistorical, with a truncated standard view of legitimacy: legitimacy is seen only as matter of rights protection. There is rarely discussion in these arguments that the legitimacy of the state over persistent minorities is questionable; rarely does the persistent lack of equal or decent concern or regard for certain groups arise as a reason to question the legitimacy of the liberal state. That indigenous peoples can readily be seen as just one more minority group within the US by prominent feminists is surely telling. It certainly ignores how many Native Americans view themselves; and while one might think Native Americans are just another minority group, this must be argued and not assumed.

There is also scant understanding that the implementation of rights will do little to help these groups overcome the challenges they face. While many liberals look at Native American tribes and see rights violations and patriarchy, only a few have patrilineal descent. A main discussion for membership within the tribes is whether blood or residence is the better criterion.[79] Surely when one thinks of the

---

[78] Susan Moller Okin, "Is Multiculturalism Bad for Women?," *Boston Review* (1997), 9.
[79] I am unsure of the number of patrilineal tribes, but my reading of the literature on Native Americans suggests the number is very small. (And there are a small number of matrilineal tribes.) For the current membership issues among the tribes, see Carole Goldberg, "Members Only? Designing Citizenship Requirements for Indian Nations," *University of Kansas Law Review* 50 (2001): 437–72.

challenges faced by the millions of Native Americans, the issue of patrilineal descent is but a small one. Why the patriarchal structure of a few tribes stands out to liberal and feminist theorists is a good question: it may be that Supreme Court cases provide fodder for political theorists, and that once a conversation gets going on a topic, it moves its way through scholarly discourse. I do not want to downplay the importance of rights violations when they occur, yet clearly it makes more sense to look at the conditions of indigenous peoples, as well as Indian and Israeli Muslims, through a broader lens, one that balances the partial legitimacy of many liberal states with the importance of protecting individual rights.

6 | *Elusive justice*

Many scholars writing about historical injustice suggest that if the larger political community just understands the past better, the injustice can be undone. These arguments are rarely accompanied by an argument about how to move past the injustice, and so the assumption seems to be that if the roadblocks are dismantled, then liberal justice can simply triumph. But this is often simply not the case.[1] The idea of progress is implicit in many of these arguments, the idea that liberalism can uplift all. Another set of scholars suggests that past injustice needs to be undone, usually when the matter is land, which can be returned. Yet matters are not so simple. When we think of enduring injustice, we will often have to think of tragic narratives. The shift in gaze I am urging here involves altering our view of progress. When we begin in the past, and move progressively toward the future, the idea of a narrative of progress follows readily enough. When we begin in the present and look toward the past with an eye toward the future, the structure of our quest does not always match a progressive narrative. David Scott argues: "For tragedy, history is not leading us anywhere in particular. And if the past is a wound, it is one that may not heal."[2] While I borrow Scott's argument about certain narratives being read as tragedy instead of romance (in which matters improve),

---

[1] One exception to this assumption is Duncan Ivison, who explicitly argues that liberal justice will often not fit indigenous peoples. Ivison argues that instead what is needed in the face of disagreement about justice is an agreement about procedures to settle disputes that is free from one party dominating the other. Ivison, *Postcolonial Liberalism* (Cambridge University Press, 2002), 110–11. Unsurprisingly, Native American scholars also take exception to the idea of liberal justice. See Dale Turner, *This is Not a Peace Pipe: Towards a Critical Indigenous Philosophy* (University of Toronto Press, 2006); Alfred Taiaiake, *Peace, Power, Righteousness: An Indigenous Manifesto* (Oxford University Press, 1999).

[2] David Scott, *Conscripts of Modernity: The Tragedy of Colonial Enlightenment* (Durham: Duke University Press, 2004), 166.

his pessimism is not always warranted. The future does not triumphantly grow out of the past, but we cannot let a tragic history render us helpless and hopeless about the future. What I mean by tragedy is that we must often make trade-offs between different goods for matters to improve; that we might make the wrong compromises and while we should work toward a better future for victims of enduring injustice, we should do so with the humility that we cannot be sure of how to do so; and that the future is open-ended. My argument is ultimately couched in terms established by Isaiah Berlin: that regimes will often have to balance different goods.[3] The shadow of an enduring injustice will affect how we should try to balance these goods.

The dominant argument within liberal democratic theory is that one value trumps all others, or that key liberal values can be assembled together harmoniously. Rawls sees few unsolvable conflicts in a just society; Habermas argues that a rationally discovered consensus can be found within a political community on all key principles; Will Kymlicka argues that individual autonomy is the pinnacle liberal value, while Chandran Kukathas argues that it is toleration; Martha Nussbaum washes away possible conflicts in her capabilities approach.[4] My argument in this chapter suggests not only a tension between different liberal values, but between democracy and liberalism. Many liberals argue, correctly enough, that liberal values are often best realized through democratic procedures; but this does not mean that democracy ensures liberal values.[5] Democratic publics can often be guided toward liberalism through constitutions, laws,

[3] Isaiah Berlin, *Four Essays on Liberty* (Oxford University Press, 1969); William A. Galston, *Liberal Pluralism: The Implications of Value Pluralism for Political Theory and Practice* (Cambridge University Press, 2002).

[4] Jürgen Habermas, *Between Facts and Norms: Contributions to a Discourse Theory of Law and Democracy*, trans. William Rehg (Cambridge, MA: MIT Press, 1998); Chandran Kukathas, *Liberal Archipelago: A Theory of Diversity and Freedom* (Oxford University Press, 2003); Will Kymlicka, *Multicultural Citizenship: A Liberal Theory of Minority Rights* (Oxford University Press, 1995); Martha C. Nussbaum, *Women and Human Development: the Capabilities Approach* (Cambridge University Press, 2000); John Rawls, *A Theory of Justice*, revised edn. (Cambridge, MA: Harvard University Press, 1999; reprint 1999).

[5] I expand upon this argument in Jeff Spinner-Halev, "The Trouble With Diversity," in Jonathan S. Davies and David L. Imbroscio, eds., *Critical Urban Studies: New Directions* (Albany: SUNY, 2010), 107–20.

educational policies, and so on. Yet there may be times when democracy comes at the expense of liberal justice.

I begin this chapter by looking at the dilemma that arises when groups use their autonomy in ways that violate individual rights. I then revisit the idea of legitimacy, but this time I ask what makes the rule of an oppressed group legitimate. In the previous chapter I argued that the authority of the liberal states over victims of enduring injustice might only be partial. Yet this says little about the legitimacy of the group's authority. Just because the liberal state's legitimacy is partial does not mean that the legitimacy of the group's ruling structure should be unquestioned, as Sarah Song has argued. I argue here that the partial authority of victimized groups is legitimate if it is really representative of the group as a whole. Since the authority of these groups will only be partial, there are still many things the liberal state can do to help ensure that the members of these groups are treated with decent regard. The hybridity of authority in these cases complicates the issue of legitimacy, but I hope to make sense of these complications here. My argument that rules of different communities must adhere to a democracy constraint, however, accepts the idea that these rules may not cohere with liberal justice.

I conclude by arguing that restitutive justice – one way to repair an enduring injustice, by replacing what was lost – does not necessarily mean the realization of liberal justice. I argue that satisfying the terms of restitutive justice assumes the past matters morally, since the idea behind it is to restore some past set of circumstances. Yet here I argue against an important assumption made by those who argue for repairing past injustice by suggesting there is no reason to think that restoring a previous condition – by returning sacred land, for example – will usher in liberal justice. This is not a reason to oppose restitutive justice, but I will contend that many advocates of repairing past injustice are apt to romanticize the victims, and assume that reversing a past injustice means the triumph of justice. Repairing an injustice, however, does not necessarily mean the unfolding of liberal justice – or sometimes of any kind of justice. It is common to think of justice and injustice as two different halves of the same coin – overturning an injustice, it is commonly thought, means the onset of justice – but toward the end of this chapter I argue that this is sometimes not the case.

6.1 Beyond rights

I now discuss a set of cases I discussed in the last chapter: how can we think of ways to overcome enduring injustices in cases where the victims have (or perhaps could have) some amount of autonomy? (Obviously, there are other cases of enduring injustice, but I set those aside here.) Liberal states do not have the legitimacy to simply change the rules of groups that are victims of enduring injustice because it finds their rules unjust. What enduring injustice sometimes shows is how a liberal regime of rights is not the ideal goal – at least not in the foreseeable future – and might even undermine attempts to overcome the enduring injustice. I complicate my argument by looking at cases where group autonomy may be used to violate individual rights. Should the liberal state do nothing in the face of injustice, or on the restriction of individual rights, within groups on its territory or shared territory, even in cases of enduring injustice?

One possible solution rests on the idea of exit: that as long as group members can leave, liberals need not worry so much about the group's internal practices. While this view has long been the standard liberal view on religious associations, it is criticized for underestimating how hard it is to leave groups, and the unfair cost it presents to members, who must choose between their beliefs and their group.[6] One liberal response is to say that exit from religious associations, along with a certain level of education for group members, is enough to secure individual autonomy while preventing the liberal state from over-reaching its legitimate bounds.[7] Yet are the religious groups I have discussed here, Israeli and Indian Muslims, and Native Americans, typical religious groups?

---

[6] Daniel Weinstock, "'Exit Rights': Reframing the Debate," in Avigail Eisenberg and Jeff Spinner-Halev, eds., *Minorities within Minorities: Equality, Rights and Diversity* (Cambridge University Press, 2004), 227–48 and Susan Moller Okin, "'Mistresses of Their Own Destiny': Group Rights, Gender, and Realistic Rights of Exit," *Ethics* 112, no. 2 (2002): 205–30; Oonagh Reitman, "On Exit," in Eisenberg and Jeff Spinner-Halev, eds., *Minorities within Minorities*, 189–208; Ayelet Shachar, *Multicultural Jurisdictions: Cultural Differences and Women's Rights* (Cambridge University Press, 2001), ch. 2.

[7] Jeff Spinner-Halev, "Autonomy, Association and Pluralism," in Eisenberg and Spinner-Halev, eds., *Minorities within Minorities*, 157–71; Jeff Spinner-Halev, *Surviving Diversity: Religion and Democratic Citizenship* (Baltimore: Johns Hopkins University Press, 2000); Jeff Spinner-Halev, "Liberalism and Religion: Against Congruence," *Theoretical Inquiries in Law* 9, no. 2 (2008): 554–72.

The right to exit rests on the idea that groups are voluntary associations, that people can leave if they wish, and enter if they are accepted by the group's members. Being dispersed in the state, Indian and Israeli Muslims have freedom of mobility and they can avail themselves of any state institutions, just as others in the state can. Personal laws are limited to matters of property and family. It is the case that personal law systems almost always apply to groups that are geographically dispersed, so their scope is limited. Israeli and Indian Muslims cannot, for example, have jurisdiction over criminal or contract law, since they have no territory to govern. Still, people in India and Israel cannot easily leave the family law system. Even if their scope is limited to family law, to be trapped in a terrible marriage or to be discarded by your husband after decades of marriage with little or no alimony, is to suffer a horribly unjust fate.

The issue of exit for Native Americans is more complicated, since tribal members can in fact leave, as they are dual citizens. Still, leaving a tribe will sometimes mean leaving the group that is an integral part of one's identity to go to live in the oppressor state. Catholics, Methodists, and Baptists who leave their Church can choose, as they often do, to join another Church or to form a new one. But tribal members cannot easily do so. They cannot simply join another or form another tribe. Some tribes in the US have jurisdiction over territory and are officially recognized by the US government, which enables them to have certain benefits. Tribal members can leave their tribe, but tribes are a hybrid political entity. They can be seen as sovereign but they are also deeply enmeshed with the larger government that sits alongside them. In the US, many tribes created constitutions for themselves in the 1930s at the urging of the US government, which were then approved by the Secretary of Interior. Many of these constitutions grant veto power to the Secretary of Interior. Membership rules, which may have been loose and amorphous before the 1930s, were then codified at the urging of the US government, which wanted ways to restrict tribal membership.[8] Tribal membership is sought after in large part because of the federal benefits that come with membership, though casino wealth is also a lure in some tribes. Some tribes lobby

---

[8] Judith Resnik, "Dependent Sovereigns: Indian Tribes, States, and the Federal Courts," *University of Chicago Law Review* 56, no. 2 (1989): 671–759. See too Sarah Song, *Justice, Gender, and the Politics of Multiculturalism* (Cambridge University Press, 2007), ch. 5.

the US government, and make political contributions to office seekers. Moreover, many tribes are simply too small to be self-sustaining and so even under better circumstances most tribal communities will be intertwined with the United States in many ways.[9]

State involvement in the construction and maintenance of personal laws for Indian and Israeli Muslims is just as deep as for Native Americans. India's personal laws are interpreted by state courts, which often defer to traditional Islamic interpretations of the relevant law. Israel's personal laws are governed by state-funded religious courts. The Islamic judges, while nominated by an internal process, are officially appointed by the Israeli state. Islamic personal law, though, is not monolithic: there are different branches of Islam, and different schools of interpretation of Islamic law within these branches. When the state sanctions personal laws, it must also sanction a particular interpretation of the law.

A problem with the current state involvement for Israeli and Indian Muslims is that it undermines the chances for internal reform. Any reform of personal law must currently be state-assisted, given the state involvement in personal laws. If a reform movement arose in the Indian Muslim community, the state would have to decide either to recognize this movement's proposals or ignore them. Since state-assisted reform is of questionable legitimacy and effectiveness, possible reform of personal law is remote, even if a majority of the community in question wishes it. If some members of the community went to the state to demand reform, there would be counter-demands, and questions of who really represents the community would arise. While sometimes the majority voice is clear, trying to sort out who

---

[9] In a previous version of this argument, I did argue that exit was sufficient for indigenous peoples. Now, however, my view is that indigenous peoples should be subject to a democracy constraint. I previously applied this argument only to Israeli and Indian Muslims; here I am expanding the argument's scope.
My previous views, which are mostly intact, can be found in Jeff Spinner-Halev, "Feminism, Multiculturalism, Oppression, and the State," *Ethics* 112, no. 1 (2001): 84–113. My change in views about indigenous peoples is in response to several thoughtful criticisms of my argument. See Monique Deveaux, *Gender and Justice in Multicultural Liberal States* (Oxford University Press, 2006); Monique Deveaux, "A Deliberative Approach to Conflicts of Culture," *Political Theory* 31, no. 6 (2003): 780–807; Marilyn Friedman, "Women's Rights, Oppressed Minorities, and the Liberal State," in Barbara Arneil *et al.*, eds., *Sexual Justice/Cultural Justice: Critical Perspectives in Political Theory and Practice* (New York: Routledge, 2007), 89–102; Song, *Justice, Gender.*

truly represents a community among competing voices amid an
informal process for determining representation can be a quagmire.
It's hard to see how reform of personal laws for Indian and Israeli
Muslims is possible under the current situation. What many in the
Indian and Israeli Muslim communities do not want is for the state to
impose change upon it, which is different from never wanting change
at all. Of course, it may be that these communities prefer not to
change their personal laws, but they should make the decision about
whether to pursue change or not. It is the community as a whole that
ought to make this decision, not a few usually male religious elites.

What some of these communities face is internal injustice, generated
by their own rules (or a certain interpretation of them), along with
the enduring injustice visited upon them by the dominant political
community. This is a difficult predicament. My aim is to provide
some ways of thinking about how to overcome the enduring injustice
without entrenching the internal injustice. Some people argue that
the best we can hope for in this circumstance is internal reform.
Partha Chatterjee notes that the state cannot simply emancipate
minority groups. Sometimes we must choose "the harder option,
which rests on the belief that if the struggle is for progressive change
in social practices sanctioned by religion, then that struggle must be
launched and won within the religious communities themselves.
There are no historical shortcuts here."[10] Questioning state legitimacy means that change should not be imposed on oppressed
groups. Change could come through the group's leadership, but
we should not expect men steeped in tradition, like in the case of
Indian and Israeli Muslim clergy, to make their rules radically more
egalitarian without pressure to do so. This apparently leaves us with
two unappealing options: state-centered reform which is morally
dubious and of questionable effectiveness, or the state does nothing,
leaving family law in the hands of traditional male authorities who
will do little to change it.

---

[10] Partha Chatterjee, "Secularism and Tolerance," in Rajeev Bhargava, ed.,
Secularism and Its Critics (New Delhi: Oxford University Press, 1998), 377.
Nussbaum too endorses internal reform, saying an effort should be made
to "promote liberal Muslim viewpoints and to encourage internal reform of
the system of personal law." She has little to say, however, about how this
encouragement might take place. Nussbaum, *Women and Human
Development*, 230.

I agree with much of Chatterjee's argument (though I think oppressed groups are the key group, which may or may not be a religion), but Chatterjee does not recognize the ways in which the state often blocks reform within oppressed groups. The state is not merely a bystander to groups with some autonomy. It shapes the lives of women and of personal laws whether it wants to or not, and it is not inevitable that it shape these lives and laws in ways that the traditional male elite desires.

An aim of my argument is to allow for internal reform while recognizing how an enduring injustice may cast doubt on the legitimacy of the dominant political community. My argument is open-ended, since there is no clear path toward these goals, though one possible route can be simply put: groups that are victims of enduring injustice and have some autonomy ought to have their rules and laws established by the community as a whole (if small enough) or by democratically accountable representatives. This does not insist that the rules they choose are liberal. My argument does mean that instead of guessing that the Muslim community supports the current formulation of family law, or simply not caring if the community supports it or not, the larger political community should insist that the rules of the minority actually have community support.

What this means is that groups that have some forms of autonomy ought to be democratic. Their rules can be voted upon by the community as a whole, or by democratically accountable representatives. Democracy does not ensure that the community will get its rules right, or allow it to speak with one voice. But democracy ensures a fair rule-making process. Ensuring participatory rights to members means that the community's decisions have an important element of legitimacy to them.[11] Democracy does not ensure that the group or polity's laws are legitimate, but it is a necessary condition: all democracies may not be legitimate, but it is hard to imagine a government or ruling structure that is not democratic but still legitimate.

One obvious objection to the argument that the rules of victims of enduring injustice ought to be decided upon democratically is that this is merely another imposition by the liberal state, that democracy

---

[11] Timothy A. Schouls, *Shifting Boundaries: Aboriginal Identity, Pluralist Theory, and the Politics of Self-Government* (Vancouver: University of British Columbia Press, 2003), ch. 6.

imposed is not much if any better than imposing liberal justice. If the liberal state cannot legitimately impose liberal justice, why can it legitimately insist upon democratic procedures? There are several complementary answers to this objection, some of which I have already suggested. First, the state is already implicated in the decision-making rules of these communities. The constitutions of Native American tribes are partly American creations; the rules governing personal laws in Israel and India involve state judges, or judges appointed by the state. The rules governing these communities are not rooted in a long tradition that was planted centuries ago, but are partly a creation of the modern liberal state. While the state must be involved in some way in the governing structure of these communities, my argument is that the state should *reduce* its involvement. Instead of actively supporting patriarchal institutions, the state should get out of the business of deciding the rules of a community that is a victim of enduring injustice, and allow the community to decide upon its own rules.

One might say that the traditions of these communities (or some of them) are patriarchal, that these communities want to have certain men in charge, that the modern liberal state simply codified or supported long-standing traditions. The democracy procedure proposal does not insist that women are in charge, or that women must be elected. The proposal allows the communities themselves to decide how they want to shape their own traditions, instead of a few unaccountable leaders doing so. Imposing liberal justice is different than insisting upon democratic procedures; the latter provides a procedure for deciding upon the rules of the community, not the rules themselves. To be sure, to insist upon democracy is to say that a minimal standard of individual rights must be adhered to, since a democracy where all adult members have a right to vote has some overlap with liberalism.

A second reason to insist upon democracy that arises in the case of indigenous peoples is that considerable state funds are at stake. The US and Canadian (and other) governments fund health clinics for indigenous peoples, and provide considerable educational grants to tribes, along with other monies. It is a well-known recipe for corruption when unaccountable leaders receive considerable funds. Tribal leaders can define membership rules and funnel funds in ways that benefit some people at the expense of others.

Democracy is not a fool-proof way to ensure that funds are distributed fairly, but it gives fairness a much better chance than having unaccountable leaders.

Yet I do not want to put too much emphasis on the need for democratically accountable representation among Native American tribes, since nearly all tribes have democratically elected representatives. My democracy procedures proposal is already implemented in most tribes. Still, the proposal is different than what many other liberals argue, who insist that tribal sovereignty be curtailed to ensure that individual rights within tribes are protected.

A second challenge to my argument is to ask what kind of a gap there really is between democracy and liberalism. The minimal version of democracy that I argue for here is certainly far more robust than Athenian democracy, where women and slaves did not receive the vote, and where foreigners could rarely become citizens. There is no question that a modern minimal democracy will have some overlap between it and liberalism, but there is still a gap between the two. A democracy constraint does insist that a standard of individual rights be protected, but there is no reason to think that this standard completely coincides with liberal justice.[12] Participatory rights are a subset of liberal rights; they are not the whole of liberal rights.

One set of restrictions that fall in this gap are freedoms that are usually allowed in a liberal state, but that the political community votes to restrict to all citizens. This injunction may mean that these laws at least appeal to the egalitarian instincts of liberals, but a democratically instituted law that applies to all may still be illiberal. A polity may democratically decide to severely restrict or even ban alcohol sales on tribal land, while courts in liberal states would probably find a ban or too many restrictions illegal. Yet given the abuse of alcohol within many tribes, such a ban or restriction may be perfectly sensible. Laws that restrict or ban property sales to non-tribal members may violate our usual understanding of liberal laws; liberalism generally allows for people to sell land to whomever they choose. Such a democratically instituted law may apply to all citizens, and be perfectly understandable as a way to protect a small tribe from cultural dilution that outsiders may cause if property sales are

---

[12] Deveaux, *Gender and Justice*, 91.

unrestricted.[13] It is illegal in Germany to belong to the Nazi party or to deny the Holocaust. These are generally legal in other liberal democracies, as these are clear restrictions on free speech and association. But Germany's history makes such a ban in this particular case seem perfectly reasonable to many.

A second set of restrictions that are generally illiberal are those that apply to only some members of the polity. Some tribes may have rules that allow only members who belong to the indigenous religion to hold certain offices. And then a group may have both democracy and patriarchal family law, as Indian and Israeli Muslims and a few tribes do. A restriction on language use falls between these two sets of restrictions. On the one hand, language restrictions can apply to all, but they clearly favor some people over others. A law, for example, that all signs must have larger print in French than in English favors French speakers, even if the law is applied equally. Besides this sign law, Quebec has a variety of laws designed to ensure the supremacy of French in Quebec, many of which restrict people's liberty in some way. In all these examples, democratic votes may undermine liberal rights. We often associate liberalism and democracy with each other; a democracy must protect a certain minimum of rights. Yet democracies need not have the full measure of liberal rights, and they can vote for illiberal laws; there is still a gap between democratic and liberal rights.

6.2 Democratic legitimacy

One objection to my argument is to point out that in the previous chapter I rested the case for legitimacy on the ideas of protection of rights and of treating members of the political community with decent regard or concern. Yet here I emphasize democratically accountable procedures and democratic participation more than the protection of rights in the case of communities that are victims of enduring injustice. My argument is seemingly paradoxical: when liberal democracies fail their own liberal standards of legitimacy, they should allow non-liberal communities to establish or maintain their non-liberal rules that may also violate liberal standards of legitimacy. If this is the case,

---

[13] This is an important theme in Kymlicka's work. See Will Kymlicka, *Liberalism, Community and Culture* (Oxford University Press, 1989); Kymlicka, *Multicultural Citizenship*.

however, why is it legitimate to allow some communities to enforce rules that may violate the rights of their members, or fail to show equal or decent regard for all of them?

There are two answers to this objection. First, these communities must treat all their members with some regard. Democratically just procedures mean that a political equality be maintained within these communities; decisions by the community that affect all members should be made by all members, or by their elected and accountable representatives. The right to vote must be given to all adults, while free speech should be guaranteed to all. Democratic accountability does not mean that all liberal rights are protected; it only insists that participatory rights are ensured to all.

Still, minorities within these groups can be ignored or disregarded. It may be harder to ignore persistent minorities within smaller groups than larger ones, but it is not impossible to do so. If some group is not treated with decent regard, then it too is partially legitimate. Democratic procedures ensure at least a partial legitimacy over the community's decisions, but no more than that; of course, the larger political community is partially legitimate as well. In some ways this is a trade-off between different concepts of partial legitimacy; the liberal state has partial legitimacy, and democratic procedures give the groups in question a partial legitimacy. There are reasons, however, to recognize the partial legitimacy of victims of enduring injustice. This legitimacy may appear partial to liberals, but giving the community power over some of its internal affairs will mean that the decision-making process will be more legitimate to the members of the community. Part of what I am urging here is that we – we liberals, we members of the dominant community – try to see matters from the point of view of the victims of enduring injustice. They don't see the larger liberal state as fully legitimate. This does not mean that they agree with all the rules of their communities, but this does not mean they want these rules changed from the outside. What Timothy Schouls found, going through the testimony of many Aboriginal youth and women within Canada (who often feel disempowered within their communities) is that they don't want the larger state to impose its view of rights and justice; what they do want are "participatory rights to shape the present and future identity of their community."[14]

---

[14] Schouls, *Shifting Boundaries*, 172.

Second, the liberal state still has considerable power over the community's members, and in many ways it can work harder to treat them with decent, if not equal, regard. That Israeli and Indian Muslims have power over their family law still leaves a myriad of issues that the state ought to address: the educational achievements of each community, the economic opportunities they ought to have, the discrimination they face, and so on. Indeed, if the state were to address these issues successfully and fairly, then it might have more legitimacy to intrude into matters of personal law. Or, rather, it would then become more likely that an increasing number of people within the community would demand – and be able to act on the demand – to be treated justly within their communities if they thought their community's norms or rules were unjust.

Part of what it means to overcome the enduring injustice in the case of indigenous peoples is to ensure that they have the tools to determine, as much as possible, their own future. Several scholars argue that indigenous peoples have different conceptions of justice than liberal states do.[15] Yet since what justice in traditional communities means in the modern world is a little unclear, Jonathan Lear's formulation is more on the mark. Lear argues that the radical hope that Plenty Coups held out for the Crow was that they would, at some point, "get the good back."[16] Hope now means giving the Crow the ability to reformulate their own new conception of the good. This does not mean that they do so in isolation, but it does mean that they do it mostly on their own, in due time. It means too that we liberals should not assume that their conception of good will be a liberal one, though it may be. It is almost certain that their conception of the good will at the least be influenced by liberal democratic principles. One may suggest that there is little point in tribal sovereignty if their conception of the good is a liberal one, but there are other reasons for group autonomy, self-respect among them. Relatedly, is the idea

---

[15] Burke A. Hendrix, *Ownership, Authority, and Self-Determination: Moral Principles and Indigenous Rights Claim* (Pennsylvania State University Press, 2008); Ivison, *Postcolonial Liberalism*; Andrew Sharp, *Justice and the Māori: The Philosophy and Practice of Māori Claims in New Zealand Since the 1970s* (Oxford University Press, 1997); Taiaiake, *Peace, Power, Righteousness*; Turner, *This is Not a Peace Pipe*.

[16] Jonathan Lear, *Radical Hope: Ethics in the Face of Cultural Devastation* (Cambridge, MA: Harvard University Press, 2006), 94.

that victims of enduring injustice ought to be in charge of the direction of their own lives; they should be the authors of their actions, and not just be directed by others. Timothy Schouls argues that tribal sovereignty is always a process, not a specific result. Aboriginal communities will change over time, and so will their political forms. What is important is the process, the form of self-determination that indigenous peoples receive.[17]

Yet it is also the case that many indigenous peoples will not be able to get the good back. There are over five hundred federally recognized tribes in both the United States and Canada. Some have tens of thousands of members, but others have a few hundred. How small tribes of a few hundred people or even a few thousand will survive in advanced industrial states is an open question. Certainly, the idea that they have full sovereignty over their own affairs without much help from the US and Canada seems out of the question. A tribe of a few hundred cannot staff a fully functioning government.[18] Some tribes may simply be too small to staff a police force and a judiciary or have a banking system. But how these matters are managed should be negotiated between the dominant community and the tribes, not simply decided by the former.

Empowering women

So too is there no assurance that more democracy will automatically lead to more gender equality. More can be done, however, to increase autonomy among women of oppressed groups than to grant the communities collective autonomy when it comes to personal laws. If the state is intent on treating all its members with decent or equal regard, it should also try to empower *all* women. Empowered women can fight to change personal laws, or, if laws permit, they can opt out of the personal laws.[19] Women can be empowered if all girls and

---

[17] Schouls, *Shifting Boundaries*, 59. [18] *Ibid.*, 127.

[19] While Indian Muslim couples can choose to use secular law and not Muslim personal law to arbitrate disputes, the fact that few couples choose this option shows that this narrow formal right to exit is not enough for at least two reasons. First, the secular law option must be chosen at the time of marriage. A spouse may not want to bring up this option for fear it is a sign of mistrust in the marriage. Since she can't change her mind after the wedding, the exit option is still severely curtailed under current Indian law. Second, the personal laws are a symbol of Muslim identity that many Muslims, including

young women receive an education. Many Indian women, Hindu and Muslim alike, are illiterate. Learning how to read would go a long way toward lessening their dependence on men. Uneducated women are more likely than the educated to rely on men for all kinds of things, including determining who to vote for. Breaking down the barriers that prevent many women, especially poor women, from working is also important. Giving these women training in agriculture or business is also crucial to empowering women. Nussbaum has been at the forefront of explaining the importance of empowering women in developing countries, particularly Asia.[20]

India has a relatively new law setting aside a third of all village council seats and village chiefs' positions for women (with a subset of these women's positions set aside from the lowest rungs of the caste system). Traditionally, almost all village council members and chiefs have been men. While some women council members defer to the male members or their husbands, there is now substantial evidence that many women are in fact exercising power, and that they are using their authority to make different choices than men in similar positions. Many Indian women find this to be an empowering experience as they learn that they can govern as well as – or often better than – men.[21] If women are empowered, they may seek changes in their community's sexist rules on their own. Simply giving women a vote

non-believers, may not want to relinquish. Eschewing Muslim marriage may even be seen as an act of treachery by other Muslims.

[20] Martha Nussbaum, *Sex and Social Justice* (Oxford University Press, 1999) and Nussbaum, *Women and Human Development*. Other important sources include Bina Agarwal, *A Field of One's Own: Gender and Land Rights in South Asia* (Cambridge University Press, 1994) and Martha Chen, "A Matter of Survival: Women's Rights to Employment in India and Bangladesh," in Martha C. Nussbaum and Jonathan Glover, eds., *Women, Culture and Development: A Study of Human Capabilities* (Oxford: Clarendon Press, 1995).

[21] Bidyut Mohanty, "Panchayat Raj Institutions and Women," in Bharati Ray and Aparnu Basu, eds., *From Independence Towards Freedom: Indian Women since 1947* (New Delhi: Oxford University Press, 1999), 19–33; Neema Kudva, "Engineering Elections: The Experiences of Women in 'Panchayati Raj' in Karnataka, India," *International Journal of Politics* 16, no. 3 (2003): 445–63; Raghabendra Chattopadhyay and Esther Duflo, "Women as Policy Makers: Evidence From a Randomized Policy Experiment in India," *Econometrica* 72, no. 5 (2004): 1409–43; Ragha Chattopadhyay and Esther Duflo, "Impact of Reservation in Panchayati Raj: Evidence From a Nationwide Randomised Experiment," *Economic and Political Weekly* 39, no. 9 (2004): 979–86.

in their communities may not mean really giving them a voice in how their communities make decisions; but empowered women are likely to exercise their voices.[22]

These two suggestions, internal democracy and empowering women, do not necessarily lead to the reform of personal laws or illiberal ways of life. These suggestions ensure a more legitimate decision process than many of these communities possess, one that recognizes the weight of history that bears down on the enduring injustice. These suggestions allow for the possibility of personal law reform; they do so in a way that will be seen as legitimate by the majority of the community and without the ill consequences of external reform. The community may decide to retain its current laws; it may decide to change them but keep elements of patriarchy; or it may decide to make its personal laws more egalitarian. Religions, it should be noted, change over time. As Nussbaum has argued, religious traditions are often quite varied, and there is no reason to think that the voices of traditional, male religious leaders are the only authentic ones.[23] Yet it may be what Nussbaum does not want to admit, that the community might choose these traditional religious leaders as the most authentic. It should be up to the religious group in question as to whose voices it decides to follow. If a group has change forced upon it, it will resent the outsiders for imposing reform upon it. The problems that often result when change is forced upon groups – anomie, despair, anger, resentment, violence – are much less likely to occur if change comes from within.

If personal laws remain patriarchal, the state can still try to ensure that divorced women or widows are cared for, either directly or by funding community organizations to do so.[24] While Muslim communities in India do try to support some of the indigent in their communities, the organizations that do so have little money. If they had more money through state support then Shah Bano would have had financial recourse through the Muslim community after her husband divorced her. Supplying more support for widows and divorced women is far from ideal, since it still allows the terms of divorce to be

---

[22] See generally Deveaux, *Gender and Justice*.
[23] Nussbaum, *Women and Human Development*, ch. 3.
[24] Bhikhu Parekh, "The Cultural Particularity of Liberal Democracy," in David Held, ed., *Prospects for Democracy: North, South, East, West* (Cambridge: Polity Press, 1993), 171.

dictated by men, and it allows other sorts of gender discrimination to remain. Nonetheless, in some cases this may be the best that can be hoped for.

6.3 The gap between injustice and (liberal) justice

Overcoming an enduring injustice sometimes means being on an uncertain path; the relationship between liberal justice and overcoming enduring injustice is often indeterminate. Before I explain that argument, however, I want to briefly discuss a common liberal approach to cultural group rights that mistakenly assumes that ending injustice means the flourishing of (liberal) justice. While my focus is on liberal justice, I will extend my argument by contending that ending an enduring injustice does not ensure any kind of justice. My focus is of course on enduring injustice, but my argument applies to injustice generally.

In Will Kymlicka's well-known formulation of group-differentiated rights (one that is echoed by others), there is an implicit liberal view of progress when it comes to minority cultural groups. Kymlicka contends that national minorities ought to be provided with external protections from outsiders. This means that indigenous peoples ought to be able to restrict land sales to non-indigenous peoples, for example. Kymlicka does not want tribes to use their autonomy to implement what he calls internal restrictions (violations of liberal rights and equality), but his argument allows for this possibility, since he is unwilling to have the state ensure that national minority groups do not impose internal restrictions. Kymlicka says that these groups should not have internal restrictions, an idea he hopes they agree with.[25] He also argues that there is no good reason why these groups cannot drop whatever internal restrictions they might have. He readily agrees that doing so might change their culture, but Kymlicka argues

---

[25] This leaves groups that receive rights the ability to do what they want, except in cases of systematic and gross human violations, like slavery or genocide, which Kymlicka argues are the same grounds for intervention in states as well. Kymlicka, *Multicultural Citizenship*, ch. 3, 169–70. Other theorists who assume that groups will or should become liberal over time include Shachar, *Multicultural Jurisdictions*; Song, *Justice, Gender*. A contrary view is Ranjoo Herr, "A Third World Feminist Defense of Multiculturalism," *Social Theory and Practice* 30, no. 1 (2004): 73–103 and Monique Deveaux, *Cultural Pluralism and Dilemmas of Justice* (Ithaca, NY: Cornell University Press, 2000).

that all cultures change over time, and there is no reason to think that one particular change will transform the culture into something else altogether. Kymlicka, for example, recognizes that certain tribes like the Pueblo want to discriminate against their Christian members, which he views as a violation of individual rights. Kymlicka argues, however, that the Pueblo would continue to exist even with an organized Protestant minority, and so he hopes that they will become more tolerant over time.[26]

Commentators debate whether the internal logic of Kymlicka's argument leads to more forceful intervention in illiberal culture than he concedes, or whether his argument grants too much latitude to illiberal practices.[27] My interest is in the teleological nature of Kymlicka's argument, the idea that eventually we will all be liberals; this idea that liberalism will triumph, that progress means the triumph of individual rights and toleration over all else allows Kymlicka to evade the hard trade-offs that liberals must make in cases like the Pueblo. We can give or protect the autonomy of illiberal groups, Kymlicka suggests, and we can expect that over time they will become liberal. If we end injustice, Kymlicka seems to suggest, then (liberal) justice will ensue. It is this logic, intuitive as it may seem, that I want to resist.

Following Rawls, Kymlicka argues that self-respect is an important liberal good, since individual autonomy – the ability to construct and pursue life plans – is very hard to do without self-respect. If our group is denigrated by others, or our culture is in disarray, then it is hard to maintain our self-respect. So, Kymlicka concludes, the integrity of what he calls societal cultures is necessary for people's self-respect, which is necessary for individual autonomy. Kymlicka says that societal cultures are large enough to provide not only shared memories and values, but also common institutions and practices. Societal cultures should be able to provide their members "with the meaningful ways of life across the full range of human activities, including social, educational, religious, recreational and economic life, encompassing

---

[26] Will Kymlicka, *Liberalism, Community and Culture* (Oxford University Press, 1989), 196.

[27] Chandran Kukathas, "Multiculturalism as Fairness: Will Kymlicka's Multicultural Citizenship," *Journal of Political Philosophy* 5, no. 4 (1997): 406–27; Susan Moller Okin, "Feminism and Multiculturalism: Some Tensions," *Ethics* 108, no. 4 (1998): 661–84.

both public and private spheres."[28] One important reason that societal cultures (or national cultures) are so important is that "people's
self-respect is bound up with the esteem in which their national group
is held. If a culture is not generally respected, then the dignity and self-
respect of its members will also be threatened."[29]

Members of national minorities will often find their culture overwhelmed by the majority culture, and so Kymlicka argues that they
need the state to help their cultural structure, in order to secure their
context of choice. People's self-respect is tied to their (national) group,
which leads Kymlicka (and Joseph Raz) to argue for the protection of
national groups, particularly minorities, since unlike majorities they
cannot readily rely on the state for support for their cultural structure,
without special measure.[30] But people can't make choices within just
any cultural context – they cannot be taken from one culture, dropped
into another, and expected to lead intelligible and worthwhile lives.[31]
People need a secure culture, or a "cultural structure," for people to
make meaningful choices. It is "only by being socialized into a culture
can one tap the options which give shape and content to, individual
freedom."[32] A dying culture will undermine people's self-respect and
ability to make choices, and so it may need active state support to
continue to exist. This is especially true for smaller cultures, which are
typically in danger of losing their distinctive characteristics in the face
of the larger majority.

These arguments may be correct in a narrow way – a secure cultural
context is probably needed to make choices. Even if these arguments
are correct, however, there is no reason to think that indigenous
peoples want protection for their societal cultures to enhance individual autonomy. There is no reason to think that many want their land,
or their sacred sites, or more group autonomy, for liberal reasons.
People do not want their sacred land because it enhances individual
autonomy or because it gives them more choices. People want access
to their sacred land because it is special to them – it allows them to

---

[28] Kymlicka, *Multicultural Citizenship*, 76.   [29] *Ibid.*, 89.
[30] *Ibid.*; Kymlicka, *Community and Culture*.
[31] Judith Baker, ed., *Group Rights* (University of Toronto Press, 1994); Kymlicka,
Community and Culture; Kymlicka, *Multicultural Citizenship*; Joseph Raz,
"Multiculturalism: A Liberal Perspective," in *Ethics in the Public Domain:
Essays in the Morality of Law and Politics* (Oxford University Press, 1994).
[32] Raz, "Ethics in the Public Domain," 178.

perform rituals, fulfill commandments, talk to their ancestors. It allows them to reach their good (at least partly), which may have little or nothing to do with liberalism. If the victims of an enduring injustice do not aspire to liberal justice, why should we assume that ensuring their self-respect will lead to liberal justice? If self-respect is a condition for liberal individual autonomy, it does not mean that self-respect must lead to autonomy. Self-respect may be a condition for several possible, even conflicting, goods. Self-respect is a good, certainly, but it is not a particularly liberal good.

Injustice

I bring this out more incisively by examining restitutive justice, which is simple and powerful: what is lost should be restored. One important challenge to restitutive (and compensatory) justice[33] is that often an injustice cannot be restored. Elizabeth Wolgast rightly argues that many injustices cannot be made right, that some wrongs cannot be undone.[34] People wrongly killed cannot be brought back to life. Slavery cannot be undone. The stunted lives of many Dalits and lower-caste Indians cannot readily be made whole. Some indigenous languages that were forcibly stamped out will not be able to be brought back. The upending of traditional cultures decades ago and longer cannot simply be reversed. The context in which those cultures thrived no longer exists, so when the oppressor government stops its oppressive policies, how the culture is reconstituted is an open question. If someone's rights are unjustly violated, then justice means the end of the violation. Yet if the violation changes the structure of the society, or the ability to regain your life as it was before the violation, then reversing the violation may not mean justice. The hunting and fishing societies of many indigenous peoples that were destroyed cannot be brought back to life. Sometimes, restitution in a meaningful way is not possible.

---

[33] Restitution means giving back what was taken; compensatory justice gives something that is of equal or near value to what was taken.

[34] In her rich and insightful book Wolgast is concerned with individual wrongdoing and the reasons for punishment (which she argues cannot be done for reasons of justice), which are not my concerns here. Elizabeth Hankins Wolgast, *The Grammar of Justice* (Ithaca, NY: Cornell University Press, 1987).

Even if not every piece of land can be restored, however, if some parts of lost land or group autonomy can be restored, we can consider it to be restitutive justice. Some theorists argue that where possible, land should be returned to indigenous peoples (or they should be given the first opportunity to purchase their former land when it is for sale).[35] My aim here is not to argue for or against restitutive justice as a general principle. The idea of return – of land, from exile – is sometimes impossible, sometimes can create a new set of injustices, but can sometimes be powerful and right. Even if full restitution is rarely possible, sometimes partial restitution is a possible and the just response to an enduring injustice.

Overcoming the enduring injustice through restitutive justice, however, does not mean the triumph of liberal justice. Restitutive justice can coincide with liberal justice, but it need not. Restitutive justice may restore a set of conditions that were themselves unjust. This is not an argument against restitutive justice, so much as a warning about romanticizing the victims of enduring injustice, and a reminder that justice is ever elusive. It is an argument too that ending (enduring) injustice does not mean the onset of liberal justice.

Over the last several decades, with the pace increasing recently, many Han Chinese have moved into Tibet, which has greatly undermined Tibetan culture. Most people in the Western world think that China's treatment of Tibet is unjust in many ways: taking over Tibet in the1950s; barring the Dalai Lama from Tibet; and importing many Han Chinese into Tibet. These actions are readily seen as unjust in the West, for good reason. One injustice is the way that Tibetan culture is being wrenched and overcome by the large number of Han Chinese entering Tibet in a short period of time. A second injustice is the way in which the Tibetan people are not determining their own fate. While the same could be said of China as a whole, the Han Chinese can see the Chinese government as their own in ways that are not the case for the Tibetans. It is not the Han Chinese and the Tibetans that rise up together in occasional violence against the government in Tibet; it is the Tibetans alone. Many Han Chinese think they are helping to modernize Tibet; the Tibetans see things very differently.

---

[35] Hendrix, *Ownership, Authority, and Self-Determination*; Renée A. Hill, "Compensatory Justice: Over Time and Between Groups," *Journal of Political Philosophy* 10, no. 4 (2002).

These two kinds of injustice I described are both different aspects of what it means not to be at home in the world – the Tibetans are becoming like foreigners in their own homeland.

From the point of view of the Tibetans, justice may be a restoration of their lands, or the expulsion of the Han Chinese. If an injustice occurs, isn't it just to reverse the injustice if that is possible? Even if a way of life cannot be restored, and the dead cannot be brought back to life, the land of a people can be returned. Perhaps Tibet must now be shared with the Han Chinese. The Tibetans can be granted self-determination, so the terms of this sharing can be established by the Tibetans, who would have control over their land. Yet ending the injustice faced by the Tibetans does not ensure that (liberal) justice will reign; it will not ensure equality among the Tibetans or individual liberty. It will not ensure mutual or equal respect among them. It may make mutual respect possible, but this is different than ensuring mutual respect. Here we see how liberal justice and enduring injustice move on different planes. It is not so much a failure of liberal justice that is the issue, but that it does not speak to some issues; to feel at home in the world does not mean the home must be liberal. If we are unsure whether the Tibetans would live by liberal justice, would liberals today then say the Han Chinese are not being unjust by undermining Tibetan culture?

If we assume that the end of the Chinese policies in Tibet would mean the flourishing of Tibetan culture, and that Tibetan self-determination would become a real possibility, this has little to do with liberal justice. Whether individual rights would be protected, whether women would face considerable discrimination, is a different matter from the radical injustice facing the Tibetans. Restoring Tibetan autonomy does not ensure justice, at least not liberal justice, in any way. The Dalai Lama is not a democratically elected leader; liberal justice is quite far from Tibet's traditions. None of this means that Tibet would not approach liberal justice in some form. It might do so, but there is no assurance that it will. The end of the injustice of cultural imperialism or ending the denial of self-determination does not mean an era of justice will reign. The enduring injustice in Tibet does not take place within a liberal democracy, but my point is that if China stopped its current Tibetan policies, justice would not be ensured in Tibet. It would only mean that a radical injustice, soon to become an enduring injustice, would end.

Liberal justice also does not speak to the issue of exile. Facilitating the return of the Tatars to the Crimea might not interfere with a liberal regime in the Crimea, if there was one. It is not necessarily contrary to liberal principles to facilitate return. To be sure, it would be contrary to liberalism to expel the current residents from their homes. But taxes can be raised to buy tracts of land to be given to returning exiles in ways that are compatible with liberalism.[36] What I want to highlight, however, is that liberal justice does not insist upon return from exile. Kymlicka's version of liberal nationalism does not speak to exile: he focuses his argument on the idea of societal cultures, cultures that are institutionally embodied and whose members live more or less contiguously. The context of choice argument also does not fit the Tatars. What many of them want is to be removed from their current context of choice, and be placed in a new context; and perhaps reconstruct their context.

There are more examples of peoples wanting to end an injustice of exile or of being dominated that have little or nothing to do with liberal justice. If the Palestinians receive their own state on the West Bank and Gaza, there is no reason to think that liberal justice will reign there. Israeli control of these territories may be unjust, but this does not mean that Palestinian control will mean justice, or equality, or liberty for the Palestinian people. Serbian control of Kosovo may have been unjust, but whether an independent Kosovo is a liberal democracy remains to be seen.

One might say that the end of these enduring injustices may not mean the flourishing of liberal justice, but that justice of *some* kind is assured. Liberal justice does not encompass all possible views of justice, of course. Perhaps the end of cruelty means that a non-liberal version of justice will ensue. This idea is mostly mistaken, however. The absence of cruelty is just that; it may create the possibility for justice, but no more than that. Hovering over my argument is an idea that Jonathan Allen expresses: "We do not know what a perfectly just society would be like to live in, but we do know – some of us know from everyday experience – what it is to live in an unjust, or cruel, or humiliating society."[37] It is often easier to determine what is wrong

---

[36] Hendrix, *Ownership, Authority, and Self-Determination*, 49.
[37] Jonathan Allen, "The Place of Negative Morality in Political Theory," *Political Theory* 29, no. 3 (2001), 350.

than what is right; injustice may be easy to see, and we may be moved to try to end it. The disjuncture between justice and injustice occurs because it is easier to get agreement on a subset of what is unjust than on what is just. This subset makes the possibility of justice impossible.

Judith Shklar criticizes political theorists and moral philosophers for ignoring injustice, for not giving injustice its due, but perhaps there is little to say that is theoretically interesting about severe injustices, since there is widespread agreement about them.[38] What moral philosophers and political theorists disagree about is what should take the place of injustice. It is these disagreements that keep political theorists writing and arguing with one another.

This is not to say that political theorists (and others) always agree on the nature of injustice. They do not. Some people think that taxes above a certain rate are unjust; others argue that the state's resources (meaning, in part, tax revenue) must be directed to a variety of programs to ensure the kind of equal regard and respect demanded by justice. Disagreements about justice will necessarily mean disagreements about injustice. But certain kinds of severe injustices do evoke widespread agreement. Liberals of all kinds, communitarians, postmodernists, and religious conservatives can all agree that certain oppressive regimes are unjust: all would agree that North Korea or Burma of 2011 is unjust, while most or all would agree that Iran or Saudi Arabia of 2011 are also unjust. These regimes point to the first kind of injustice that most can agree upon: the oppression of these regimes makes it impossible for any vision of justice to be realized. Whatever vision of justice one has – communitarian, liberal, and so on – cannot be realized in these regimes, not even in a significant partial way. While these regimes may invoke the ideal of community in their rule, it is clear that their rule is self-interested, and is about power and stability. Western communitarians do not support these regimes, since the community at large is not involved in constructing the community. Furthermore, these regimes make it impossible or near impossible for subjects to even discuss their visions of justice, much less try to implement them. Indeed, that the members of these communities are better thought of as subjects rather than citizens is telling, and is suggestive about the nature of the regime's deep injustice. When

---

[38] Judith N. Shklar, *The Faces of Injustice* (New Haven: Yale University Press, 1990).

there is a regime of subjects where justice is not its aim, where it is likely that open discussions of justice are forbidden, it is probable that removing the injustice will not usher in an era of justice. How could it, when discussions of justice can hardly take place? Removing the injustice allows the society to discuss the rules it wants to have; it can then try to determine what sort of justice it wants to achieve.

The second kind of injustice about which there is less though still large agreement is one which I have discussed at length in this book, the injustice of a people not being able to direct their collective lives. This encompasses the injustice of "not being at home in the world" – which means not being treated with equal or even decent regard by the institutions of the state and many fellow citizens, or it can mean that one's group is treated as a ward of the state, that the group's life is directed by others. This is of course similar to the modern civic republican idea of being dominated by others. Some liberals object to this kind of formulation, which moves beyond the formal strictures of the individual. If we see indigenous peoples simply as citizens of the larger state, then they are not victims of a particularly severe injustice,[39] a view that I have obviously taken issue with in this book.

Being at home in the world, however (in the narrow sense I describe in Chapter 1), does not ensure that justice will thrive. Ending the injustice that allows people to be at home in the world, will often make it possible, once again, for justice to be discussed, debated, and perhaps implemented. But ending these injustices does not ensure that this will happen. To be sure, in some cases, ending the enduring injustice will mean in some important way that justice ensues. When certain groups are treated with severe discrimination, when they are not treated with equal or even decent regard, then removing the injustice will mean that justice, at least in a partial way, will ensue. There will be times when nonideal theory is a transition to an ideally just society; we just cannot assume that this will always be the case.

6.4 The danger of romantic narratives

Since enduring injustices are so painful, it becomes easy to romanticize the victims. When a group has suffered terribly, there is an

---

[39] Tom Flanagan, *First Nations? Second Thoughts* (Montreal: McGill-Queen's University Press, 2008).

understandable urge to focus on ending the suffering. Yet doing so should not lead us to assume that ending a group's oppression translates into the triumph of justice. That a group suffered and suffers greatly does not tell us much about the group itself. One recent book on Tibet, for example, acknowledges the feudal character of traditional Tibetan society, but then declares (without any citations) "all accounts speak of the peaceful nature of Tibetan society and the happiness of the Tibetan people" before the Chinese invaded.[40] Tibetan feudal society may have been gentler than the European version, but statements like these obviously exaggerate the harmony of Tibetan society. Indeed, two pages previously the author notes the tensions in the 1920s and 1930s between the Dalai Lama and large estate holders over the Dalai Lama's desire to increase taxes to support a larger army, which led to the Panchen Lama fleeing to China, where he stayed in exile for thirteen years until his death. So it was not always peaceful and happy in Tibet – which would surely be surprising if it was the case.

It is also easy to romanticize the lost Native American way of life. The Native American's relationship to the environment was different, and some would say better, than the relationship of Europeans and their descendants to the environment. (One can think of the old anti-pollution public service announcement, showing a Native American man on a canoe, surrounded by smokestacks billowing out pollution, litter in the water, and then more litter on shore.)[41] While the relationship of indigenous peoples to the land and their surroundings may be admirable, it is also the case that many indigenous peoples were patriarchal cultures. Here's a short description of the Crow: "War was not the concern of a class nor even of the male sex, but of the whole population, from cradle to grave.... Women danced wearing scalps, derived honor from their husband's deeds." A hero's death was celebrated: "Old age is a thing of evil, it is well for a young man to die in battle."[42] The Crow were not the only warrior culture: after

---

[40] Warren W. Smith Jr., *China's Tibet? Autonomy Or Assimilation* (Lanham, MD: Rowman & Littlefield, 2008), 14.

[41] The narrator states: "Some people have an abiding respect for the land, and some people don't," as a person, presumably white, throws his trash out of the car at the feet of the Native American man, who is by now crying at the desecration of the land.

[42] Lear, *Radical Hope*, 12.

they obtained the horse, the Comanche pushed aside many peoples, sometimes cruelly, building what one historian calls an empire.[43]

Nor are all indigenous communities today completely praiseworthy. Since the Civil War, former Black Cherokee slaves and their descendants (the Freedmen) have fought to retain their membership within the tribe.[44] The recent history is of the Cherokee political leadership fighting to deny the Freedmen citizenship; when a Cherokee court reversed the elected officials, the latter called a general referendum, where Cherokee citizens then voted to deny citizenship to the Freedmen. The Cherokee courts have again recently insisted that the Freedmen are Cherokee citizens (they were granted citizenship by treaty with the US shortly after the Civil War, which the courts have declared is unalterable), though it is unclear if this is the last word on the subject.[45] As this and the Martinez case show, we should not assume that all tribes will treat membership in a fair way.

Few advocates of repairing past injustice through restitution say much about what ensues after the enduring injustice ends. A focus on returning or restoring land or honoring past treaties simply sidesteps the issue of justice within these communities. The idea left lingering from these accounts is that certain communities were victims of a past injustice, and if this injustice were repaired all would be well. Similarly, multicultural arguments that focus on group autonomy often simply hope that groups will become liberal over time. Yet those of us who want liberal states to work harder to overcome enduring injustices need to realize that doing so does not ensure liberal justice. Ending some kinds of injustice and ushering in an era of justice are often two different matters.

Romantic narratives may also be an obstacle to coming to a fair compromise when there is an enduring injustice. Those who argue for

[43] Pekka Hamalainen, *The Comanche Empire* (New Haven: Yale University Press, 2009).

[44] The history can be found in Circe Sturm, *Blood Politics: Race, Culture, and Identity in the Cherokee Nation of Oklahoma* (University of California Press, 2002).

[45] A recent Cherokee court decision is described in Rochelle Hines, "Tribal Court Rules Against Cherokee Freedmen Amendment," *Native American Times* (2011). www.nativetimes.com/index.php?option=com_content&view= article&id=4822:tribal-court-rules-against-cherokee-freedmen-amendment& catid=54&Itemid=30.

the importance of remembering rarely note that collective memory does not always lead to solutions of injustice, but may make matters harder to resolve. Israeli Jews and Palestinian Arabs have two different collective narratives that are intertwined, but often do not overlap much. Similar events are recounted by each side but often in very different ways. Some narratives on each side present a victim and an oppressor, but one-sided narratives like this make it harder for each side to see the harm suffered by the other; it is hard to compromise when one thinks that all of truth is on one side. But this is very rarely the case. What is true is that negotiations and compromises will often have to occur to repair enduring injustices. I have discussed here the absence of justice when land is returned, but it is often the case that not all of a land can be returned without committing more injustices, as Jeremy Waldron has argued.[46] While the Tatars were gone, people have moved in. When the Jews were expelled from Palestine, others moved in (as did some Jews); when some Palestinians were forced out, others moved in as well.

None of this means that people are better off forgetting rather than remembering. People and peoples have collective narratives, and suggesting that one simply forgets is not sensible advice. But we can ask that each side in a conflict should listen to the collective narrative of the other. This will not be easy, but those outside the conflict can certainly urge or insist that each side should do so. In these cases of clashing narratives that result in reasonable competing claims, there probably is not a just solution to the conflict. There may be plausible arguments for giving both considerable land to the Jews and considerable land to the Palestinians, but these goals conflict. Maximizing the chances that an enduring injustice will not again be visited upon the Jews may mean being unfair or unjust to the Palestinians. And maximizing the chances that the Palestinians will not be victims of an injustice may mean being unfair or unjust to the Israeli Jews. Reducing the chances of injustice to one side as much as possible may simply be unfair to the other. Negotiations and compromises will have to take place in order to come up with a fair agreement. This fair agreement may seem like it contains justice within it: one might say that justice

[46] Jeremy Waldron, "Superseding Historic Injustice," *Ethics* 103, no. 4 (1992): 4–28.

means a Palestinian state. Yet as I have already argued a Palestinian state may be a just state, but it may not be. A Palestinian state, however, would allow many Palestinians to feel at home in the world. This does not ensure justice, but it does allow for the possibility, something that cannot occur while the Palestinians live under foreign domination.

7 | *A chastened liberalism*

Theories of justice can readily be elegant and unitary, but this is not the case for theories of enduring injustice. There are many kinds of injustice, many endure, for which there is no single reason or set of reasons. One could lay the blame, as some do, at the doorstep of liberalism. Certainly the ideas of civilization and progress not only led many liberals to justify injustices against indigenous peoples, but also against Black Americans and many peoples in the colonial world. It is too easy, though, to suggest that liberalism is the cause of injustice. Liberals have not cornered the market on injustice. Many of the injustices I have discussed here were inherited by liberal polities, not caused by them. The expulsion of the Tatars, and much of the history of the caste system took place within non-liberal regimes. Indigenous peoples were (and are) victims of both liberal and non-liberal regimes. The cultural destruction of Tibet is caused by a clearly non-liberal regime.

This does not excuse liberalism, but it is wrong to think that there is one single core problem for which there is one solution. My goal in this book is to frame a difficult problem in a particular way, which I hope will alter our way of thinking about how to solve it, even if solutions are not easy to come by. The framework of group or cultural rights or liberal justice will not do much or enough to overcome many enduring injustices. The framework of liberalism cannot tell us why the past matters, but overcoming enduring injustice means taking the past into account. I have argued here, however, that using history and memory to determine responsibility for past injustices is the wrong route to take; rather, we need to use the past to help us see why some injustices exist, why some persist, and determine ways to overcome the enduring injustice. The past of liberal states can also matter as well, and help us to understand why the implementation of liberal justice is as important as its substance.

My aim in this chapter is to point out other implications my argument has for liberal theory. I begin with signs of hope, a few examples of victims of enduring injustice having some success in their struggle to move past the injustice. I argue that liberals should have less faith in progress and turn toward hope instead. Hope lacks the confidence of progress; it is part of what I call a chastened liberalism. A chastened liberalism will also be comfortable with a political community that has a dominant sense of justice that is pluralistic enough to allow for some smaller communities to diverge from this dominant view. To accommodate this divergence, I argue that liberals should accept the idea of overlapping communities. A more plural liberalism will also be skeptical of certain kinds of post-national cosmopolitanism. Partly working through Habermas, I argue that liberal polities that acknowledge their enduring injustices should not readily embrace post-nationalism. I end the book by arguing that ending many enduring injustices will mean that many liberal citizens will have to rethink what it means to feel at home in the world. This will clearly not be easy, and I point out the reasons why members of the dominant community will sometimes have a hard time sympathizing with victims of enduring injustice. But in order to be a decent society, much less a just one, more citizens of liberal states will have to rethink what it means to feel at home in the world.

7.1 Partial success stories

Brazil, like much of Latin America, has among the most skewed land ownership patterns in the world, a legacy of colonialism. The origins of this injustice are easily traced back to when Portugal in Brazil (and Spain in the rest of Latin America) gave enormous tracts of land to a small number of settlers. Brazilian slaves did not receive land when they became free in 1888, while indigenous peoples in Brazil have seen their land reduced since the arrival of the Portuguese. Rural land reform has been an issue in Latin America since the 1930s, often promised by various governments, though it has often been a broken promise.[1] Latin American peasants are much more likely to be indigenous or descendants of slaves than

---

[1] William C. Thiesenhusen, *Broken Promises: Agrarian Reform and the Latin American Campesino* (Boulder, CO: Westview Press, 1995).

landowners and the wealthy.[2] In Brazil, like in many Latin American countries, it is hard to disentangle race from class; and it can be hard to disentangle the peasantry from indigeneity. The lack of land for much of the poor peasantry, which is identified as indigenous or by people with darker skin, is an enduring injustice.

In the late 1970s, a group demanding land redistribution arose in Brazil. Brazil's Movement of Landless Rural Workers (MST) arose in response to the large number of landless peasants in Brazil. Aided by the Catholic Church, the MST demanded that land be redistributed to the landless; sometimes, its members simply took (often uncultivated) land.[3] The MST has had its ups and downs, but has also had some noteworthy success in gaining land for formerly landless peasants. The MST shows that an enduring injustice may be at least partially overcome. There are many reasons for the partial success of the MST. The victims of the injustice must push for it be overcome, but this is something that victims often do, and not always successfully. The struggle to overcome the injustice will often require allies to succeed. In the case of the MST, it had important help from the Catholic Church, and together they influenced the government to help with land reform. Many Brazilian governments talked about land reform, but only recently has the government actually matched its words with deeds.

There are other instances of enduring injustices being overcome, some of which I have noted in the previous pages. Both Canada and the US have given more power to Native peoples over the last two decades. In Canada, the province of Nunavut was created in 1999, giving Inuit considerable power in this sparsely populated province. In the mid-1990s, the Canadian government announced a new policy toward Aboriginal peoples designed to "ensure that Aboriginal

---

[2] "Inadequate incomes, illiteracy, landlessness or near landlessness, and dark skin are closely correlated" in Latin America. The "closer the relationship to European stock," the more likely a person in Latin America will have a "high income level, land, and education." William C. Thiesenhusen, "Human Rights, Affirmative Action and Land Reform in Latin America," in M. L. Wyzan, ed., *The Political Economy of Ethnic Discrimination and Affirmative Action: A Comparative Perspective* (New York: Praeger Publishers, 1990), 26.

[3] Sue Branford and Jan Rocha, *Cutting the Wire: The Story of the Landless Movement in Brazil* (London: Latin America Bureau, 2002); Gabriel A. Ondetti, *Land, Protest and Politics: The Landless Movement and the Stuggle for Agrarian Reform in Brazil* (University Park: Pennsylvania State University Press, 2008).

peoples have greater control over their lives."[4] The 1988 *Mabo* decision in Australia gave legitimacy to Aboriginal land claims.[5] A number of court cases have given Native American tribes the right to have casinos on their tribal lands, and the general population in the US certainly holds indigenous peoples in more respect than it did a hundred years ago. In the US generally there has been a successful renewal of tribal sovereignty.[6] The treaties between some Maori tribes and New Zealand and the reassertion of sovereignty among some Native American tribes are also partial successes at repairing enduring injustice.[7] All this is promising and important, and points to the hope that other enduring injustices may be repaired as well.

The list of partial successes at ending enduring injustices is mostly populated by indigenous tribes. Groups that face considerable discrimination within their societies – we can add the Roma (gypsies) of Europe to the groups I have discussed in the previous chapters (African Americans, Israeli Muslims, Indian Muslims) – clearly have a harder time overcoming the enduring injustice they face. I can only speculate why: it may be that the cost to the larger society of granting more sovereignty to tribes in sparsely populated areas is less than really taking on racial discrimination in a meaningful way. Treaties also give some indigenous tribes an important legal tool in courts. One can ask about the liberal detour I discussed in Chapter 5 that justifies affirmative action: what happens if the detour looks endless? What should be done if it does not seem like changes will be implemented that will help overcome the enduring injustice anytime soon? I do not have good answers to these questions. Clearly, if the path toward

---

[4] Ronald Irwin, "The Government of Canada's Approach to Implementation of the Inherent Right and the Negotiation of Aboriginal Self-Government," www.ainc-inac.gc.ca/pr/pub/sg/plcy_e.html (accessed August 8, 2010).

[5] Jeremy Webber, "Beyond Regret: Mabo's Implications for Australian Constitutionalism," in Duncan Ivison *et al.*, eds., *Political Theory and the Rights of Indigenous Peoples* (Cambridge University Press, 2000), 60–88.

[6] Samuel V. Laselva, "Aboriginal Self-Government and the Foundations of Canadian Nationhood," *BC Studies* 120 (1998): 41–54; Kevin Bruyneel, *The Third Space of Sovereignty: The Postcolonial Politics of U.S.-Indigenous Relations* (Minneapolis: University of Minnesota Press, 2007), 175.

[7] For one example of a resurgent tribal sovereignty in the US, see Valerie Lambert, *Choctaw Nation: A Story of American Indian Resurgence* (Lincoln: University of Nebraska Press, 2009). The text of the New Zealand treaties can be found at www.ots.govt.nz/.

ending these injustices is easily seen, the injustices would not be enduring. Enduring injustices are difficult to overcome, and so in many cases we cannot assume that a detour to liberal justice can readily lead to repairing the enduring injustice. Yet it is also the case that the partial success of indigenous people does not mean we should despair about other enduring injustices. A peace treaty between the Palestinians and Israel may ease the discrimination faced by Israeli Arabs, for example. That the US has an African American President may someday be seen as a sign of progress for racial relations. There has not been a swift move toward racial equality in the US like many had assumed would happen in the 1960s, but there surely has been some. The issue of discrimination against Dalits has become prominent over time in India, raising the prospect that more will be done about this issue.[8] The halting progress on these fronts may mean that we should be skeptical of assuming progress, but perhaps we can be hopeful that enduring injustices will be repaired.

7.2 From progress to hope

We cannot have the nineteenth-century confidence that progress is sure to come. This is obviously true in the case of enduring injustice, but this is also the case for other situations. The usual concepts and categories of liberalism, for example, may be an ill-fit for the challenge of climate change. Individual rights, redistribution of wealth, the idea of equal respect are probably the wrong language to use when trying to determine how to decrease greenhouse emissions, or the death or near death of many of the world's largest lakes. The nineteenth-century view that technological progress has few negative consequences and will spur on moral progress is hard to hold on to in the twentieth-first century. Technology can clearly solve many problems, but it also creates new ones. It is certainly possible to think that moral progress has occurred over the last centuries, while also thinking that it is hard now to assume that morality will only progress.

Instead of assuming progress, we will often have to hope for certain matters, including enduring injustices, to improve. Margaret Urban

---

[8] Clifford Bob, "'Dalit Rights Are Human Rights': Caste Discrimination, International Activism, and the Construction of a New Human Rights Issue," *Human Rights Quarterly* 29, no. 1 (2007): 167–93.

Walker discusses the importance of what she calls restorative justice, which is about restoring hope to the victims of the injustice and trust between the groups involved.[9] Walker argues that in cases of historical injustice what is needed is "*some* morally effective response, and that the response is not perceived as expedient or cheap."[10] I think Walker is correct, but we cannot assume that liberal or modern progress will ensure that freedom and justice will triumph. We can hope for a better future without teleology; we can try to combine a sense of tragedy with hope.

Hope is obviously different than having faith in progress – it lacks the confidence of faith in progress, and is more open-ended. It is hard today to have the same faith in progress that eighteenth- and nineteenth-century liberals had. Without denying the power and importance of individual rights and the redistribution of wealth,[11] we need to recognize when these solutions will not or should not solve certain problems. We can no longer assume that unleashing the power of individual liberty will lead to increasing progress, to all good things. I have argued for what I have called a tragic liberalism, but we can also think of a chastened liberalism.

One key difference between hope and progress is the amount and kind of struggle one engages in when trying to overcome injustice. When one believes that progress will occur (or is occurring), one fights injustice with the confidence that the injustice will be overcome. The idea of progress does not mean that one should simply let history unfold, and not engage in work for a better world. Mill did not think that progress would automatically happen, but he did think that industrialization and technological changes would enable progress to occur. But when one hopes that the struggle to overcome injustice will work out, without the confidence of having faith in progress, the struggle is psychologically harder. It can be hard to avoid hoping when one is uncertain of success, and when the struggle seems slow. One works with progress; but one struggles to overcome an enduring injustice.

---

[9] Margaret Urban Walker, *Moral Repair: Reconstructing Moral Relations After Wrongdoing* (Cambridge University Press, 2006), 209–10.

[10] *Ibid.*, 144. Italics in the original.

[11] As I write this, the gap between the wealthy and the poor in the US is increasing, pointing to the continuing importance of wealth redistribution. Larry M. Bartels, *Unequal Democracy: The Political Economy of the New Gilded Age* (Princeton University Press, 2008).

Hope and struggle move together. That there has been some success in overcoming some enduring injustices is surely hope that there can be more success. Margaret Walker argues that hope is important for action, by giving people the motivation to act. Walker rightly notes the increasing research on the effects of emotion on human action.[12] While Walker tightly connects hope to action, people can still act without hope or purpose. Pretty Shield, the Crow woman I quoted in Chapter 1, lived a life she did not understand. She lived a life without purpose, hope or a conception of the good, but she lived nonetheless. Such a life, however, is hardly a good life. People have to feel that their actions may have some efficacy in order to act with purpose; surely people will act differently, and with more motivation and energy if they have hope than without it. People will act with more efficacy if they have hope than they will without it.

Victims of enduring injustice will generally have more hope in liberal democracies than those in other countries. Liberal democracies give their citizens the space and ability to bring attention to the injustice that they suffer. If the victims are important agents in ending the injustice, as I have argued they must be, then it is those regimes that allow the victims to be agents that provide the most hope. This does not mean there is never hope in authoritarian regimes that an enduring injustice will end, but liberal democracies clearly open up a space for victims to have more hope. Liberal democracies will not always provide great hope that the enduring injustice will be overcome; political moods change and there will undoubtedly be times when political support for repairing enduring injustices will be weak. But liberal democracies allow for political struggle, which is so important for hope.

7.3 Overlapping communities

Helping to ensure hope means that some minority communities – indigenous tribes, some religious groups – will receive sovereign status of some kind or other forms of group-differentiated rights. This moves against the grain of much (but not all) political theory, which argues or assumes that political communities should be able to share a single conception of justice. Rawls wants a shared political conception of

---

[12] Walker, *Moral Repair*, 61.

justice, while Habermas wants a shared democratic culture that
enables effective communication that can lead to a rationally agreed
consensus on justice. Michael Walzer suggests that justice comes from
within a community's shared meanings and understandings about the
goods that it values.[13] These assumptions all allow for arguments and
disagreements, but they do so under narrow conditions, and these
theorists all assume that the right answer about justice can be found.
Yet sharing does not always lead to agreement. What if a connection
to land is shared, but each group wants the land for itself? What if
there is a shared history, but the history is a bloody one, of one group
oppressing, killing, and trying to taking advantage of the other?
Sometimes what is shared does not lay the groundwork for justice,
but to distrust and anger. Under such conditions, when the powerful
liberal state pushes toward a unitary framework of justice, the victims
of the enduring injustice feel more mistrust, despair, anger, and hope-
lessness. Under these conditions, it is hard to see why liberal justice is a
virtue, since it will not alleviate the enduring injustice.

One solution to this dilemma is to argue that deliberation across
group lines may lead to increased trust, and eventually perhaps to
a sense of solidarity across communities, which may lead to a unitary
sense of justice. I do not want to deny this possibility, but this will not
happen easily or readily. Sometimes deliberation leads to convergence,
sometimes it leads to more understanding about the disagreements at
hand; and sometimes it merely makes the interlocutors think that each
party is badly confused or mistaken. The history of an enduring
injustice will often weigh heavily on minority communities; the push
toward a single sense of justice will often be seen as a push toward a
liberal imperialism. While deliberation may sometimes bring different
communities together, it is also the case that the mistrust built up over
decades or centuries, and the concomitant group identities that are
created, are not readily broken down. My argument suggests that
some communities within liberal states will have different conceptions
of justice that ought to be respected – or that they might have some

---

[13] Jürgen Habermas, *Between Facts and Norms: Contributions to a Discourse
Theory of Law and Democracy*, trans. William Rehg (Cambridge, MA: MIT
Press, 1998); John Rawls, *A Theory of Justice* (Cambridge, MA: Harvard
University Press, 1971); John Rawls, *Political Liberalism* (New York: Columbia
University Press, 1993); Michael Walzer, *Spheres of Justice: A Defense of
Pluralism and Equality* (New York: Basic Books, 1983).

non-liberal conceptions, though what they might be can be unclear. Liberalism's failures mean that in some cases the liberal state – and liberal theory – ought to allow for the possibility that alternative ways of justice may fit certain communities better than liberal justice. My argument does not specify what this justice alternative might be, since it is up to the victims of enduring injustice to determine that.

The victims of enduring injustice inhabit the same political community as the dominant majority; overcoming the injustice will mean working out some understandings between members of the two communities. To acknowledge the enduring injustice means to acknowledge something shared – and something importantly shared – between the minority and the majority. It is important that the collective narratives of each community overlap. They do not have to be the same, but the overlap does need to be meaningful. My suggestion that a unitary ideal of justice may not be appropriate does not mean walls will arise within the political community. Rawls discusses an overlapping consensus; I am describing overlapping communities, where there must be – or should be – some matters that are meaningfully shared: history, many institutions (educational, political, judicial). But in some cases, alongside these shared histories and institutions, some communities may have their own institutions and their own narratives and histories. Accepting these exceptions is outside the realm of mainstream liberal theory. Seeing non-liberal fragments in a liberal world, understanding how these non-liberal fragments can exist within liberal states is a difficult task within a framework of liberal theory.[14]

Few tribes that regain their sovereignty will be completely sovereign or have the same range of institutions that most nation-states have. Size does matter. But tribes can still have considerable sovereignty, even if they live intermeshed with the larger political community that surrounds them. Sovereignty does not have to be an either/or proposition: tribes can inhabit what Kevin Bruyneel calls the "third space of sovereignty."[15] This sovereign space is not discrete, separate

---

[14] My argument about overlapping communities is not particularly novel, however. Over the last few years increasing attention has been paid to legal pluralism, to interlocking and overlapping legal jurisdictions (the European Courts and those of individual European states, for example). For a general overview of global legal pluralism, see Paul Schiff Berman, "Global Legal Pluralism," *Southern California Law Review* 80, no. 6 (2006): 1155–237.

[15] Bruyneel, *Third Space of Sovereignty*.

from the larger nation-state in which the tribes are enmeshed, but it does mean that tribes are viewed as tribes – not as a collection of individual liberal citizens, but as a sovereign entity that has claims on the larger nation-state; the two entities must cooperate in various ways, and may have interlocking governing structures.[16]

Between these overlapping communities (which include those territorially dispersed communities that have personal law systems), there will also be overlapping values. I have argued here that victims of enduring injustice, if they have or are given a partial autonomy, should meet democratic procedures, which will also mean respecting individual rights in important ways. In a world dominated by the ideal of democracy, it is hard to see how groups within liberal states will have values that are completely foreign to liberal democracies. For some of the groups I have written about here, the kind of autonomy I have defended is a partial one; the state has control over some areas of life, while the group has the authority to maintain and control certain rules. In these kinds of cases, there will obviously have to be an overlapping sense of justice, and a sense of a shared political community.

Having overlapping values and ideals is not the same as having the same single ideal of justice. How some communities try to combine tradition and modernity does not mean that they will end up with the complete set of liberal democratic ideals. Rawls argues that there is limited social space in liberal democracies available for different ways of life; the demands of liberal citizenship, he argues, may simply make some kinds of lives unavailable to citizens.[17] In many ways my argument suggests that Rawls is right; there is a limit to the ways of life that can exist within the modern state. Yet the limits that Rawls discusses are the limits imposed by a monist idea of liberal justice, and are more restrictive than need be. A liberalism that recognized its failures and its absences would enlarge its views of legitimate ideals of justice beyond liberalism itself.

One obvious objection to this argument is that it undermines the unity of the state, the "ties that bind." Of course, victims of enduring injustice rarely feel like full members of the state, so the unity of

---

[16] See too the argument of Timothy A. Schouls, *Shifting Boundaries: Aboriginal Identity, Pluralist Theory, and the Politics of Self-Government* (Vancouver: University of British Columbia Press, 2003).

[17] Rawls, *Political Liberalism*, 197.

the state is already undermined.[18] Still, one could argue that my argument does little to reverse this, and does more to reinforce the divisions within the state. Even in cases of partial autonomy, however, there is much the state can do to increase solidarity among victims of enduring injustice and others. When the smaller community is integrated economically with the larger community, there will be one single set of rules governing the economy, and the policies guiding economic justice will almost always be applicable to all the communities within the state, minority and majority alike. While economic justice is not the whole of justice, one way for liberal states to move past their history of imperialism and oppressive practices, is to help the economic conditions of many minorities improve. And then of course there are non-economic matters that can be attended to: land can be returned – the US government can negotiate to return at least some of the Black Hills, for example – sacred sites preserved, and past injustices acknowledged. None of this means that a single theory of justice will be legitimate for the whole of society, but when liberal states are attentive to the enduring injustices within their midst they may narrow the gap between liberal justice and other possible forms of justice. By trying to overcome the history of injustice, the political community will be more likely to converge, and liberal justice may feel less alien to its (former?) victims.

My argument leaves open whether the limitations of liberal justice are simply a long-term detour or the pursuit of a different path to justice. That there is good reason to think that in the foreseeable future some tensions between the protection of individual rights and group autonomy should be settled in favor of the latter still allows for the possibility that eventually individual rights and liberal justice will triumph. Similarly, the idea that ending certain kinds of enduring injustices like those in Tibet or the Crimea does not automatically lead to liberal justice certainly allows for the possibility that liberal justice could, eventually, triumph in those places. My argument does not rule out the eventual possibility of a comprehensive liberal society (though accepting the issues of homeland and sacred land as addendums to a theory of justice), but it does insist upon a certain kind of

---

[18] Will Kymlicka addresses this issue in *Multicultural Citizenship: A Liberal Theory of Minority Rights* (Oxford University Press, 1995); see too James Tully, *Strange Multiplicity: Constitutionalism in an Age of Diversity* (Cambridge University Press, 1995), ch. 6.

open-endedness about the future in some cases of enduring injustice. It is at least possible that some communities may work out ways of living that fit within a democratic framework, are not fully liberal, yet are recognizably fair and legitimate. This possibility is congruent with an underlying theme of the argument in this book, which is to defend liberal justice while striking a note of skepticism about it.

7.4 Cautionary notes about post-nationalism and liberal nationalism

Along with overlapping communities come overlapping collective narratives. Different collective narratives within a single political community can be worrisome when these narratives contradict one another on important matters. But that is not as likely as when narratives are overlapping. Victims of enduring injustice have their own narratives, but part of their narratives can and should be interwoven with those of the dominant community. This is part of what my argument for acknowledgement aims for. What I want to emphasize here are the implications of particular interwoven narratives. The New Zealand narrative ought to include the Maori narrative, for example; in the Americas, the mainstream narratives ought to incorporate parts of the narratives of indigenous peoples and descendants of slaves.

These collective narratives pose a challenge to those who want to move toward post-nationalism, a variant of cosmopolitanism. (My argument about overlapping communities applies more to territorially concentrated groups than others; here, my argument applies to all victims of enduring injustice.) Many scholars argue that the horrors of nationalism mean that we need to move past nationalism toward a post-nationalist world, where the nation-state is not a primary political unit.[19] In a way, this argument continues the idea of progress: protecting individual rights within the contours of the nation-state

---

[19] Arash Abizadeh, "Liberal Nationalist Versus Postnational Social Integration: On the Nation's Ethno-Cultural Particularity and 'Concreteness'," *Nations and Nationalism* 10, no. 3 (2004): 231–50; Jürgen Habermas, *The Inclusion of the Other: Studies in Political Theory*, trans. Ciaran Cronin (Cambridge, MA: MIT Press, 1998); Jürgen Habermas, *The Postnational Constellation: Political Essays*, trans. Max Pensky (Cambridge, MA: MIT Press, 2001); Chaim Gans, *The Limits of Nationalism* (Cambridge University Press, 2003); Andrew Mason, *Community, Solidarity and Belonging: Levels of Community and Their Normative Significance* (Cambridge University Press, 2000).

may be an advance over illiberal regimes, but to advance further, we need to think of protecting individuals as individuals, not as members of particular nations or states. Liberalism within the nation-state can be seen as a steppingstone toward a cosmopolitan liberalism.

One challenge to post-national liberalism may be the kind of over-lapping communities I have argued for here. Each liberal political community will be constructed in different ways, as it is made up of its own particular communities. Still, some argue that there is not an inherent tension between a particular political community and univer-sal principles of justice, that there can be a civic state with its own particularistic history. Kok-Chor Tan, for example, argues that cosmo-politanism and national identities can co-exist.[20] As Anna Stilz argues, liberal justice may be implemented in different ways in different states. Norway is not Sweden because its particular interpretation of freedom is its own, yet both are recognizably liberal social welfare states.[21] Habermas argues that it is the terrible pasts of nation-states that should lead us toward constitutional patriotism, a term he uses inter-changeably with post-nationalism. The horrors of exclusive national-ism should lead Germany to universalistic principles.[22] This does not mean forgetting the past. Habermas maintains that Germans today are not guilty of past misdeeds, but they are the bearers of the burden of Auschwitz: "for those born later, this divided legacy establishes neither personal merit nor personal guilt. Beyond guilt that can be ascribed to individuals, however, different contexts can mean different historical burdens."[23] The consequence of this burden is that Germans today can no longer embrace an ethnic or cultural nationalism, but must separate cultural from political identity.[24] At the same time, Habermas argues that one's constitutional principles will

[20] Kok-Chor Tan, *Justice Without Borders: Cosmopolitanism, Nationalism, and Patriotism* (Cambridge University Press, 2004).

[21] Anna Stilz, *Liberal Loyalty: Freedom, Obligation, and the State* (Princeton University Press, 2009), 160.

[22] Jürgen Habermas, *The New Conservatism: Cultural Criticism and the Historians' Debate*, trans. Shierry Weber Nicholsen (Cambridge, MA: MIT Press, 1989), 236.

[23] *Ibid.*, 251.

[24] Habermas also argues that the German past should not be normalized. Much of his writings on the past were triggered by arguments by some German historians that the Holocaust was not historically unique and that the legacy of Nazi Germany should not prevent Germans from looking upon their history with pride. *Ibid.*

express "an interpretation of constitutional principles from the perspective of the nation's historical experience."[25]

Since other nation-states have terrible pasts (at least in part), they too should move to universal principles. The Turkish government refuses to acknowledge the role of the Ottoman Empire in the Armenian genocide. Acknowledging this role hardly means that universal principles of justice are inapplicable in Turkey today. Habermas's argument suggests that the particular atrocities in our national memories differ, but the lessons citizens from different nation-states should learn from them are quite similar, and all these citizens should move toward post-nationalism.

One problem with the idea that states can be liberal in different ways (which is surely the case) is that sometimes overcoming an enduring injustice will mean moving away from liberal justice, either temporarily or for a longer term; when this happens, it will be in part because of the particular circumstances and history of the enduring injustice. Yet this might be seen as a minor amendment to post-nationalism. Both cosmopolitanism and post-nationalism argue for universal principles of justice that should be applied everywhere, and that we have robust obligations to all people in the world. Unlike some versions of cosmopolitanism, however, post-nationalism aspires to separate national or ethnic group identity from the state: "The level of the shared political culture must be uncoupled from the level of subcultures and their prepolitical identities."[26] Constitutional patriotism (or post-nationalism) attempts to bind the state around its constitution and the abstract principles and procedures of liberal democracy, moving it away from a basis in an ethnic or cultural identity. The sort of state that Habermas aims for is well explained by Andrew Mason: "In principle at least, the citizens of a state could identify with their major institutions and practices, and feel at home in them, without believing that there was any deep reason why they should associate together, of the sort which might be provided by the belief that they shared a history, religion, ethnicity, mother tongue, culture, or conception of the good."[27] If a group of people is treated well by the state,

[25] Jürgen Habermas, "Struggles for Recognition in the Democratic Constitutional State," in Amy Gutmann, ed., *Multiculturalism and the Politics of Recognition* (Princeton University Press, 1994), 122.

[26] Habermas, *Inclusion of the Other*, 118.

[27] Mason, *Community, Solidarity and Belonging*, 127.

then they may very well come to feel loyalty to the state and its institutions; they need not have much connection to one another.[28]

When Habermas turns to lessons from history, however, he speaks of states having a specific identity, with a history and a memory; when he speaks of constitutional patriotism (his version of post-nationalism) he strips the state of anything particular. Germany's nationalist past is a memory that pre-dates the current German state; it is a memory of the German *people*. The Third Reich is not the Federal Republic of Germany; and the German Republic changed shape considerably in 1990. If a post-nationalist state is made up of different identity groups, however, none of whom have their identity reflected in the state, then the memory of German nationalism and the Holocaust becomes a memory of one group among several in the German state. If this is the case, then how can the Holocaust bequeath a legacy to those living in the German state? When Habermas suggests that a large increase in immigration to the West is one reason why the nation-state is anachronistic, and he argues that we decouple group identity from politics, he seems to suggest that immigrants in Germany and their progeny need not incorporate the Holocaust as part of their legacy. Yet in an article on a Holocaust memorial in Germany, Habermas suggests that immigrants challenge the nation-state, but will become incorporated

---

[28] Habermas's conception of constitutional patriotism is under-argued in several ways. One problem for Habermas is that while he argues that nationalism provided an important integrative function for democracies, he does not suggest how this integration will be supplied in a post-national state. The reasons Habermas thinks nationalism is no longer viable – its horrible past, and the onset of immigration and globalization – do not undercut the integrative function that Habermas says nationalism performs. A good exploration of this tension in Habermas is Robert Fine and Will Smith, "Jürgen Habermas's Theory of Cosmopolitanism," *Constellations* 10, no. 4 (2003): 469–87; see also Pablo De Greiff, "Habermas on Nationalism and Cosmopolitanism," *Ratio Juris* 15, no. 4 (2002): 418–38; Patchen Markell, "Making Affect Safe for Democracy? On 'Constitutional Patriotism'," *Political Theory* 28, no. 1 (2000): 38–63; Max Pensky, "Cosmopolitanism and the Solidarity Problem: Habermas on National and Cultural Identities," *Constellations* 7, no. 1 (2000): 64–79. A second problem is how thin or thick is Habermas's conception of political culture, since sometimes he portrays it as abstract, and other times he suggests it has specific national content. A good sympathetic exploration of this issue is Cecile Laborde, "From Constitutional to Civic Patriotism," *British Journal of Political Science* 32, no. 4 (2002): 591–612. A more critical argument is Margaret Canovan, "Patriotism is Not Enough," *British Journal of Political Science* 30, no. 3 (2000): 413–32.

into it: "Nevertheless, in becoming naturalized citizens, they [immigrants] accepted a political culture in full awareness of its historical burdens. They may well regard other things as relevant and will one day leave their own mark on the cultural memory of the nation. But, for the present, they can only make their voices heard within the context which currently exists."[29] These burdens, though, are the burdens of taking on a national history on Habermas's account, not merely the burdens of citizenship.

It is one thing to argue that the nation-state should embrace universal principles of justice, though I have argued some cautionary notes about that; it is another matter to argue that identity groups should be decoupled from the state, as Habermas sometimes argues. While I have argued here that we should detach responsibility from causality, it is the case that certain political communities have the responsibility to work toward repairing particular enduring injustices. A civic state that simply inculcated a sense of belonging that was detached from any group, like some post-nationalists want, would too readily lead to forgetting about enduring injustices; it would be yet another obstacle to acknowledgement and repair. It may be that some of our obligations are global (I believe they are, but that point is far afield from my argument here), but some obligations are particular and specific. When the MST presses its claims for land reform, it is asking that the Brazilian people and government come to its aid. The political appeal that the MST makes is a Brazilian one; some of their success is surely based on the degree of solidarity among Brazilian citizens.

Habermas thinks the horrors of nationalism mean we need to move beyond the nation-state; but narratives are not free-floating. History and memories are most readily preserved when there are institutions that help enable them to do so. Nation-states preserve – or recreate or reinterpret – certain histories and narratives; museums commemorate the past; the state influences the curriculum in the schools; the state can call us to the past through its holidays. Nation-states are not natural communities of memory; instead, they have the institutional framework to interpret and maintain memories. Importantly, they contain the institutions in which debates and discussions about how

---

[29] Jürgen Habermas, *Time of Transitions*, trans. Ciaran Cronin and Max Pensky (Cambridge: Polity, 2006), 42–43.

to present history can readily take place. As Booth says: "Space and institutions are the tangible boundaries of the community, malleable but essential nevertheless."[30] The state has an important role in constructing and maintaining collective narratives, since it exerts considerable control of the space and institutions out of which these narratives come forth. These narratives will not just be of the state, but of the political community and the groups within it.

This means, undoubtedly, maintaining national memories and national identity: the memories and narratives of a political community always reach beyond the state, as the example of Germany shows. Habermas's reasons to move toward post-nationalism are certainly important, reasons that liberal nationalists and multiculturalists do not do enough to consider. These scholars base their case for group attachment on the idea of self-respect, which is more ambiguous than many liberals admit. We know from political and social psychologists that a strong group identity increases members' desire to pursue the collective good of the group, regardless of how it affects them personally. Group members tend to behave cooperatively (rather than competitively) with one another. This all sounds good, of course, but social psychologists have also found that people feel better about their ingroup and have higher collective self-esteem after they have shown favoritism toward ingroup members or, among low-status groups, after they have derogated the outgroup. Collective self-esteem is not just a reaction to positive feelings toward the ingroup but involves a comparison with an outgroup, and the outgroup often loses in the comparison. People give higher ratings to ingroup members than to outgroup members on the same tasks (ingroup favoritism); and focusing on the negative aspects of the outgroup and the positive aspects of the ingroup (which is inherently part of group differentiation) makes ingroup members feel better about their group.[31] Simply by thinking in terms of ingroup and outgroup categories, people minimize the differences among members of the same group and maximize the differences between the groups.

[30] William James Booth, *Communities of Memory: On Witness, Identity, and Justice* (Ithaca, NY: Cornell University Press, 2006), 51.

[31] Jeff Spinner-Halev and Elizabeth Theiss-Morse, "National Identity and Self-Esteem," *Perspectives on Politics* 1, no. 3 (2003): 515–32; Elizabeth Theiss-Morse, *Who Counts as an American? The Boundaries of National Identity* (Cambridge University Press, 2009).

Much of this should make us feel uneasy about group attachments; it shows in part the attraction of post-nationalism, since group attachments easily become comparative in dangerous ways. The difficulty with arguments aimed at bolstering collective self-esteem (or self-respect) is that this is often accomplished in competitive and violent ways. Liberal nationalists can, of course, distance themselves from collective self-esteem when it turns nasty in some way. But this distancing comes at a high price to their argument. Liberal nationalists cannot tell people a priori how their collective self-esteem will be shored up. Self-esteem is a psychological notion: liberal nationalists cannot pick the one way they like to have collective self-esteem secured and then inform everyone that this is how it will happen. If one wants to hold onto self-esteem, but not in its competitive or dangerous forms, then one has taken out a large part of the meaning that self-esteem holds for many people. A non-competitive, safe collective self-esteem cannot be at the core of liberal-nationalist arguments, since this type of self-esteem will not fit many people. Rawls envisions such a safe self-esteem when he argues that a people's self-respect must be grounded in mutual respect and must rest on "their common awareness of their trials during their history and of their culture with its accomplishments."[32] But these accomplishments often include the trampling upon of other peoples, and the trials remembered are often of being trampled upon.

Fueling post-nationalism are understandable worries about group identity: when groups are in control of their own collective narratives, they are likely to reinforce only a certain narrative, one that buttresses group pride. We know that many nations have great triumphs, and have overcome adversity; we also know that many of these same nations have committed great harms to others, sometimes interwoven with their achievements. Yet getting rid of group identities is an impossible task, and should not, even ideally, be our goal. It is not accidental that nearly all (or perhaps all) successful states have what Rogers Smith calls "ethically constitutive stories."[33] These stories explain the worth of the people, why the particular traits they have are so important, and often legitimate the authority of the rulers; these

---

[32] John Rawls, *The Law of Peoples* (Cambridge, MA: Harvard University Press, 1999), 34.

[33] Rogers M. Smith, *Stories of Peoplehood: The Politics and Morals of Political Membership* (Cambridge University Press, 2003).

stories bind together the ruler with the dominant community in the state. Smith suggests that most of us have a need to believe some ethically constitutive story – we need communities that endure and identities that feel secure, an argument that is backed by considerable psychological research.[34]

Better than getting rid of or privatizing group identities is to politicize and problematize them. This is what my argument for acknowledgement aims, in part, to do. Since we cannot get rid of group identity, we should try to make it an object of discussion and contestation.[35] Habermas is right when he says: "In the public process of transmitting a culture we decide which of our traditions we want to continue and which we do not. The debate of this rages all the more intensely the less we can rely on a triumphal national history, on the unbroken normality of what has come to prevail, and the more clearly we become conscious of the ambivalence in every tradition."[36] Liberal states should teach citizens about the triumphs of the nation, and its tragedies, and aim to curb the excesses of nationality by teaching its ambivalences, rather than try to reach the impossible goal of getting rid of group identity. This means, certainly, teaching the histories of enduring injustices. It may mean teaching about other injustices as well. And not just teaching, of course, but incorporating the histories of enduring injustices into the larger collective narrative through museums, symbolic actions, and policies as well. It means integrating the narratives of the victims of enduring injustices with the narratives of the larger political community.

All this should be compatible with national identity as a source of pride. One can be proud of one's political community, while recognizing that its history is flawed. The idea that a political community is flawless is surely odd. There is unsurprisingly a tendency to say that these flaws are in the past, that now the political community has come to triumph over these unfortunate lapses and mistakes. It is certainly uncomfortable to say that the political community that one is so proud of is also flawed. Yet decency will often suggest that this is what we must do.

---

[34] The pyschological evidence for this view is reviewed in Spinner-Halev and Theiss-Morse, "National Identity and Self-Esteem."

[35] Laborde, "Civic Patriotism"; Smith, *Stories of Peoplehood.*

[36] Habermas, *The New Conservatism,* 263. See too Smith, *Stories of Peoplehood.*

7.5 Moving forward, uncomfortably

Repairing enduring injustice is not only hard to do, but will often make many uncomfortable. Those in the majority, those who see the state as legitimate, will sometimes (and perhaps often) have a hard time understanding why others find the state illegitimate. They will have what Russell Hardin calls the "epistemological comforts of home" – they are at home in the world.[37] When you are proud of your country, it is uncomfortable to listen to those narratives that may make you feel shameful. If you live on a Native American reservation, however, impoverished, modernity has passed you by, and liberalism has been of little help. It is understandable if you look to the past to see how you have arrived at this point. If you are a Dalit in a small Indian village living a subordinate and poor life while seeing parts of India prosper, you will likely ponder the conditions that have circumscribed your life. Slavery, expulsion, massacres – the past will often loom large in the collective narratives of victims of enduring injustice. Members of oppressed groups are "simultaneously connected with their history of marginalization and with the experience of other group members."[38] And indeed, many of the advocates of repairing historical injustices argue that the past ought to loom large in the collective narratives of dominant communities, that since these communities are shaped by the past they should take responsibility for it. Lawrie Balfour argues that the "story of reparations is centrally a story of memory's suppression" – meaning that most Americans have suppressed the memory of slavery, which explains their opposition to reparations.[39] McCarthy argues that part of the cure of racism "lies in broadening and deepening the public memory of slavery and segregation."[40]

Yet dominant communities in modern societies often look toward the future. The mind of the person on the Native American reservation

---

[37] Russell Hardin, *One for All: The Logic of Group Conflict* (Princeton University Press, 1995), 217.

[38] Melissa Williams, *Voice, Trust and Memory: Marginalized Groups and the Failings of Liberal Representation* (Princeton University Press, 1998), 183.

[39] Lawrie Balfour, "Unreconstructed Democracy: W. E. B. Du Bois and the Case for Reparations," *American Political Science Review* 97, no. 1 (2003), 40.

[40] Thomas McCarthy, "Vergangenheitsbewaltigung in the USA: On the Politics of the Memory of Slavery," *Political Theory* 30, no. 5 (2002), 641.

may understandably drift back to the past. But the person in Times Square, or Los Angeles or Chicago or Toronto or, increasingly, Bangalore, will often look around and wonder what the future brings. The churning of modernity often means the past for many people is left in the past. It is not just that many want bygones to be bygones; it is that they see their lives structured by future possibilities as much if not more than the inheritance of the past. Some argue that the importance of memory and history came to the fore in nineteenth-century Europe because of modernity; the dislocations that many felt meant that people no longer took the past for granted, or assumed that the present would be like the future and the past. Instead, as they consciously changed the world they lived in, they looked upon the past as much different than the present, in contrast to earlier eras when the past and present were seen to be considerably more continuous.[41] A common complaint made against American citizens is that they know so little history. In a constantly changing world, however, how much history does one need to know to move into the future?

The charge that Americans (or others) are forgetful does not answer the question of why people living in modernity should remember the injustices of the past. When you live in a world where change is perhaps not constant but frequent, the ties of the past do not seem particularly alluring. Moreover, collective narratives do not begin in the past and move forward, but are constructed to make sense of today. If a people's present seems good, and the future holds out promise, the collective narrative will be shaped to lead up to these points. It will be a narrative on an upward trajectory. Those who present a narrative of pessimism will often be dismissed. This is not because the majority finds the past uninteresting. People have interest in the roots of their families, many people are keenly interested in history, and so on. Nonetheless, the narrative of a dominant group will be shaped by its present and its view of the future.

Modern societies do not forget the past, but there is a challenge of asymmetrical collective narratives. The dominant community may focus less on the past than the victims of enduring injustice, and perhaps more importantly, it will focus on the past in different ways. Collective narratives are packages of stories that a people tell

---

[41] Peter Fritzsche, *Stranded in the Present: Modern Time and the Melancholy of History* (Cambridge, MA: Harvard University Press, 2004).

themselves, and that try to make sense of their place today, and where they hope to go in the future. Our narratives of the past are constructed through the lens of the present. When groups have different views of the present and different perceptions of the future, their collective narratives will differ in many ways. If two stories "end" on a very different note, then the stories themselves, even if they contain some of the same events, will be told in very different ways. Different events will be emphasized in the two narratives; the same events will sometimes be interpreted in different ways. When the victims of the enduring injustice are rarely seen – if they live on isolated reservations, or they live in exile – then their collective narrative is even more likely to be overlooked by the dominant political community.

Convincing dominant communities to see the exceptions to progress will not be easy. One way to start is to reconceive the problem of historical injustice as one of enduring injustice. The point is not to convince the wider political community to acknowledge the injustices of the past in order to try to make for a better present and future. The point is to convince the political community to acknowledge that some current injustices are enduring, and that repairing them may mean understanding the history of these injustices better.

To get many in the dominant community to see the importance of repairing enduring injustice will often mean making them uncomfortable, since it will mean re-conceptualizing their worldview. This is not easy or comfortable to do. The MST does not politely ask for land reform; if it did, it would not get very far. Black nationalism undoubtedly makes many liberal citizens uncomfortable – the idea that a particular group of citizens must band together to the exclusion of others will strike at some liberal sensibilities. I do not think there is a way around this edgy feeling: when your world is constructed so you are epistemologically at home, it can be hard to sympathize with those who are not. But they are uncomfortable with their world, and there is no easy, comfortable way forward for all involved in a partially legitimate state with an enduring injustice (or injustices). It does seem like folly, however, to bewail the lack of historical knowledge that many people have. While it is important for political communities to acknowledge enduring injustices, what should fuel this acknowledgement is that the injustice exists today. It is not just a matter of remembering the past better; it is a matter of trying to make the future better for those victims of injustice today.

Some people are at home in the world, while others are not; the former may have to feel less comfortable for the latter to feel at home in the world. This may seem like a seesaw, where both groups cannot be at home simultaneously; if one is up, then the other is down. But if one group is at one in the world at the expense of another, then a way should be found so both can feel at home. This should not be an insurmountable obstacle. If one feels at home in the world partly because of an injustice – say, white supremacy – then one feels at home in the world because one is on top of the world. This is, however, not necessary for one to be an empowered agent. There is more than one way to feel at home in the world, and one should be able to feel at home without dominating others. To be an empowered agent, to feel like one's voice is heard, that one has a say in the political process, that one is efficacious in one's life, does not mean that one's political community must comport with all of one's desires, particularly if they mean dominating others.

One may feel at home in an unjust political community – or a partly just one. If that is the case, then one ought to work toward a better society so all can feel at home. It is likely that many will feel uncomfortable during this transition time. When one feels at home in the world, making room for others will mean seeing one's political community from other points of view; it will mean revising one's collective narrative to incorporate others; it will mean acknowledging the enduring injustices that exist within one's political community. For many, doing this will be an uncomfortable undertaking; yet this does not mean one will no longer be at home in the world. My argument here does not suggest a revolution in liberal societies; it does suggest an expansion of liberal democracy's horizons. It may mean that at times one sees the world through a variegated lens rather than a unitary one. It means paying attention to liberalism's failures, but my claims do not suggest we overlook liberalism's many successes either. A chastened liberalism is not a failed liberalism; it is a liberalism with some failures. My argument may make some who feel at home in the world uncomfortable, but they should be less comfortable while enduring injustices persist.

Liberals too may be uncomfortable with some of the solutions I have suggested here: group autonomy in some cases, a defense of communal solidarity, a warning about the ethos of cosmopolitanism, an argument about plural conceptions of justice possibly co-existing are all outside what is epistemologically comfortable for liberals. But enduring injustices are moral failures of liberal societies, ones that demand a meaningful response. To insist on a liberal justice that does not repair enduring injustices simply falls short. Trying to correct these failures will not necessarily mean justice for all, nor will correcting these failures be easy to do. This is in part why I argue for acknowledgement instead of apology. The liberal promise of justice will sometimes be hard to reach when it comes to enduring injustices, and while this may mean a modesty with respect to liberal goals, this should not stop us from trying to become, at the very least, decent societies.

Bibliography

Abdel-Nour, Farid. "National Responsibility," *Political Theory* 31, no. 5 (2003): 693–719.

Abizadeh, Arash. "Liberal Nationalist Versus Postnational Social Integration: On the Nation's Ethno-Cultural Particularity and 'Concreteness'," *Nations and Nationalism* 10, no. 3 (2004): 231–50.

Adams, David Wallace. *Education for Extinction: American Indians and the Boarding School Experience 1875–1928*. University Press of Kansas, 1997.

Agarwal, Bina. *A Field of One's Own: Gender and Land Rights in South Asia*. Cambridge University Press, 1994.

Ahmad, Imtiaz. *Caste and Social Stratification among Muslims in India*. 2nd edn. New Delhi: Manohar, 1978.

Allen, Jonathan. "The Place of Negative Morality in Political Theory," *Political Theory* 29, no. 3 (2001): 337–63.

Anderson, Benedict. *Imagined Communities: Reflections on the Origins and Spread of Nationalism*. 2nd edn. London: Verso, 1991.

Anderson, Elizabeth S. *The Imperative of Integration*. Princeton University Press, 2010.

Anderson, Terry L., and Dominic P. Parker. "Sovereignty, Credible Commitments, and Economic Prosperity on American Indian Reservations," *The Journal of Law and Economics* 51, no. 41 (2008): 641–66.

Appiah, Kwame Anthony, and Amy Gutmann. *Color Conscious*. Princeton University Press, 1998.

Associated Press. "Records: Percentage of Mormons in Utah Declines." 2008. www.azcentral.com/news/articles/2008/11/20/20081120 fewer-mormons1120-ON.html. (Accessed July 30, 2010).

Australian Human Rights Commission. "Report of the National Inquiry into the Separation of Aboriginal and Torres Strait Islander Children from Their Families. Bringing Them Home." April 1997. www.hreoc.gov.au/social_justice/bth_report/report/index.html. (Accessed August 10, 2010.)

Baker, Judith, ed. *Group Rights*. University of Toronto Press, 1994.

Balagangadhara, S. N., and Jakob De Roover. "The Secular State and Religious Conflict: Liberal Neutrality and the Indian Case of Pluralism," *Journal of Political Philosophy* 15, no. 1 (2007): 67–92.

Baldwin, Peter. *Reworking the Past: Hitler, the Holocaust, and the Historians' Debate*. Boston: Beacon Press, 1990.

Balfour, Lawrie. "Unreconstructed Democracy: W. E. B. Du Bois and the Case for Reparations," *American Political Science Review* 97, no. 1 (2003): 33–44.

Bancroft, Angus. *Roma and Gypsy – Travellers in Europe: Modernity, Race, Space and Exclusion*. Aldershot: Ashgate Publishing, 2005.

Banner, Stuart. *How the Indians Lost Their Land: Law and Power on the Frontier*. Cambridge, MA: Belknap Press of Harvard University Press, 2005.

Barkan, Elazar, and Alexander Karn. "Group Apology as Ethical Imperative," in Elazar Barkan and Alexander Karn, eds.,*Taking Wrongs Seriously: Apologies and Reconciliation*. Stanford University Press, 2006, 3–32.

Barkan, Elazar, and Alexander Karn, eds. *Taking Wrongs Seriously: Apologies and Reconciliation*. Stanford University Press, 2006

Barry, Brian M. *Culture & Equality: An Egalitarian Critique of Multiculturalism*. Cambridge, MA: Harvard University Press, 2001.

Bartels, Larry M. *Unequal Democracy: The Political Economy of the New Gilded Age*. Princeton University Press, 2008.

Beiner, Ronald, ed. *Theorizing Nationalism*. Albany, NY: State University of New York Press, 1999.

Berlin, Isaiah. *The Crooked Timber of Humanity: Chapters in the History of Ideas*. New York: Knopf, 1991.

Four Essays on Liberty. Oxford University Press, 1969.

Berman, Paul Schiff. "Global Legal Pluralism," *Southern California Law Review* 80, no. 6 (2006): 1155–237.

Birnbaum, Bruce. "A Family Deposition: Should Egypt Receive Reparations for the Exodus?" 2004. www.theatlantic.com/doc/200401/birnbaum. (Accessed 5 July, 2011.)

Blaikie, Piers, Terry Cannon, Ian Davis, and Ben Wisner. *At Risk: Natural Hazards, People's Vulnerability and Disasters*. New York: Routledge, 2003.

Blatz, Craig, Karina Schumann, and Michael Ross. "Government Apologies for Historical Injustices," *Political Psychology* 30, no. 2 (2009): 219–41.

Blustein, Jeffrey. *The Moral Demands of Memory*. Cambridge University Press, 2008.

Bob, Clifford. "'Dalit Rights Are Human Rights:' Caste Discrimination, International Activism, and the Construction of a New Human Rights Issue," *Human Rights Quarterly* 29, no. 1 (2007): 167–93.

Booth, William James. *Communities of Memory: On Witness, Identity, and Justice*. Ithaca, NY: Cornell University Press, 2006.

Borrows, John. "Re-Living the Present: Title, Treaties, and the Trickster in British Columbia," *BC Studies* 120 (1998): 99–108.

Bowen, William G., and Derek Bok. *The Shape of the River*. Princeton University Press, 2000.

Boxill, Bernard. "A Lockean Argument for Black Reparations," *The Journal of Ethics* 7, no. 1 (2003): 63–91.

"The Morality of Reparations," *Social Theory and Practice* 2, no. 1 (1972): 113–24.

Branford, Sue, and Jan Rocha. *Cutting the Wire: The Story of the Landless Movement in Brazil*. London: Latin America Bureau, 2002.

Broadfoot, Barry. *Years of Sorrow, Years of Shame: The Story of the Japanese Canadians in World War II*. Toronto: Doubleday Canada, 1977.

Brooks, Roy L. *Atonement and Forgiveness: A New Model for Black Reparations*. Berkeley: University of California Press, 2004.

"The New Patriotism and Apology for Slavery," in Elazar Barkan and Alexander Karn, eds., *Taking Wrongs Seriously: Apologies and Reconciliation*. Stanford University Press, 2006, 213–33.

Brophy, Alfred L. *Reparations: Pro and Con*. Oxford University Press, 2008.

Brubaker, Rogers. *Citizenship and Nationhood in France and Germany*. Cambridge, MA: Harvard University Press, 1992.

Bruyneel, Kevin. *The Third Space of Sovereignty: The Postcolonial Politics of U.S.–Indigenous Relations*. Minneapolis: University of Minnesota Press, 2007.

Buchanan, Allen. "Political Legitimacy and Democracy," *Ethics* 112, no. 4 (2002): 689–719.

Bury, J. B. *The Idea of Progress: An Inquiry Into Its Origin and Growth*. New York: Cosimo Press, 2011 [1920].

Butt, Daniel. "On Benefiting From Injustice," *Canadian Journal of Philosophy* 37, no. 1 (2007): 129–52.

Rectifying International Injustice: Principles of Compensation and Restitution Between Nations. New York: Oxford University Press, 2009.

Canovan, Margaret. *Nationhood and Political Theory*. Cheltenham: Edward Elgar, 1996.

"Patriotism is Not Enough," *British Journal of Political Science* 30, no. 3 (2000): 413–32.

Casal, Paula. "Is Multiculturalism Bad for Animals?," *Journal of Political Philosophy* 11, no. 1 (2003): 1–22.

Celermajer, Danielle. "The Apology in Australia: Re-Covenanting the National Imaginary," in Elazar Barkan and Alexander Karn, eds.,

Taking Wrongs Seriously: Apologies and Reconciliation. Stanford University Press, 2006, 153–84.

The Sins of the Nation and the Ritual of Apologies. Cambridge University Press, 2009.

Chatterjee, Partha. "Secularism and Tolerance," in Rajeev Bhargava, ed., *Secularism and Its Critics.* New Delhi: Oxford University Press, 1998, 345–79.

Chattopadhyay, Ragha, and Esther Duflo. "Impact of Reservation in Panchayati Raj: Evidence From a Nationwide Randomised Experiment," *Economic and Political Weekly* 39, no. 9 (2004): 979–86.

"Women as Policy Makers: Evidence From a Randomized Policy Experiment in India," *Econometrica* 72, no. 5 (2004): 1409–43.

Chen, Jack. *The Chinese of America.* San Francisco: Harper & Row, 1980.

Chen, Martha. "A Matter of Survival: Women's Rights to Employment in India and Bangladesh," in Martha C. Nussbaum and Jonathan Glover, eds., *Women, Culture and Development: A Study of Human Capabilities.* Oxford: Clarendon Press, 1995, 37–57.

Christiano, Thomas. *The Constitution of Equality: Democratic Authority and Its Limits.* Oxford University Press, 2008.

Cohen, Andrew I. "Compensation for Historic Injustices: Completing the Boxill and Sher Argument," *Philosophy and Public Affairs* 37, no. 1 (2009): 81–102.

Coicaud, Jean-Marc, and Jibecke Jonsson. "Elements of a Road Map for a Politics of Apology," in Mark Gibney, Rhoda E. Howard-Hassmann, Jean-Marc Coicaud, and Niklaus Steiner, eds., *The Age of Apology: Facing Up to the Past.* Philadelphia: University of Pennsylvania Press, 2008, 77–91.

Cole, David. "Can Our Shameful Prisons be Reformed?" *The New York Review of Books* 56, no. 18 (2009). www.nybooks.com/articles/archives/2009/nov/19/can-our-shameful-prisons-be-reformed/ (Accessed January 5, 2010.)

Congress, *Public Law 110–82 110th.* www.usmint.gov/mint_programs/nativeamerican/Legislation.pdf. (Accessed August 2, 2010.)

Copp, David. "The Idea of a Legitimate State," *Philosophy and Public Affairs* 28, no. 1 (1999): 3–45.

Dalrymple, William. *From the Holy Mountain: a Journey Among the Christians of the Middle East.* New York: Henry Holt, 1998.

De Greiff, Pablo. "Habermas on Nationalism and Cosmopolitanism," *Ratio Juris* 15, no. 4 (2002): 418–38.

Derrett, Duncan J. *Religion, Law and the State in India.* New Delhi: Oxford University Press, 1999.

Deveaux, Monique. *Cultural Pluralism and Dilemmas of Justice.* Ithaca, NY: Cornell University Press, 2000.

"A Deliberative Approach to Conflicts of Culture," *Political Theory* 31, no. 6 (2003): 780–807.

Gender and Justice in Multicultural Liberal States. Oxford University Press, 2006.

Dienstag, Joshua Foa. *Pessimism: Philosophy, Ethic, Spirit.* Princeton University Press, 2006.

Dworkin, Ronald. *Sovereign Virtue: The Theory and Practice of Equality.* Cambridge, MA: Harvard University Press, 2002.

Edelman, Martin. *Courts, Politics, and Culture in Israel.* Charlottesville: University Press of Virginia, 1994.

Edmunds, R. David. "Native Americans, New Voices: American Indian History, 1895–1995," *The American Historical Review* 100, no. 3 (1995): 717–40.

Estlund, David M. *Democratic Authority: A Philosophical Framework.* Princeton University Press, 2009.

Fette, Julie. "The Apology Moment: Vichy Memories in 1990s France," in Elazar Barkan and Alexander Karn, eds., *Taking Wrongs Seriously: Apologies and Reconciliation.* Stanford University Press, 2006, 259–87.

Fine, Robert, and Will Smith. "Jurgen Habermas's Theory of Cosmopolitanism," *Constellations* 10, no. 4 (2003): 469–87.

Fitzhugh, George. *Cannibals All! Or, Slaves Without Masters.* Richmond, VA: A. Morris, 1857.

Flanagan, Tom. *First Nations? Second Thoughts.* Montreal: McGill-Queen's University Press, 2008.

Flood, Gavin. *An Introduction to Hinduism.* Cambridge University Press, 1996.

Foner, Philip S. *The Great Labor Uprising of 1877.* New York: Monad Press, 1977.

Freeman, Michael. "Historical Injustice and Liberal Political Theory," in Mark Gibney, Rhoda E. Howard-Hassmann, Jean-Marc Coicaud, and Niklaus Steiner, eds., *The Age of Apology: Facing Up to the Past.* Philadelphia: University of Pennsylvania Press, 2008, 31–44.

Friedman, Marilyn. "Women's Rights, Oppressed Minorities, and the Liberal State," in Barbara Arneil, Monique Deveaux, Rita Dhamoon, and Avigail Eisenberg, eds., *Sexual Justice/Cultural Justice: Critical Perspectives in Political Theory and Practice.* New York: Routledge, 2007, 89–102.

Fritzsche, Peter. *Stranded in the Present: Modern Time and the Melancholy of History.* Cambridge, MA: Harvard University Press, 2004.

Galanter, Marc. "Secularism, East and West," in Rajeev Bhargava, ed., *Secularism and Its Critics*. Oxford University Press, 1998, 234–67.

Galston, William A. *Liberal Pluralism: The Implications of Value Pluralism for Political Theory and Practice*. Cambridge University Press, 2002.

Gans, Chaim. *The Limits of Nationalism*. Cambridge University Press, 2003.

Gellner, Ernest. *Nations and Nationalism*. Ithaca, NY: Cornell University Press, 1983.

Gibney, Mark, and Erik Roxstrom. "The Status of State Apologies," *Human Rights Quarterly* 23, no. 4 (2001): 911–39.

Gibney, Mark, Rhoda E. Howard-Hassmann, Jean-Marc Coicaud, and Niklaus Steiner, eds. *The Age of Apology: Facing Up to the Past*. Philadelphia: University of Pennsylvania Press, 2008.

Gill, Kathleen. "The Moral Functions of an Apology," *The Philosophical Forum* 31, no. 1 (2000): 11–27.

Goldberg, Carole. "Members Only? Designing Citizenship Requirements for Indian Nations," *University of Kansas Law Review* 50 (2001): 437–72.

Goodridge v. Department of Public Health. 440 Mass. 309, 798 N.E.2d 941 (Mass. 2003).

Gover, Kevin. "*Remarks of Kevin Gover.*" 2000. www.tahtonka.com/apology. html. (Accessed June 29, 2011.)

Govier, Trudy, and Wilhelm Verwoerd. "The Promise and Pitfalls of Apology," *Journal of Social Philosophy* 33, no. 1 (2002): 67–82.

Habermas, Jürgen. *Between Facts and Norms: Contributions to a Discourse Theory of Law and Democracy*, trans. William Rehg. Cambridge, MA: MIT Press, 1998.

   The Inclusion of the Other: Studies in Political Theory, trans. Ciaran Cronin. Cambridge, MA: MIT Press, 1998.

   The New Conservatism: Cultural Criticism and the Historians' Debate, trans. Shierry Weber Nicholsen. Cambridge, MA: MIT Press, 1989.

   The Postnational Constellation: Political Essays, trans. Max Pensky. Cambridge, MA: MIT Press, 2001.

   "Struggles for Recognition in the Democratic Constitutional State," in Amy Gutmann, ed., *Multiculturalism and the Politics of Recognition*. Princeton University Press, 1994, 106–48.

   Time of Transitions, trans. Ciaran Cronin and Max Pensky. Cambridge: Polity, 2006.

Hacker, Andrew. *Two Nations: Black and White, Separate, Hostile, Unequal*. New York: Touchstone, 2003.

Hamalainen, Pekka. *The Comanche Empire*. New Haven: Yale University Press, 2009.

Hammarberg, Thomas. *Human Rights Report: Turkey.* Strasbourg: Commissioner for Human Rights of the Council of Europe, 2009.

Hansen, Thomas Blom. *The Saffron Wave: Democracy and Hindu Nationalism in Modern India.* Princeton University Press, 1999.

Hardimon, Michael O. "The Project of Reconciliation: Hegel's Social Philosophy," *Philosophy and Public Affairs* 21, no. 2 (1992): 165–95.

Hardin, Russell. *One for All: The Logic of Group Conflict.* Princeton University Press, 1995.

Hartlyn, Jonathan, and Arturo Valenzuela. "Democracy in Latin America Since 1930," in Leslie Bethell, ed., *Latin America: Politics and Society Since 1930.* Cambridge University Press, 1998, 3–66.

Headley, John M. *The Europeanization of the World: On the Origins of Human Rights and Democracy.* Princeton University Press, 2007.

Heinze, Eric A. *Waging Humanitarian War: The Ethics, Law, and Politics of Humanitarian Intervention.* Albany, NY: State University of New York Press, 2010.

Helling, Amy, and David Sawicki. "Race and Residential Accessibility to Shopping and Services," *Housing Policy Debate* 14, no. 1 (2003): 69–101.

Hendrix, Burke A. "Memory in Native American Land Claims," *Political Theory* 33, no. 6 (2005): 763–85.

Ownership, Authority, and Self-Determination: Moral Principles and Indigenous Rights Claim. Pennsylvania State University Press, 2008.

Herr, Ranjoo. "A Third World Feminist Defense of Multiculturalism," *Social Theory and Practice* 30, no. 1 (2004): 73–103.

Herzog, Don. *Happy Slaves: A Critique of Consent Theory.* University of Chicago Press, 1989.

Higham, John. *Strangers in the Land: Patterns of American Nativism, 1860–1925.* New York: Atheneum, 1963.

Hill, Renée A. "Compensatory Justice: Over Time and Between Groups," *Journal of Political Philosophy* 10, no. 4 (2002): 392–415.

Hines, Rochelle. "Tribal Court Rules Against Cherokee Freedmen Amendment," *Native American Times.* 2011. www.nativetimes.com/index.php?option=com_content&view=article&id=4822:tribal-court-rules-against-cherokee-freedmen-amendment&catid=54&Itemid=30. (Accessed June 8, 2011.)

Hirschman, Albert O. *Exit, Voice, and Loyalty; Responses to Decline in Firms, Organizations, and States.* Cambridge, MA: Harvard University Press, 1970.

Hobbes, Thomas. *Leviathan.* Indianapolis: Hackett, 1994 [1651].

Hooker, Juliet. *Race and the Politics of Solidarity.* Oxford University Press, 2009.

Hoxie, Frederick E. *A Final Promise: The Campaign to Assimilate the Indians, 1880–1920*. Lincoln: University of Nebraska Press, 1984.

Hume, David. *Essays: Moral, Political and Literary*. Indianapolis: Liberty Press, 1985 [1742].

Irwin, Ronald. *The Government of Canada's Approach to Implementation of the Inherent Right and the Negotiation of Aboriginal Self-Government*. 1995. www.aadnc-aandc.gc.ca/eng/1100100031843. (Accessed August 8, 2010.)

Ivison, Duncan. *Postcolonial Liberalism*. Cambridge University Press, 2002.

Jayal, Niraja Gopal. *Democracy and the State*. New Delhi: Oxford University Press, 1999.

Jordan, Kay K. "Devadasi Reform: Driving the Priestesses Or the Prostitutes Out of Hindu Temples?," in Robert Baird, ed., *Religion and Law in Independent India*. New Delhi: Manohar, 1993, 257–78.

Kershnar, Stephen. "Are the Descendants of Slaves Owed Compensation for Slavery?," *Journal of Applied Philosophy* 16, no. 1 (1999): 95–101.

Khory, Kativa R. "The Shah Bano Case: Some Political Implications," in Robert D. Baird, *Religion and Law in Independent India*. New Delhi: Manohar Publishers, 1993, 121–38.

Kinsley, Michael. "Essay: Rally Round the Flag, Boys." 1988. www.time.com/time/printout/0,8816,968407,00.html. (Accessed August 2, 2010.)

Kudva, Neema. "Engineering Elections: The Experiences of Women in 'Panchayati Raj' in Karnataka, India," *International Journal of Politics, Culture and Society* 16, no. 3 (2003): 445–63.

Kukathas, Chandran. *Liberal Archipelago: A Theory of Diversity and Freedom*. Oxford University Press, 2003.

"Multiculturalism as Fairness: Will Kymlicka's Multicultural Citizenship," *Journal of Political Philosophy* 5, no. 4 (1997): 406–27.

"Responsibility for the Past: How to Shift the Burden," *Politics, Philosophy and Economics* 2, no. 2 (2003): 165–90.

Kurban, Dilek, Çelik, Ayse Betul, and Denis Yükseker. "Overcoming a Legacy of Mistrust: Towards Reconciliation Between the State and the Displaced." Geneva: IDMC, 2006.

Kymlicka, Will. "An Update From the Multiculturalism Wars: Comments on Shachar and Spinner-Halev," in Steve Lukes and Christian Joppke, eds., *Multicultural Questions*. Oxford University Press, 1999, 112–29.

Contemporary Political Philosophy: An Introduction. Oxford University Press, 2001.

Liberalism, Community and Culture. Oxford University Press, 1989.

Multicultural Citizenship: A Liberal Theory of Minority Rights. Oxford University Press, 1995.

Laborde, Cecile. "From Constitutional to Civic Patriotism," *British Journal of Political Science* 32, no. 4 (2002): 591–612.

Lambert, Valerie. *Choctaw Nation: A Story of American Indian Resurgence.* Lincoln: University of Nebraska Press, 2009.

Laselva, Samuel V. "Aboriginal Self-Government and the Foundations of Canadian Nationhood," *BC Studies* 120 (1998): 41–54.

Lazarus, Edward. *Black Hills/White Justice: The Sioux Nation Versus the United States: 1775 to the Present.* New York: HarperCollins, 1991.

Lear, Jonathan. *Radical Hope: Ethics in the Face of Cultural Devastation.* Cambridge, MA: Harvard University Press, 2006.

Levy, Jacob. *The Multiculturalism of Fear.* Oxford University Press, 2000.

Lind, Jennifer. *Sorry States: Apologies in International Politics.* Ithaca, NY: Cornell University Press, 2010.

Locke, John. *The Second Treatise of Government.* Indianapolis: Hackett, 1980 [1689].

Lovett, Frank. "Cultural Accommodation and Domination," *Political Theory* 38, no. 2 (2010): 243–67.

Lowenthal, David. *The Past is a Foreign Country.* Cambridge University Press, 1999.

Lowrance, Sherry. "Identity, Grievances, and Political Action: Recent Evidence From the Palestinian Community in Israel," *International Political Science Review/ Revue internationale de science politique* 27, no. 2 (2006): 167–90.

Lyons, David. "The New Indian Claims and Original Rights to Land," *Social Theory and Practice* 4, no. 3 (1977): 249–71.

MacCormick, Neil. "Liberalism, Nationalism, and the Post-Sovereign State," *Political Studies* 44, no. 4 (1996): 553–67.

"Nation and Nationalism," in Ronald Beiner, ed., *Theorizing Nationalism.* Albany, NY: SUNY Press, 1999, 189–204.

Macedo, Stephen. *Diversity and Distrust: Public Schooling and American Liberalism.* Cambridge, MA: Harvard University Press, 1993.

"Transformative Constitutionalism and the Case of Religion: Defending the Moderate Hegemony of Liberalism," *Political Theory* 26, no. 1 (1998): 280–304.

Maddox, Lucy. *Citizen Indians: Native American Intellectuals, Race, and Reform.* Ithaca, NY: Cornell University Press, 2005.

Magee, Rhonda V. "The Master's Tools, From the Bottom Up: Responses to African-American Reparations Theory in Mainstream and Outsider Remedies Discourse," *Virginia Law Review* 79 (1993): 863–916.

Mahmood, Tahir. *Personal Laws in Crisis.* New Delhi: Metropolitan Book Co., 1986.

Mann, Michael. *The Dark Side of Democracy: Explaining Ethnic Cleansing*. Cambridge University Press, 2005.

Margalit, Avishai. *The Decent Society*. Cambridge, MA: Harvard University Press, 1996.

The Ethics of Memory. Cambridge, MA: Harvard University Press, 2002.

Margalit, Avishai, and Joseph Raz. "National Self-Determination," *Journal of Philosophy* 87, no. 9 (1990): 439–61.

Markell, Patchen. "Making Affect Safe for Democracy? On 'Constitutional Patriotism'," *Political Theory* 28, no. 1 (2000): 38–63.

Marneffe, Peter de. *Liberalism and Prostitution*. New York: Oxford University Press, 2009.

Marrus, Michael R. "Official Apologies and the Quest for Historical Justice," *Journal of Human Rights* 6, no. 1 (2007): 75–105.

Marx, Karl, and Friedrich Engels. *Capital: a Critique of Political Economy*. Vol. I, Moscow: Progress Publishers, 1978.

Mason, Andrew. *Community, Solidarity and Belonging: Levels of Community and Their Normative Significance*. Cambridge University Press, 2000.

McCarthy, Thomas. "Coming to Terms With Our Past, Part II: On the Morality and Politics of Reparations for Slavery," *Political Theory* 32, no. 6 (2004): 750–72.

Race, Empire, and the Idea of Human Development. Cambridge University Press, 2009.

"Vergangenheitsbewaltigung in the USA: On the Politics of the Memory of Slavery," *Political Theory* 30, no. 5 (2002): 623–48.

Mehta, Uday Singh. *Liberalism and Empire: A Study in Nineteenth-Century British Liberal Thought*. University of Chicago Press, 1999.

Meisels, Tamar. "Can Corrective Justice Ground Claims to Territory?," *Journal of Political Philosophy* 11, no. 1 (2003): 65–88.

Michaels, Walter Benn. "'You Who Never Was There': Slavery and the New Historicism, Deconstruction and the Holocaust," *Narrative* 4, no. 1 (1996): 1–16.

Mill, John Stuart. "Civilization," in *Essays on Politics and Culture*, ed. Gertrude Himmelfarb. New York: Anchor Books, 1963 [1836], 45–76.

"Considerations on Representative Government," in *On Liberty and Other Essays*. Oxford University Press, 1991 [1861], 205–467.

Principles of Political Economy, With Some of Their Applications to Social Philosophy, ed. J. M. Robson. 33 vols., Vol. III, *Collected Works*. University of Toronto, 1965 [1848].

"The Spirit of the Age," in *Essays on Politics and Culture*, ed. Gertrude Himmelfarb. New York: Anchor Books, 1963 [1831], 1–44.

"Utilitarianism," in *Utilitarianism and Other Essays*. Penguin: Harmondsworth, 1987 [1861], 131–201.

Miller, David. "Distributing Responsibilities," *Journal of Political Philosophy* 9, no. 4 (2001): 453–71.

On Nationality. Oxford University Press, 1995.

Miller, William Ian. *Faking It*. Cambridge University Press, 2003.

Mohanty, Bidyut. "Panchayat Raj Institutions and Women," in Bharati Ray and Aparnu Basu, eds., *From Independence Towards Freedom: Indian Women since 1947*. New Delhi: Oxford University Press, 1999, 19–33.

Moore, Margaret. *The Ethics of Nationalism*. Oxford University Press, 2001.

Morris, Christopher W. "Existential Limits to the Rectification of Past Wrongs," *American Philosophical Quarterly* 21, no. 2 (1984): 175–82.

Muthu, Sankar. *Enlightenment Against Empire*. Princeton University Press, 2003.

Nielsen, Kai. "Liberal Nationalism and Secession," in Margaret Moore, ed., *National Self-Determination and Secession*. Oxford University Press, 1998, 103–33.

Nisbet, Robert. *History of the Idea of Progress*. New Brunswick: Transaction Publishers, 1994.

Nobles, Melissa. *The Politics of Official Apologies*. Cambridge University Press, 2008.

Nozick, Robert. *Anarchy, State, and Utopia*. New York: Basic Books, 1974.

Nussbaum, Martha C. *The Clash Within: Democracy, Religious Violence, and India's Future*. Cambridge, MA: Harvard University Press, 2009.

Sex and Social Justice. Oxford University Press, 1999.

Women and Human Development: the Capabilities Approach. Cambridge University Press, 2000.

Nussbaum, Martha C., and Jonathan Glover, eds. *Women, Culture and Development: A Study of Human Capabilities*. Oxford: Clarendon Press, 1995.

Okin, Susan Moller. "Feminism and Multiculturalism: Some Tensions," *Ethics* 108, no. 4 (1998): 661–84.

"Is Multiculturalism Bad for Women?," *Boston Review* (1997).

"'Mistresses of Their Own Destiny': Group Rights, Gender, and Realistic Rights of Exit," *Ethics* 112, no. 2 (2002): 205–30.

"Multiculturalism and Feminism: No Simple Question, No Simple Answers," in Avigail Eisenberg and Jeff Spinner-Halev, eds., *Minorities within Minorities: Equality, Rights and Diversity*. Cambridge University Press, 2004, 67–89.

Okun, Barbara, and Dov Friedlander. "Educational Stratification Among Arabs and Jews in Israel: Historical Disadvantage, Discrimination, and Opportunity," *Population Studies* 59, no. 2 (2005): 163–80.

Olick, Jeffrey K. *The Politics of Regret: On Collective Memory and Historical Responsibility.* New York: Routledge, 2007.

Ondetti, Gabriel A. *Land, Protest and Politics: The Landless Movement and the Stuggle for Agrarian Reform in Brazil.* University Park: Pennsylvania State University Press, 2008.

Papke, David Ray. *The Pullman Case: The Clash of Labor and Capital in Industrial America.* Lawrence: University Press of Kansas, 1999.

Parekh, Bhikhu. "The Cultural Particularity of Liberal Democracy," in David Held, ed., *Prospects for Democracy: North, South, East, West.* Cambridge: Polity Press, 1993, 156–75.

Parker, Linda S. *Native American Estate: The Struggle Over Indian and Hawaiian Lands.* Honolulu: University of Hawaii Press, 1989.

Pearce, Roy Harvey. *The Savages of America: A Study of the Indian and the Idea of Civilization.* Baltimore: Johns Hopkins Press, 1953.

Pearson, Noel. "Contradictions Cloud the Apology to the Stolen Generations." 2008. www.theaustralian.com.au/news/features/when-words-arent-enough/story-e6frg6z6–1111115528371. (Accessed May 28, 2010.)

Pensky, Max. "Cosmopolitanism and the Solidarity Problem: Habermas on National and Cultural Identities," *Constellations* 7, no. 1 (2000): 64–79.

Perdue, Theda, and Michael Green. *The Cherokee Nation and the Trail of Tears.* New York: Viking Press, 2007.

Perez, Nahshon. "On Compensation and Return: Can the 'Continuing Injustice Argument' for Compensating Historical Injustices Justify Compensation for Such Injustices Or the Return of Property?," *Journal of Applied Philosophy* 28, no. 2 (2011): 151–68.

   "Should Multiculturalists Oppress the Oppressed?," *Critical Review of International Social and Political Philosophy* 5, no. 3 (2002): 51–79.

Pettit, Philip. *Republicanism: A Theory of Freedom and Government.* Oxford University Press, 1999.

Pfaelzer, Jean. *Driven Out: The Forgotten War Against Chinese Americans.* New York: Random House, 2007.

Pitts, Jennifer. *A Turn to Empire: The Rise of Imperial Liberalism in Britain and France.* Princeton University Press, 2005.

Plank, Geoffrey Gilbert. *An Unsettled Conquest: The British Campaign Against the Peoples of Acadia.* Philadelphia: University of Pennsylvania Press, 2001.

Pohl, J. Otto. "Stalin's Genocide Against Repressed Peoples," *Journal of Genocide Research* 2, no. 2 (2000): 267–93.

Pommersheim, Frank. "The Black Hills Case: On the Cusp of History," *Wicazo Sa Review* 4, no. 1 (1988): 18–23.

Prucha, Francis Paul. *The Great Father: The United States Government and the American Indians*. Abridged edn. Lincoln: University of Nebraska Press, 1986.

Rawls, John. *The Law of Peoples*. Cambridge, MA: Harvard University Press, 1999.

Political Liberalism. New York: Columbia University Press, 1993.

A Theory of Justice. Revised edn. Cambridge, MA: Harvard University Press, 1999.

Rayner, Jay. *Eating Crow*. New York: Simon & Schuster, 2004.

Raz, Joseph. "Multiculturalism: A Liberal Perspective," in *Ethics in the Public Domain: Essays in the Morality of Law and Politics*. Oxford University Press, 1994, 170–91.

Reitman, Oonagh. "On Exit," in Avigail Eisenberg and Jeff Spinner-Halev, eds., *Minorities within Minorities: Equality, Rights and Diversity*. Cambridge University Press, 2004, 189–208.

Resnik, Judith. "Dependent Sovereigns: Indian Tribes, States, and the Federal Courts," *University Chicago Law Review* 56, no. 2 (1989): 671–759.

Ridge, Michael. "Giving the Dead Their Due," *Ethics* 114, no. 1 (2003): 38–59.

Robinson, Randall. *The Debt: What America Owes to Blacks*. New York: Penguin, 2001.

Rosin, Hanna. "*The End of Men*." 2010. www.theatlantic.com/magazine/archive/2010/07/the-end-of-men/8135. (Accessed July 29, 2010.)

Ross, Dorothy. "Grand Narrative in American Historical Writing: From Romance to Uncertainty," *The American Historical Review* 100, no. 3 (1995): 651–77.

Sachs, Susan. "Egypt's Women Win Equal Rights to Divorce," *New York Times*, March 1, 2000.

Savage, Lon. *Thunder in the Mountains: The West Virginia Mine War, 1920–21*. University of Pittsburgh Press, 1990.

Schouls, Timothy A. *Shifting Boundaries: Aboriginal Identity, Pluralist Theory, and the Politics of Self-Government*. Vancouver: University of British Columbia Press, 2003.

Scott, David. *Conscripts of Modernity: The Tragedy of Colonial Enlightenment*. Durham: Duke University Press, 2004.

Shachar, Ayelet. "Group Identity and Women's Rights in Family Law: The Perils of Multicultural Accommodation," *Journal of Political Philosophy* 6, no. 3 (1998): 285–305.

Multicultural Jurisdictions: Cultural Differences and Women's Rights. Cambridge University Press, 2001.

Sharp, Andrew. *Justice and the Māori: The Philosophy and Practice of Māori Claims in New Zealand Since the 1970s*. Oxford University Press, 1997.

Shelby, Tommie. "Justice, Deviance, and the Dark Ghetto," *Philosophy and Public Affairs* 35, no. 2 (2007): 126–60.

We Who Are Dark: The Philosophical Foundations of Black Solidarity. Cambridge, MA: Harvard University Press, 2007.

Sher, George. "Transgenerational Compensation," *Philosophy and Public Affairs* 33, no. 2 (2005): 181–200.

Shklar, Judith N. *The Faces of Injustice.* New Haven: Yale University Press, 1990.

Shue, Henry. *Basic Rights: Subsistence, Affluence and U.S. Foreign Policy.* 2nd edn. Princeton University Press, 1996.

Simmons, A. John. "Historical Rights and Fair Shares," *Law and Philosophy* 14, no. 2 (1995): 149–84.

"Ideal and Non-Ideal Theory," *Philosophy and Public Affairs* 38, no. 1 (2010): 5–36.

Moral Principles and Political Obligations. Princeton University Press, 1979.

Smith, Donald Eugene. *India as a Secular State.* Princeton University Press, 1963.

Smith, Nick. *I Was Wrong: The Meanings of Apologies.* Cambridge University Press, 2008.

Smith, Rogers M. *Stories of Peoplehood: The Politics and Morals of Political Membership.* Cambridge University Press, 2003.

Smith, Jr., Warren W. *China's Tibet? Autonomy Or Assimilation.* Lanham, MD: Rowman & Littlefield, 2008.

Song, Sarah. *Justice, Gender, and the Politics of Multiculturalism.* Cambridge University Press, 2007.

Spadafora, David. *The Idea of Progress in Eighteenth-Century Britain.* New Haven: Yale University Press, 1990.

Sparrow, Robert. "History and Collective Responsibility," *Australasian Journal of Philosophy* 78, no. 3 (2000): 346–59.

Spinner, Jeff. *The Boundaries of Citizenship: Race, Ethnicity and Nationality in the Liberal State.* Baltimore: Johns Hopkins University Press, 1994.

Spinner-Halev, Jeff. "Autonomy, Association and Pluralism," in Avigail Eisenberg and Jeff Spinner-Halev, eds., *Minorities within Minorities: Equality, Rights and Diversity.* Cambridge University Press, 2005, 157–71.

"Democracy, Solidarity and Post-Nationalism," *Political Studies* 56, no. 3 (2008): 604–28.

"Feminism, Multiculturalism, Oppression, and the State," *Ethics* 112, no. 1 (2001): 84–113.

"From Historical to Enduring Injustice," *Political Theory* 35, no. 5 (2007): 550–73.

"Hinduism, Christianity, and Liberal Religious Toleration," *Political Theory* 33, no. 1 (2005): 28–57.

"Liberalism and Religion: Against Congruence," *Theoretical Inquiries in Law* 9, no. 2 (2008): 554–72.

Surviving Diversity: Religion and Democratic Citizenship. Baltimore: Johns Hopkins University Press, 2000.

"The Trouble With Diversity," in Jonathan S. Davies and David L. Imbroscio, eds., *Critical Urban Studies: New Directions.* Albany, NY: SUNY, 2010, 107–20.

Spinner-Halev, Jeff, and Elizabeth Theiss-Morse. "National Identity and Self-Esteem," *Perspectives on Politics* 1, no. 3 (2003): 515–32.

Staal, Frits. *Rules Without Meaning: Ritual, Mantras, and the Human Sciences.* New York: Peter Lang, 1989.

Steinberg, Ted. *Acts of God: The Unnatural History of Natural Disaster in America.* New York: Oxford University Press, 2006.

Stilz, Anna. *Liberal Loyalty: Freedom, Obligation, and the State.* Princeton University Press, 2009.

Stowell, David O. *The Great Strikes of 1877.* Urbana: University of Illinois Press, 2008.

Streich, Gregory W. "Is There a Right to Forget? Historical Injustices, Race, Memory, and Identity," *New Political Science* 24, no. 4 (2002): 525–42.

Sturm, Circe. *Blood Politics: Race, Culture, and Identity in the Cherokee Nation of Oklahoma.* University of California Press, 2002.

Szelenyi, Ivan, and Janos Ladanyi. *Patterns of Exclusion: Constructing Gypsy Ethnicity and the Making of an Underclass in Transitional Societies of Europe.* Boulder, CO: East European Monographs, 2006.

Taiaiake, Alfred. *Peace, Power, Righteousness: An Indigenous Manifesto.* Oxford University Press, 1999.

Tamir, Yael. *Liberal Nationalism.* Princeton University Press, 1993.

Tan, Kok-Chor. *Justice Without Borders: Cosmopolitanism, Nationalism, and Patriotism.* Cambridge University Press, 2004.

Tavuchis, Nicholas. *Mea Culpa: A Sociology of Apology and Reconciliation.* Stanford University Press, 1991.

Taylor, Charles. "Nationalism and Modernity," in Ronald Beiner, ed., *Theorizing Nationalism.* Albany, NY: SUNY Press, 1999, 219–46.

Theiss-Morse, Elizabeth. *Who Counts as an American? The Boundaries of National Identity.* Cambridge University Press, 2009.

Thiesenhusen, William C. *Broken Promises: Agrarian Reform and the Latin American Campesino.* Boulder, CO: Westview Press, 1995.

"Human Rights, Affirmative Action and Land Reform in Latin America," in M. L. Wyzan, ed., *The Political Economy of Ethnic Discrimination and Affirmative Action: A Comparative Perspective.* New York: Praeger Publishers, 1990, 25–48.

Thompson, Janna. "Apology, Justice and Respect," in Mark Gibney, Rhoda E. Howard-Hassmann, Jean-Marc Coicaud, and Niklaus Steiner, eds., *The Age of Apology: Facing Up to the Past.* Philadelphia: University of Pennsylvania Press, 2008, 31–44.

"The Apology Paradox," *The Philosophical Quarterly* 50, no. 201 (2000): 470–75.

Taking Responsibility for the Past: Reparation and Historical Injustice. Cambridge: Polity, 2002.

Till, Karen E. *The New Berlin: Memory, Politics, Place.* Minneapolis: University of Minnesota Press, 2005.

Trehan, Nidhi, and Nando Sigona. *Romani Politics in Contemporary Europe: Poverty, Ethnic Mobilization, and the Neo-Liberal Order.* Basingstoke: Palgrave Macmillan, 2010.

Trudeau, Pierre. "Remarks on Aborginal and Treaty Rights. Excerpts From a Speech Given August 8th, 1969," in Peter A. Cumming and Neil H. Mickenberg, eds., *Native Rights in Canada.* Toronto: Indian-Eskimo Association of Canada in association with General Pub. Co., 1972, 331–32.

Tsosie, Rebecca. "The BIA's Apology to Native Americans: An Essay on Collective Memory and Collective Conscience," in Elazar Barkan and Alexander Karn, eds., *Taking Wrongs Seriously: Apologies and Reconciliation.* Stanford University Press, 2006, 185–212.

Tully, James. *Public Philosophy in a New Key: Vol. I, Democracy and Civic Freedom.* Cambridge University Press, 2008.

Public Philosophy in a New Key: Vol. II, Imperialism and Civic Freedom. Cambridge University Press, 2008.

Strange Multiplicity: Constitutionalism in an Age of Diversity. Cambridge University Press, 1995.

Turner, Dale. *This is Not a Peace Pipe: Towards a Critical Indigenous Philosophy.* University of Toronto Press, 2006.

Uehling, Greta Lynn. *Beyond Memory: The Crimean Tatars' Deportation and Return.* New York: Palgrave Macmillan, 2004.

UNESCO. *World Heritage.* 2006. http://whc.unesco.org/en/about/.

US Supreme Court. "United States v. Sioux Nation of Indians." 448 *US* (1980): 371.

Valls, Andrew. "Reconsidering the Case for Black Reparations," in Jon Miller and Rahul Kumar, eds., *Reparations: Interdisciplinary Inquiries.* Oxford University Press, 2007, 114–29.

Vernon, Richard. "Against Restitution," *Political Studies* 51, no. 3 (2003): 542–57.

Waldron, Jeremy. "Special Ties and Natural Duties," *Philosophy and Public Affairs* 22, no. 1 (1993): 3–30.

"Superseding Historic Injustice," *Ethics* 103, no. 4 (1992): 4–28.

Walker, Margaret Urban. *Moral Repair: Reconstructing Moral Relations After Wrongdoing.* Cambridge University Press, 2006.

Walls, Melissa, Les Whitbeck, Dan Hoyt, and Kurt Johnson. "Early-Onset Alcohol Use Among Native American Youth: Examining Female Caretaker Influence," *Journal of Marriage and Family* 69, no. 2 (2007): 451–64.

Walzer, Michael. *Just and Unjust Wars: a Moral Argument With Historical Illustrations.* New York: Basic Books, 1977.

Spheres of Justice: A Defense of Pluralism and Equality. New York: Basic Books, 1983.

Webber, Jeremy. "Beyond Regret: Mabo's Implications for Australian Constitutionalism," in Duncan Ivison, Paul Patton, and Will Sanders, eds., *Political Theory and the Rights of Indigenous Peoples.* Cambridge University Press, 2000, 60–88.

Weiner, Brian A. *Sins of the Parents: The Politics of National Apologies in the United States.* Philadelphia: Temple University Press, 2005.

Weinstock, Daniel. "'Exit Rights': Reframing the Debate," in Avigail Eisenberg and Jeff Spinner-Halev, eds., *Minorities within Minorities: Equality, Rights and Diversity.* Cambridge University Press, 2004, 227–48.

Wenar, Leif. "Reparations for the Future," *Journal of Social Philosophy* 37, no. 3 (2006): 396–405.

Westley, Robert. "Many Billions Gone: Is it Time to Reconsider the Case for Black Reparations?," *Boston College Third World Law Journal* 19 (1998): 429–76.

Wheeler III, Samuel C. "Reparations Reconstructed," *American Philosophical Quarterly* 34, no. 3 (1997): 301–18.

Wilkins, David E. *American Indian Politics and the American Political System.* Lanham, MD: Rowman & Littlefield Publishers, 2007.

Williams, Melissa. *Voice, Trust and Memory: Marginalized Groups and the Failings of Liberal Representation.* Princeton University Press, 1998.

Williams, Rina Verma. *Postcolonial Politics and Personal Laws: Colonial Legal Legacies and the Indian State.* New Delhi: Oxford University Press, 2006.

Wolford, Wendy. "Land Reform in the Time of Neoliberalism: A Many-Splendored Thing," *Antipode* 39, no. 3 (2007): 550–70.

Wolgast, Elizabeth Hankins. *The Grammar of Justice.* Ithaca, NY: Cornell University Press, 1987.

Wood, Allen W. "The Marxian Critique of Justice," *Philosophy and Public Affairs* 1, no. 3 (1972): 244–82.

Yack, Bernard. "Popular Sovereignty and Nationalism," *Political Theory* 29, no. 4 (2001): 517–36.

Yashar, Deborah J. *Contesting Citizenship in Latin America: The Rise of Indigenous Movements and the Postliberal Challenge.* Cambridge University Press, 2005.

Yoo, Aileen. "*Kosovo: the Jerusalem of Serbia.*" 1999. www.washingtonpost.com/wp-srv/inatl/longterm/balkans/overview/kosovo.htm. (Accessed July 8, 2011.)

Yoshida, Takashi. *The Making of the "Rape of Nanking": History and Memory in Japan, China, and the United States.* Oxford University Press, 2006.

Young, Iris Marion. *Justice and the Politics of Difference.* Princeton University Press, 1990.

Zagorin, Perez. *How the Idea of Religious Toleration Came to the West.* Princeton University Press, 2003.

Zerubavel, Eviatar. *Time Maps: Collective Memory and the Social Shape of the Past.* University of Chicago Press, 2003.

Index